Radical Economics and Labor

To celebrate the centenary of the most radical union in North America – The Industrial Workers of the World – this collection examines radical economics and the labor movement in the twentieth century. The union advocates direct action to raise wages and increase job control, and it envisions the eventual abolition of capitalism and the wage system through the general strike.

The contributors to this volume speak both to economists and to those in the labor movement, and point to fruitful ways in which these radical heterodox traditions have engaged and continue to engage with each other and with the labor movement. In view of the current crisis of organized labor and the beleaguered state of the working class – phenomena which are global in scope – the book is both timely and important. Representing a significant contribution to the non-mainstream literature on labor economics, the book reactivates a marginalized analytical tradition which can shed a great deal of light on the origins and evolution of the difficulties confronting workers throughout the world.

This volume will be of most interest to students and scholars of heterodox economics, those involved with or researching the Industrial Workers of the World, as well as anyone interested in the more radical side of unions, anarchism and labor organizations in an economic context.

Frederic S. Lee is Professor of Economics at University of Missouri-Kansas City, USA and **Jon Bekken** is Associate Professor of Communications at Albright College, USA and former General Secretary-Treasurer of the Industrial Workers of the World.

Routledge Advances in Heterodox Economics

Edited by Frederic S. Lee

University of Missouri-Kansas City

Over the past two decades, the intellectual agendas of heterodox economists have taken a decidedly pluralist turn. Leading thinkers have begun to move beyond the established paradigms of Austrian, feminist Institutional-evolutionary, Marxian, Post Keynesian, radical, social, and Sraffian economics – opening up new lines of analysis, criticism, and dialogue among dissenting schools of thought. This cross-fertilization of ideas is creating a new generation of scholarship in which novel combinations of heterodox ideas are being brought to bear on important contemporary and historical problems.

Routledge Advances in Heterodox Economics aims to promote this new scholarship by publishing innovative books in heterodox economic theory, policy, philosophy, intellectual history, institutional history, and pedagogy. Syntheses or critical engagement of two or more heterodox traditions are especially encouraged.

1. **Ontology and Economics:**
Tony Lawson and his critics
Edited by Edward Fullbrook

2. **Currencies, Capital Flows and Crises**
A post Keynesian analysis of exchange rate determination
John T. Harvey

3. **Radical Economics and Labor**
Essays inspired by the IWW Centennial
Frederic Lee and Jon Bekken

This series was previously published by The University of Michigan Press and the following books are available (please contact UMP for more information):

Economics in Real Time
A theoretical reconstruction
John McDermott

Liberating Economics
Feminist perspectives on families, work, and globalization
Drucilla K. Barker and Susan F. Feiner

Socialism After Hayek
Theodore A. Burczak

Future Directors for Heterodox Economics
Edited by John T. Harvey and Robert F. Garnett, Jr.

Radical Economics and Labor

Essays inspired by the IWW Centennial

Edited by
Frederic S. Lee and Jon Bekken

Routledge
Taylor & Francis Group
LONDON AND NEW YORK

First published 2009
by Routledge
2 Park Square, Milton Park, Abingdon, Oxon OX14 4RN

Simultaneously published in the USA and Canada
by Routledge
270 Madison Avenue, New York, NY 10016

Routledge is an imprint of the Taylor & Francis Group, an informa business

Typeset in Times New Roman by
Keystroke, 28 High Street, Tettenhall, Wolverhampton
Printed in the UK by
the MPG Books Group

British Library Cataloguing in Publication Data
A catalogue record for this book is available from the British Library

Library of Congress Cataloging in Publication Data
Radical economics and labor/[edited by] Frederic S. Lee and Jon Bekken.
p. cm.
Includes bibliographical references.
1. Labor movement—History. 2. Radical economics—History.
I. Lee, Frederic S., 1949– II. Bekken, Jon, 1960–
HD4851.R27 2009
331.88—dc22 2008033870

ISBN10: 0–415–77723–2 (hbk)
ISBN10: 0–203–88255–5 (ebk)

ISBN13: 978–0–415–77723–0 (hbk)
ISBN13: 978–0–203–88255–9 (ebk)

Contents

Illustrations

Figure

Tables

Contributors

Tony Aspromourgos is Professor of Economics at the University of Sydney and author of *On the Origins of Classical Economics: Distribution and Value from William Petty to Adam Smith* (Routledge, 1996). His publications have appeared in a wide variety of journals including *History of Economic Ideas* and the *Review of Political Economy*. He is a member of the editorial board of the *European Journal of the History of Economic Thought.*

Jon Bekken is Associate Professor at Albright College, co-author of *The IWW: Its First 100 Years*, and former editor of the monthly *Industrial Worker*. He served two terms as General Secretary-Treasurer of the Industrial Workers of the World, and has published scholarly articles on the political economy of the retail book industry and on the history of the labor press, newsboy unions, foreign-language newspapers, and Chicago journalism. He is on the editorial boards of *Anarcho-Syndicalist Review* and *Journalism History*.

Mathew Forstater is Associate Professor of Economics and Director of the Center for Full Employment and Price Stability at the University of Missouri-Kansas City. His publications have appeared in *Review of Political Economy, Journal of Economics Issues, Journal of Post Keynesian Economics, Review of Social Economy*, and many other journals; and has co-edited, with Edward Nell, *Reinventing Functional Finance* (Elgar, 2003).

José Ricardo Barbosa Gonçalves is Professor of Economics at the Instituto de Economia at the University of Campinas, Brazil, and author of *The Utopia of the Social Order*. His recent publications include *After Financial Deregulation and Social Exclusion: Expectations from Micro-credit Proposals in Brazil; Corporate Social Responsibility: Credit and Banking Inclusion in Brazil;* and *Labor Conditions and Syndicalism in the Brazilian Banking Sector.*

Michael Hillard is Professor of Economics at the University of Southern Maine. He teaches and writes about U.S. labor history, radical labor economics, and the history of industrial relations. His essay "Labor at Mother Warren" won *Labor History*'s "Best Essay, U.S. Topic" prize for 2004. He is currently writing a book about the labor history of Maine paper workers and woodcutters.

José Dari Krein is Professor and researcher at CESIT (Center of Studies on Labor and Syndicalism), Instituto de Economia, University of Campinas, Brazil. He taught at the School for Trade Union Activists-CUT. His recent publications include *Labor Conditions and Syndicalism in the Brazilian Banking Sector.*

Frederic S. Lee is Professor of Economics at University of Missouri-Kansas City, and is the editor of the book series "Routledge Advances in Heterodox Economics" and the editor of the *Heterodox Economics Newsletter.* His publications include "To be a Heterodox Economist: The Contested Landscape of American Economics, 1960s and 70s," *Journal of Economic Issues* (2004); "History and Identity: The Case of Radical Economics and Radical Economists, 1945–1970," *Review of Radical Political Economics* (2004); *Post Keynesian Price Theory* (1998); and many other articles and books.

Maria Alejandra Caporale Madi is Professor of Economics at the Instituto de Economia at the University of Campinas, Brazil, and author of *Monetary Policy in Brazil: A Post Keynesian Interpretation.* Her recent publications include *After Financial Deregulation and Social Exclusion: Expectations from Micro-credit Proposals in Brazil*; *Corporate Social Responsibility: Credit and Banking Inclusion in Brazil*; and *Labor Conditions and Syndicalism in the Brazilian Banking Sector.*

John Marangos is Associate Professor at the Department of Economics at the University of Crete. His main research interests are transition economics, political economy, and teaching economics. He is a graduate of ASOEE, Greece, with a major in Economic Analysis, he received his Masters from Monash University in Melbourne, Australia, and his PhD from LaTrobe University, Melbourne, Australia. He has taught at the University of Melbourne, Monash University, University of Ballarat in Australia, and Colorado State University. He is the editor of the *Forum of Social Economics*, a journal sponsored by the Association for Social Economics, and section editor of International Economics and Development Studies for the *Global Business and Economic Review.* He was also a member of the editorial board of the *Journal of Economic Issues.*

Richard McIntyre is Director of the Honors Center and Professor of Economics at the University of Rhode Island. He edits the *New Political Economy* book series for Routledge and is the author of *Are Labor Rights Human Rights (and does it matter if they are)?* (forthcoming from the University of Michigan Press).

Spencer J. Pack is Professor of Economics at Connecticut College. His publications include *Reconstructing Marxian Economics: Marx Based upon a Sraffian Commodity Theory of Value* (1985); *Capitalism as a Moral System: Adam Smith's Critique of the Free Market Economy* (1991); and many articles in the history of economic thought. His current project is tentatively entitled *Aristotle, Adam Smith, and Karl Marx on Some Fundamental Issues in Political Economy: Exchange Value, Money, Capital; Character, Government, Change.*

Claude Pottier is a researcher at the French National Center for Scientific Research and University of Paris 10, working on the multinationals' organization of production. His publications include: “Le développement des pays émergents sous la contrainte des multinationales,” *Recherches Internationales* (2004) *Les multinationales et la mise en concurrence des salariés* (L’Harmattan, 2003) and “La division du travail entre les pays développés et les pays à bas salaires impact de l’organisation des multinationales,” *Economies et Sociétés* (2003).

Noel Thompson is Professor of History and Head of the School of Humanities at the University of Swansea. His publications include *The Real Rights of Man: Political Economies for the Working Class, 1775–1850* (1998), *Left in the Wilderness, the Political Economy of British Democratic Socialism since 1979* (2002), and *Political Economy and the Labour Party* (2nd edn, 2006).

Introduction

Radical economics and the labor movement

Frederic S. Lee and Jon Bekken

The year 2005 was the one hundredth anniversary of the founding of the Industrial Workers of the World (IWW), the most radical union in North America. To commemorate the anniversary, a conference on radical economics and the labor movement in the twentieth century was hosted by Fred Lee and Jon Bekken (both members of the IWW) and held at University of Missouri-Kansas City from September 15–17, 2005. The conference theme was the role of radical economics in the labor movement in the United States and around the world. For some, radical economics refers to one of many theoretical approaches that constitute heterodox economics. However, a closer look reveals that radical modifies a number of them. Therefore for the purpose of the conference, radical economics included but was not restricted to anarchism, Marxism, syndicalism, radical institutionalism, left-wing Keynesianism, and plain old-fashioned radical economics. Hence, in this broader context radical economics is "heterodox" in that it draws together different radical approaches and promotes theoretical engagement between them. Over fifty conference participants listen to twenty presentations ranging from the birth of syndicalist political economy, Sraffa and organized labor, to struggles for economic democracy and union organizing on commission. The ten papers included in this volume were selected from those presentations to illustrate how the different approaches of radical economics can contribute in many ways to the labor movement in general (not just to the IWW), and in turn to suggest ways in which that engagement can contribute to radical economic analysis and thus to the advancement of heterodox economics.

Historically, radical economics arose in dialogue with contemporary radical workers' movements. From Senex's letters in the radical press of his day to the many columns labor newspapers used to devote to radical economic analysis, labor activists and radical economists informed each others' analyses, challenging mainstream economists both in the academy and in popular discourse. The IWW press, too, frequently published articles and pamphlets critiquing capitalist economics and sketching an alternative vision of a society based on abolition of the wage system and the alienation of the working class not only from the product of its labor but also from its direction and planning through workers' control of the means of production. At a moment when both socialism, however defined, and the labor movement are increasingly embattled, the IWW centenary offered an opportunity to reflect on a century of radical workers' struggles and thinking, and to explore ways in which this crucial dialogue might be reinvigorated, strengthening both the labor movement and radical hence heterodox economic analysis.

History of the Industrial Workers of the World[1]

The origins of the Industrial Workers of the World may be traced back to the period from the 1870s to the turn of the century; a period when economic, social, and political unrest dominated the United States landscape. On the one hand, there was a growing interest in socialism, anarchism, and syndicalism among workers coupled with the great labor uprising in 1877, the Haymarket incident in 1886, the Pullman strike in 1894, and the bloody strikes among the western miners in the 1890s. In contrast, many contemporary unions, such as represented by the American Federation of Labor which the IWW derided as the "American Separation of Labor," were becoming increasingly conservative and craft-oriented. The AFL was controlled by a cast of officials increasingly aloof from their members; discriminatory towards women, blacks, and various ethnic groups; supportive of demobilizing myths such as labor-management cooperation and economic isolationism; and guilty of wasting members' dues on pro-employer politicians. Into this explosive mix emerged the Industrial Workers of the World. It was founded in Chicago in June 1905 by nearly 200 delegates representing the Western Federation of Miners and various smaller unions and socialist organizations. Organized in opposition to capitalism and conservative unionism, the IWW mission statement was and remains radical:

> The working class and the employing class have nothing in common. There can be no peace so long as hunger and want are found among millions of working people and the few, who make up the employing class, have all the good things in life. Between these two classes a struggle must go on until the workers of the world organize as a class, take possession of the means of production, abolish the wage system, and live in harmony with the earth . . . . Instead of the conservative motto, "A fair day's wage for a fair day's work," we must inscribe on our banner the revolutionary watchword, "Abolition of the wage system."[2]

To fulfill its mission statement, the IWW adopted two concepts: revolutionary industrial unionism and "One Big Union" that combined commitment to industrial unionism, direct action, and building a union controlled by its members. IWW organizers believed that such a union would organize workers' power more effectively to battle for better conditions on the job and ultimately bring an end to capitalism which would occur through the combination of increasing job control and the general strike.

The IWW got off to a rocky start, arguing over ideology, organizing strategies, and the wisdom of fighting for higher wages. Nevertheless, the union did engage in a number of industrial actions, such as conducting in 1906 the first documented sit-down strike in American history at General Electric's factory in Schenectady, New York. From 1911 to 1917, the IWW grew in reputation and membership (peaking at around 100,000 members in the United States, with autonomous administrations in Latin America and elsewhere) through engaging in the high-publicity Lawrence textile (1912) and Paterson silk (1913) strikes, and organizing integrated locals in the South, migratory farm workers on the Great Plains, oil and mine workers in the Southwest, housemaids in Denver, and construction and timber crews across the West.

The success of the IWW provoked much opposition. Its rhetoric of class war, the overthrow of capitalism, and sabotage (which most Wobblies, as IWW members came to be called, defined to mean deliberate inefficiency rather than destruction) frightened employers, social elites, and the state. Local ordinances were passed to limit public demonstrations and the freedom of speech; these ordinances led to "free speech" fights around the United States and contributed to the freedom of speech that Americans take for granted today. In addition, various states passed criminal syndicalism laws that labeled the IWW as a subversive organization and justified official crackdowns on the union; while the federal government carried out its own attack on the IWW in part because of its opposition to World War I and in part because it simply wanted to destroy the union. Finally, local officials turned a blind eye to (or even abetted) numerous acts of vigilante violence that resulted in the deaths of many Wobblies, including union organizer Frank Little and the unknown number killed in the Everett massacre, and that railroaded many thousands to jails and deportation.

Federal, state, and local government attacks on the IWW led to a near total disruption of the union and a steady decline in membership from 1917 onwards. Moreover, inspired by the 1917 Bolshevik Revolution in Russia, many Wobblies left the union and joined the Communist Party. Yet, the IWW was still active in the 1920s, 1930s, and into the 1940s; but in 1949 it was put on the U.S. Attorney General's List of Subversive Organizations and in 1950 it lost National Labor Relations Board representation rights.

Down to a handful of members in the 1950s, the IWW was near extinction when it was revived by an influx of young workers radicalized by the civil rights and antiwar movements during the 1960s. By the 1980s, the IWW had established job control in several small and mid-sized firms primarily in the printing, recycling, retail, and social services sector. Today the IWW has more than 1,000 dues-paying members, most in the United States and Canada, but also in the United Kingdom, Australia, Germany, and other countries.[3] Its mission statement is still the same after 100 years: to promote workers' control, to abolish the wage system, and to help usher in a new classless society through direct action, industrial unionism, and the general strike.

Over its history, the IWW never measured its success or its influence by grand spectacles. The columns of the IWW's many newspapers were filled with reports on daily struggles such as winning better food, forcing a foreman to treat workers more respectfully, or gaining 50 cents a day on a job. Those struggles were fundamentally over power relations on the job; that is, job control. When timber workers burned their bed rolls in 1917 and adopted the eight-hour day by the simple expedient of blowing a whistle at the end of eight hours and halting work, they were not presenting a grievance or seeking an agreement with the boss; they were acting collectively to assert their dignity, and their determination henceforth to live a very different sort of life. In short, for the IWW job control was and is central to transforming capitalism. Hence it is central to its revolutionary vision where workers through their own actions can make a better world out of the old.

Today the IWW continues its efforts through a "solidarity unionism" model. In addition to representing workers in a number of workplaces (including foodstuffs distributors, print shops, recycling facilities, restaurants, retail outlets, and social service agencies) where it has won formal union recognition, the IWW has recently focused on campaigns to organize workers and achieve gains in industries and workplaces characterized by high employee turnover and poor conditions. For example, immigrant truck drivers on the West Coast, paid by the haul, turned to the IWW in 2004 to help them organize against long wait times, the blacklisting of militant workers, and rates that had not been adjusted to deal with skyrocketing fuel prices. In Chicago and elsewhere, the IWW is organizing bike messengers, building shop committees and initiating short job actions to address pressing grievances. In both cases, many employers sought to define workers as independent contractors in order to escape obligations ranging from workers' compensation to minimum wages and overtime pay (reflecting an international trend that moves workers into precarious, nonstandard work arrangements and shifts much of the cost of employment to workers). IWW organizers have, with much success, confronted this by campaigning against firms considering the independent-contractor model, taking direct action against particular manifestations of this approach, and supporting individual workers' claims for benefits and legal protections before regulatory agencies.

In New York City, the IWW is working with immigrant workers' centers to organize the foodstuffs industry, winning majorities at several shops, and building strong committees at others (including several Starbucks outlets) that can take union action regardless of formal recognition. Elsewhere, the IWW has launched campaigns to organize entire retail strips, helping low-wage workers to deal with grievances while working to raise the regional floor for pay and working conditions. In several instances in recent years, the IWW has drawn upon its sections in Australia, the British Isles, and Canada to organize solidarity actions against transnational employers engaged in violating IWW members' rights in the United States (just as U.S. IWW members are active in supporting the struggles of their fellow workers abroad).

The IWW thus continues a long heritage of direct-action unionism in which workers build the instruments of their power through job actions. Moreover, by struggling to exercise an ever greater degree of control over their jobs, Wobblies are also contesting broader social and economic power. A similar vision once animated the broader labor movement, and it continues to be relevant. Without a vision of autonomy and self-actualization that lead to increasing job control and the transformation of capitalism through the general strike, unions are limited to defensive struggles that leave the employers' control of working lives, and of society, unchallenged.

About the book

Embedded in the IWW's preamble and its general heterodox discourse is a Marxist-anarchist-syndicalist critique of capitalism. This outlook advocates direct action to raise wages and increase job control, and it envisions the eventual abolition of capitalism and the wage system through the general strike. The first two chapters of this book provide some historical background to this critique. In his chapter on the "Letters on Associated Labour" (which may be found at http://www.iww.org/culture/senex), Noel Thompson explores the origins of a neo-syndicalist political economy published in the British working-class newspaper, *The Pioneer*, in 1834. He argues that the "Letters" articulated a socialist, almost proto-Marxian, political economy that was radically different from the dominant contemporary strain of communitarianism socialism, emphasized the socialization of the means of production and the decentralization of economic decision-making, and most significantly emphasized the active role of the working class in its own emancipation through the medium of trade unions. These three contributions became central components of the IWW critiques of capitalism, its view that it is the working class in One Big Union that would overthrow capitalism, and the utopian vision that the new society would enable all workers to have control over their working lives. Chapter 2, by Jon Bekken, is concerned with anarchist ideas shortly before the formation of the IWW, in particular, Peter Kropotkin's critique of capitalism and his anarchist economics for the new society. Bekken first delineates Kropotkin's critique of the labor theory of value and then his critiques of capitalism as an economic system, such as its deliberate inability to be productive, its wage slavery, and its emphasis on private property when production is a social, communal activity. The second part of the chapter discusses Kropotkin's anarchist economics for a new society, especially his views on shorter working hours and on work as a positive activity, and the ways these evolved through Kropotkin's engagement with revolutionary workers' movements of his day. While the IWW did not accept Kropotkin's critique of the labor theory of value, it did embrace his critique of capitalism and wage slavery, and his view that when workers controlled and organized production in their own interests, working hours would be shorter and work itself would be an enjoyable social activity.

In Chapter 3, Mathew Forstater takes the discussion of anarchist economics into the twentieth century. He poses the question "Is there an anarchist economics beyond simply a critique of capitalism?" and answers it affirmatively. Drawing on a wide literature, Forstater delineates many of anarchism's core principles: decentralization, bioregionalism, and municipal confederation; division of labor and work; appropriate technology; and reciprocity and mutualism. He concludes with a most significant discussion of the potential links between anarchism and heterodox economics. Frederic Lee and Tony Aspromourgos (chapters 4 and 5) critically examine radical labor's critique of capitalism from contemporary heterodox theoretical perspectives. Lee reviews the IWW's Marxian critique of capitalism and its justification of direct action for increasing wages and job control and of the general strike for abolishing capitalism and the wage system. However, because of theoretical problems with Marxism, relying on it to justify direct action for job control and the general strike for revolution is problematic. Thus Lee substitutes heterodox economic theory and its disaggregated micro-macro model of the economy. The model is used first to examine from a heterodox perspective the wage-profit nexus so central to traditional IWW arguments and then to re-establish on a firmer basis the traditional IWW tactics of job control and revolution. As a result he links together radical labor traditions with radical heterodox theory emanating from the post-Keynesian and Marxist traditions. Aspromourgos considers the capacity of organized labor to influence economic outcomes, from the standpoint of Piero Sraffa's reconstruction of the classical approach to distribution under capitalism. In particular, he argues that Sraffa's system of price equations was intended to convey a strong substantive claim about the possibilities for social forces, beyond competition, to influence the distribution of the surplus in a capitalist society. By implication, such a conception of how capitalism functions provides space for organized labor to have impact, as an element of those social forces. Thus, Aspromourgos considers the question of the capacities for organized labor to influence outcomes in such societies. All this raises the question of the relationship between economic science and political belief which he discusses and relates to wider issues of science, postmodernism, and the Left.

Chapters 6 and 7 deal with the role of radical economics, big business, and the contemporary labor movement in the United States. In Chapter 6, Spencer Pack re-evaluates Galbraith's *New Industrial State* from a radical perspective. He argues that Galbraith's vision of a humane, liberal welfare form of capitalism, where big business is largely controlled and tamed by the countervailing powers of big government and big labor, has been undermined during the past forty years: government in the U.S. now largely serves the needs of big business, and big labor is no longer so big. The reason for the failure of Galbraith's vision and hope to materialize is that he paid insufficient attention to two major Wobbly themes: the intensity of the class struggle between workers and the owners of the means of production; and the fact that capitalism is inherently a worldwide system. Richard McIntyre and Michael Hillard (Chapter 7) offer a radical critique and alternative to the traditional study of industrial relations (IR) in the U.S. The argument builds on their earlier critiques of the IR field, which stresses the importance of understanding class both in the workplace and in the household, including how crises in class relations in both sites can become intertwined. They combine a critical history of the field and its relationship to recent heterodox thinking (radical, Marxist, and feminist) with analyses of the rise of immaterial labor and crises in the household. They conclude by suggesting a provocative image: that of a new opportunity to "stand the IWW on its head" by pursuing a new and very different set of gender identities and class conflicts as the basis for a new solidarity.

Chapters 8, 9, and 10 utilize radical institutional, Marxian, regulationalist, and post-Keynesian approaches to examine particular labor issues: labor in transition economies, offshoring and outsourcing production, and the impact of the restructuring of the Brazilian banking industry on the Bank Workers' Union movement. In Chapter 8, John Marangos argues that institutional changes in labor relations, employment policy, and labor law were crucial for a successful transition from a centrally administered economy to a market economy in Russia, the former Soviet Union, and Eastern Europe. Concurrently with economic restructuring, the labor market in the transition economies has been characterized by rising unemployment, declining real wages, increasing polarization of income and wealth, growing poverty, and a reduction in life expectancy. Marangos adopts a radical institutional approach to develop an understanding of the changing workers' rights and working conditions during the transition process. The introduction of market relations and the development of a foreign-corporate-dominated economy required the simultaneous development of myth and emulation in supporting the ceremonial and pecuniary side of the institutional dichotomy. A process of disembeddedment had to be initiated in the transition economies to allow market economic relationships to displace custom, trust, morals, and culture. Therefore, the key elements of the economic system of culture, history, working rules, conflict, power, inequality, and government are important in determining labor's position during transition.

Claude Pottier (Chapter 9) analyzes the expansion of offshore production and its impact on the situation of labor. He argues that standard analyses of neoliberalism take insufficient account of the impact of globalization on labor and the effects of global organization of firms. Pottier advances and develops the hypothesis that outsourcing and offshoring is really a form of global labor arbitrage and it represents a new era of capitalism; and he then presents evidence to support the hypothesis Given that multinationals use global labor arbitrage to manage their workforce Pottier concludes the chapter with a review of worker-friendly alternatives to oppose that strategy. Finally, in Chapter 10, Maria Madi, José Ricardo Gonçalves, and José Dari Krein argue that the recent transformations in labor relations enhanced challenges to collective negotiations in the Brazilian Bank Workers' Union movement that has always played a strong role in protecting workers' interests during the modernization process. The authors explore and develop an interpretation of the impacts of the recent structural changes in Brazilian banking industry on Brazilian society and particularly on the Brazilian Bank Workers' Union. Since the 1990s, the banking industry has adopted flexibilization strategies, such as outsourcing, organizational innovations, and a new policy of labor relations. As a result, the industry has been characterized by job reduction, high turnover, redefinition of bank workers' abilities and skills, besides the emergence of new forms of labor control and remuneration patterns centered on individual performance. In a framework of changing social conditions, Madi, Gonçalves, and Krein point out that the Bank Workers' Union Movement in contemporary Brazil faces a process of redefinition of the strategies inside the category of bank workers. The tensions observed between the changing labor relations and the trends in the collective negotiations characterize the current role and scope of the Brazilian Bank Workers' Union movement.

There is, of course, much more that could be written on the subject. For example, the labor process and social structures of accumulation traditions, which were absent at the conference, have much to contribute. Moreover, the conference from which this collection emerged included analysis of contemporary efforts to bring radical economics into contemporary labor struggles and popular education, explored the implications of economic theory for union structure and cross-border organizing, and explored other radical traditions within heterodox economics. We have striven here to collect papers that can speak both to economists and to those in the labor movement, and that point to fruitful ways in which these radical heterodox traditions have engaged and continue to engage each other and with the labor movement. Both kinds of engagement will lead to further theoretical development and to the broadening of the community of heterodox economics so that its membership will include professional economists as well as labor educators, union negotiators, and rank-and-file workers. These twin developments would clearly constitute advancement in heterodox economics. But advancing heterodox economics is not enough; the world needs to be changed as well. We hope that the chapters in this volume do both.

Notes

1 The leading histories of the IWW include Paul Brissenden, *The IWW: A Study of American Syndicalism* (New York: Columbia University Press 1919); Joseph R. Conlin (ed.), *At the Point of Production: The Local History of the IWW* (Westport: Greenwood Press 1981); Melvyn Dubofsky, *We Shall Be All* (Chicago: Quadrangle 1969); Philip Foner, *The Industrial Workers of the World, History of the Labor Movement, Vol. 4* (New York: International Publishers 1966); Patrick Renshaw, *The Wobblies* (New York: Doubleday 1967); and Salvatore Salerno, *Red November, Black November: Culture and Community in the IWW* (Albany: State University of New York Press 1989). The IWW tells its own story in Fred Thompson and Jon Bekken, *The IWW: Its First 100 Years* (Cincinnati: Industrial Workers of the World 2006).

2 This is the current language of the IWW Preamble, which has been amended twice since the union's founding. The original 1905 language spoke of the need for workers to "take and hold that which they produced by their labor, through an economic organization of the working class without affiliation with any political party." This was amended in 1908 to read: "a struggle must go on until the workers of the world organize as a class, take possession of the earth and the machinery of production, and abolish the wage system." Eight decades later, the Preamble was amended to the form quoted in the text in response to growing ecological concerns.

3 The address of the IWW is P.O. Box 23085, Cincinnati, Ohio 45223, U.S.A. Its website is http://www.iww.org (accessed February 20, 2008).

1 Senex's *Letters on Associated Labour* and *The Pioneer*, 1834

A syndicalist political economy in the making

Noel Thompson

It is often assumed that British syndicalism had its roots in the late nineteenth and early twentieth centuries and, in terms of its organization and institutional expression, that cannot be disputed.[1] Yet the articulation of a neo-syndicalist political economy can be found much earlier in a remarkable series of fourteen short pieces entitled *Letters on Associated Labour* in a working-class paper – *The Pioneer; or Grand National Consolidated Trades' Union Magazine* – which ran from March 15 to July 5, 1834.[2] *The Pioneer* itself was published weekly from September 7, 1833 to July 5, 1834 and its peak circulation of *c*. 20,000 far outstripped that of most stamped and unstamped papers of the period.[3]

The paper, and the *Letters*, were published during a period of acute industrial and political tension and unrest. Specifically, the period saw an increasing power over workshops and independent producers by capitalist middlemen through their control of credit, the supply of material and semi-finished goods and the distribution of finished products; a control that seems to have produced an alteration in "the tempo and quality of workshop life" (Joyce 1990: 155). It was also the case that if the mechanization associated with rapid industrialization in the early nineteenth century did not always, indeed rarely, displaced labor, it did, at the same time, exert significant downward pressure on prices and wages as well as forcing an acceleration in the pace of production within the putting-out system: something that created major problems for certain groups, most notably handloom weavers, in the silk, cotton, and wool industries and the framework knitters in that of hosiery (Samuel 1977: 17). These problems were also further exacerbated by the economic instability that was an endemic feature of British capitalism during the three decades that followed the end of the Napoleonic wars.[4]

In such a context the growth of a manufacturing system still characterized by small workshops, and the "putting out" of work to independent producers, seems to have made for the proliferation of "dishonorable" or "scurf" masters and middle-men who sweated their workforce with increasing intensity and who sought to remove or circumvent legislative restrictions that had previously been placed on their activities as regards prices, wages, apprentices, and female labor.[5] More specifically, the Napoleonic and immediate post-Napoleonic War period witnessed a dismantling of that regulatory, legislative framework that had governed many trades since the Statute of Artificers of 1563. Its wage regulation and apprenticeship clauses were repealed in 1813 and 1814 respectively, while the Spitalfields Act of 1773, that had regulated wages and prices in the London silk-weaving industry, did not long survive the end of the Wars, being repealed in 1824.[6] Such developments not only adversely affected remuneration but also eroded the independence, status, security, respectability, and self-respect that many artisans had previously enjoyed (Prothero 1979: 27).

The early 1830s in particular were also years of economic depression and were marked too by a sense of betrayal among those of the working class who had supported the movement for political reform, only to find that the Great Reform Act of 1832 left the vast majority of the population disenfranchised. Moreover, this period also saw the rapid growth of a cooperative movement inspired by Owenite ideas, of "equitable labour exchanges" in London, Manchester, and Glasgow where goods were denominated and exchanged according to labor time, a communitarianism that received both theoretical and practical expression,[7] the emergence of a vibrant, illegal, "unstamped" working-class press, and trade union activity on a scale, and of a kind, that had not been seen before and was not to be seen again in Britain until the new unionism of the late 1880s and early 1890s.[8]

In this latter regard the period saw the emergence of national and general unions such as the National Association for the Protection of Labour of the cotton textile workers, the Operative Builders' Union, the Potters' Union, and the Grand National Consolidated Trades Union. And while the phenomenon of general unions was not altogether new, what distinguished these working-class organizations was their geographical extent and organizational sophistication.[9]

Further, proponents of these trade unions, when reflecting on the causes of, and remedies for, their discontents, drew increasingly upon an anti-capitalist and socialist political economy that found expression in the work of writers such as John Gray, Robert Owen, William Thompson, Thomas Hodgskin, "Bronterre" O'Brien, and others, and also through the medium of working-class papers such as *The Pioneer*, the *Poor Man's Guardian*, the *Crisis*, the *Voice of the West Riding*, the *Herald to the Rights of Industry* and the *Voice of the People*.[10] That said, while the *Letters on Associated Labour* reflect elements of the critique of capitalism formulated by these writers, they are nonetheless distinctive in terms of the force, precision, and emphasis of that critique and, more obviously, in terms of their particular conception of a socialist alternative.

The immediate context of the *Letters on Associated Labour* was a prolonged struggle (1833 to 1834) of the silk weavers of Derby, who were locked out by their employers for refusing to abjure membership of a trade union; this being one aspect of a counterattack by employers and the state which also saw the imprisonment and subsequent deportation of six Dorchester laborers (the Tolpuddle martyrs) for membership of a trade union of agricultural workers. The struggle of the Derby weavers was ultimately unsuccessful but it was the cause of major social antagonism. "War! War! War!" declared one headline in *The Pioneer* (January 25, 1834), "Labor has declared war against capital." And it was a struggle too which elicited considerable support from workers and trade unionists in other parts of the country.

The *Letters* were published under the name of "Senex" and many commentators have speculated as to the identity of the author. A strong case has been made for James Morrison, the editor of *The Pioneer*,[11] but it has also been suggested that they may have been written by J.E. "Shepherd" Smith, the editor of the Owenite paper *The Crisis* (Stunt 2004). The problem with these suggestions is that in Letter XII the author refers to him/herself as having a life "now counted more than three score years,"[12] whereas the birth dates of J.E. Smith (1801) and James Morrison (1802) put them in their early thirties when the pieces were written. In consequence, one writer has argued that the *Letters* were jointly written by Morrison and Smith who combined their ages to provide the requisite three score (Oliver 1954: 364). However, for a number of reasons this is not altogether convincing.

First, the *Letters* display a remarkable internal coherence and consistency that militate against the notion of joint authorship. Second, there seems no obvious reason why the "fiction" of single authorship should be maintained to a point that involved such elaborate subterfuge. Third, while it is possible to detect in the writing of Morrison ideas, particularly on the prescriptive side, that clearly parallel those to be found in the *Letters*,[13] the same cannot be said of the work of J.E. Smith. It is also the case that the author of the letters refers in one to an incapacitating illness and Morrison died in 1835 shortly after the paper folded.

That said, there is a letter written by Smith on March 28, 1834 that refers to an article "respecting *Blackwoods*" as having been penned by Morrison but "concocted" by the two men, and the second letter does indeed open with an attack on *Blackwoods Magazine*. The article also contains the sole reference to *Blackwoods* in *The Pioneer* around this time.[14] So it may be the case that the *Letters* were the product of two minds and one pen; though the problem still remains as to why Morrison felt he needed to portray himself as a sexagenarian and embrace the pseudonym of "Senex."[15]

But questions of authorship aside, what of the political economy of the *Letters*? The first thing to note is that the pieces are informed by a particular periodization of history and a distinctive understanding of the forces making for historical progress; progress seen in terms of the extension of humanity's productive power. Thus "there [we]re three states of labor – 'enslaved or compulsory labour,' 'hireling or marketable labour' and 'free or associated labour.'"[16] As to this progression, the primary focus of Senex was on the contemporary transition from "hireling" to "associated labor" and this was seen as the "natural" outcome of the economic forces which were precipitating the demise of the former. As Senex wrote (May 24, 1834, Letter IX, *The Pioneer*),

> labour is at the present period in its transition between hireling labour – in which the life of a man is sold piecemeal, by the day or the week, at or below the market price, and associated labour – in which men will, and must, act together for the mutual benefit of the whole body of the association.

It was

> a revolution silently going on, which is preparing us [the working class] to take our turn . . . in the affairs of the world; and we are watching its progress ready to seize upon every advantage it may offer us. Let it proceed quietly – we are not impatient – we know our turn is coming, and *must come*.
>
> (June 28, 1834, Letter XIV)

Like later syndicalists, therefore, Senex saw human progress in terms of the abolition of the wages system and an end to the commodification of labor.

The transition from "hireling" to "associated" labor was ineluctable. The "system of associated labor is the natural and regular offspring of the times in which we live; it is the unavoidable result of the concurrence of circumstances which belong to the present state of civilization" (April 5, 1834, Letter III). This was so because the existing economic and institutional structures that characterized "hireling labor" were simply not equipped to cope with contemporary developments that were enhancing the productive power available to humanity. As Senex put it,

> the plenty producible by the industry and ingenuity of man, acting by means of machinery, continually improving in creative power, has no assignable limit; but the profit derivable to individual capitalists, in the creation of such plenty, has its limit – a limit at which the capital of the kingdom has long since arrived, and where it is struggling by every sort of temporary manoeuvre to save itself from being crushed and crumbled to atoms.

In consequence,

> manufacture, with its increased powers of production, and its daily extending powers of communication, will go on in a course of temporary employment, diminished profits, depressed wages, misery, ruin and discontent, until the generous and Christian system of Associated Labour shall be generally adopted, or turbulent revolution overwhelm the civilized world.[17]

The contemporary economy was characterized by glutted markets, mass unemployment, falling profits, underutilized productive capacity, and the impoverishment of significant sections of the working class. Only a system of "associated labour" would enable this state of affairs to be rectified, and allow increased powers of production, particularly those furnished by mechanization, to be fully utilized for the benefit of the community. It was "now easily demonstrable . . . that more commodities . . . can be produced with facility in the country, or brought into it by means of commerce, than all its inhabitants can consume" (May 24, 1834, Letter IX). But such potential abundance could only be realized once economic activity was organized on the basis of "associated labour."

The more general critique of contemporary economic and social arrangements embedded in the *Letters* is less distinctive and parallels that to be found in the work of a number of early nineteenth-century socialist and anti-capitalist writers.

Thus labor was considered to be the sole source of value. Capital, both fixed and circulating, was seen as necessary for production, but was the product of labor:

> We know that the operative manufacturer, and, in fact, the labourer of every description, requires sustenance, raw materials and tools. These are derived from the reserved produce of former labour which is termed capital. The amount of capital in this country is very great; but, brethren, it was you that gave it existence.[18]

Yet if labor gave existence to capital, and if it was the source of all wealth, its ownership and control was in the hands of others. And in the *Letters* of Senex one finds as powerfully expressed as anywhere in the anti-capitalist and socialist literature of the period the idea of the commoditization of labor. "Wages," he wrote "is a term of purchase; it means the piece meal purchase of your blood, and bones, and brains at weekly payments; it is the present name for the *Saturday's market purchase of man woman and child*!" (June 14, 1834, Letter XII). Moreover, "capitalists," and the term is used by Senex consistently throughout the *Letters*, "only b[ought] so much of a man as they can make any profit of; they will have the best joints, the best days of his life; all the rest may be thrown to the dogs; or rot in a ditch, or a workhouse, just as it may happen" and they "combine[d] together in order to compel you to dispose of your labour at the lowest possible price."[19]

It was this commoditization that gave capitalists their power over labor and it was only once it had been ended that labor could be liberated. That would require the economic powerlessness of labor to be addressed; something which Senex was clear could not be done by political means. In this regard he was to distance himself from those who advocated universal suffrage, not because he was opposed to such an extension of the franchise, but because he believed that it became effectual only once economic power resided with the working class. He was therefore adamant that "social must precede political liberty." Until that occurred the House of Commons would remain what it was, namely a "market-clerk," administering and regulating "a market of which the profitmongering capitalists have control" (June 14, 1834, Letter XII).

Mere political revolutions had done nothing to improve the material condition of labor. Those of 1688 and 1789 did not advance

> the real interests of the labouring classes, in either France or England; and were one of these government revolutions to take place at the present period . . . the producers would not . . . be benefited by it . . . whether this party holds the helm of power, or that party with large promises of attention to the interests of the people endeavours by our assistance to seize upon the management of the same helm, we must continue as we were before – the ill-paid servants, the hard-working slaves of the consuming and non-productive classes of the state.
> (June 28, 1834, Letter XIV)

The aftermath of 1832 also seemed to confirm this view that little could be expected from simply widening the franchise, eliminating rotten boroughs, and removing government pensioners and placemen. Such activity merely "reform[ed] the decorative parts of society, whilst the foundation is suffered to remain unsound and rotten."[20]

What also comes across powerfully in the *Letters* is a conception of class antagonism and a concept of class that is economically rooted. The historiography of the struggles of early nineteenth-century labor has tended, over the past three decades, to question the emergence of a language of class during this period. Rather, many intellectual and social historians have emphasized the continuities with the discourse of late eighteenth-century political radicalism that are to be found in the language of those who articulated the interests of the laboring classes; a language which, such commentators have argued, defined these interests against those of a corrupt political establishment rather than against those of a capitalist class (see Jones 1983).

Yet such a denial of the existence of an early nineteenth-century language of class is one that is difficult to reconcile with what one finds in *The Pioneer* in general and the *Letters* in particular. For the latter are certainly characterized by the notion of an emerging class identity and growing class antagonism; ideas which became ever more prominent as the industrial conflict of the 1833 to 1834 period increased in intensity and moved towards its climax. Thus capitalist employers were seen as having "a close instinctive sense of their own interest" and as acting in "combination" "to depreciate and keep down wages" (May 10, 1834, Letter VII).

Labor too was seen as acquiring an increasing sense of its common interests, though the nature of its economic position often militated against the kind of reflection necessary to engender this. For, with laborers "compelled to sell their time for the purpose of labour, in order to subsist, at the very lowest price they can obtain, they have none left for those mental improvements by which men are principally distinguished from the inferior animals" (ibid.). It was this absence of the opportunity for reflection, this "want of the habit of thinking and of considering the proper means of benefiting his condition," which was seen as "the chief reason" why many among the working classes had failed to join the unions that were emerging and which were seen by Senex as both the catalyst and the agents for the transformation of society. But he was also adamant that, "as knowledge extends, the habit of thinking and of acting with the majority of the class to which we belong" would "extend . . . in a greater ratio . . . As intelligence spreads this feeling of the necessity of men who have the same interests acting with one mind, spreads also" (ibid.). Another contributor to *The Pioneer* was equally sanguine that a consciousness of its common interest and historic destiny was emerging among the working class. "Your class is the first which has arisen in the majesty of its strength to assert its own independence."[21]

Those comprising other classes could not be trusted. The Reform Act of 1832 was one indication, but only one, that while the middle classes might join with the working class to pursue their political and other interests, once these had been realized, antipathy and antagonism would again prevail. Only through its own efforts, therefore, could the working class effect a transformation of its social position.

> Did any of you ever know a rich man speak of you respectfully? Did any of you ever hear a man of power applaud a single virtue you possess. . . . In any struggle who befriends us? In any danger who protects us? In any ignominy who pities us? Trust none who is a grade above our class . . . trust none of them.[22]

It is difficult to reconcile all this with the notion of a "continuity of discourse."

The idea of a class struggle, increasing in intensity, was also purveyed in the *Letters* and *The Pioneer* more generally. Thus:

> the capitalist [was] continually accumulating and the working man continually going down; and this will continue to operate until the injured labourer, galled by intolerable oppression, shall rise with a determination that nothing can quell, and effect a dreadful revolution.[23]

The gulf between classes was unbridgeable; the interests of capital and labor irreconcilable. Capital and labor were locked into a conflict that could only be resolved by the victory of one over the other. "The struggle between profits and wages" would not "cease until wages are completely victorious, or the manufactory is to the productive labourers the same thing as the workhouse."[24] As we have seen, for Senex, natural forces were at work which would ensure that labor would indeed prevail.

It was the activity of the working class seizing the opportunities provided by these natural forces which would effect the transition to a system of associated labor. Specifically, during the course of the strikes and lockouts that characterized the 1833 to 1834 period, particularly in the textile industry, trade unions had resorted to employing some of their members to produce articles for sale. Moreover, there was evidence of "combinations form[ing] . . . to produce for themselves and each other, and modes of exchange arranged to prevent the capitalist cheating them out of the fruits of their labour."[25] Initially these were seen as providing financial support for those who were out of work and as a means of securing some return on that outlay. But it was such practical expression of working-class solidarity that undoubtedly suggested the possibility of trade unions acting in concert to create what would, in effect, be a parallel economy; an economy in which enterprises would be owned and managed by workers and produce goods that would be exchanged with and consumed by other trade unionists.

This idea of an economy constituted on a radically different basis from that which existed is clearly expressed at a number of points in the *Letters*. We must," wrote Senex, "begin with founding manufactories and trades; we must open shops, and deal entirely with one another; and we shall afterwards proceed to the building of ships, and to both the cultivation and importation of corn." Elsewhere Senex wrote of his vision of "large partnership manufactories and trad[ing] among [them]selves, upon a pure republican principle."[26] These would create the basis for that system of "free or associated labor" which Senex viewed as the next stage in humanity's exploitation of the material world for the satisfaction of its needs. The vision then is essentially a syndicalist one, of a decentralized, socialist economy where decision-making resided with trade unionists in the enterprises and trades over which they had established ownership and control.

Such a vision of the socialist commonwealth was in marked contrast to that purveyed by many Owenite socialists of the period, and in particular by Robert Owen himself. Thus writers such as Owen and William Thompson (1830) conceived of socialism in essentially communitarian terms; communities that were to be largely self-sufficient and, therefore, primarily agrarian; "new moral worlds" whose autarky would protect them from most of the corruptions of competitive capitalism. They might exchange with other communities whatever surpluses they produced but such exchanges would be relatively unimportant in relation to the satisfaction of their total needs and, in this context, it was rare among such communitarian socialists for much consideration to be given to the business, and possible benefits, of international trade (see Thompson 1988: 86–102). Indeed such trade, in necessitating contact with the old immoral world, was, as far as possible, to be eschewed.

In marked contrast the vision of Senex manifestly encompassed the benefits that could be derived from large-scale industrial production, the social division of labor and domestic and international commerce. Even where trade unionists where exhorted to "get land [and] withdraw [them]selves from large towns," it was not to establish autarkic, agrarian, cooperative communities but to become "*manufacturing* colonists."[27] The advantages of the social and international division of labor were identified and embraced. In this regard Senex's socialism was outward-looking, even entrepreneurial, rather than inward-looking and autarkic. It was also a vision of socialism that was more in keeping with the emerging industrial realities of early nineteenth-century Britain than that advanced by many writers of the period.

It was, indeed, with an eye to the benefits of such an economy that Senex discussed, and at some length, the means by which an expansion of equitable exchanges between producer-owned enterprises might take place. Here he highlighted the need for trade unionists to "establish a bank and circulating medium."[28]

> The labourers of the country who create everything, ought also to create the money, and then they could always have a sufficient quantity to give them a free exchange of labour. . . . If the productive classes would have their own paper money to represent the value of the various kinds of wealth actually made, and to enable them without difficulty to exchange one sort for another, they would raise their condition in six months, to a higher state of comfort and prosperity than was ever before experienced in the world.[29]

In effect, a socialized banking system would play a vital role in integrating the various productive units and enterprises which would constitute a socialist economy characterized by decentralized decision-making.

Such ideas were not entirely original. John Gray (1831), in his *The social system, a treatise on the principle of exchange*, had mooted the possibility of just such a banking system and medium of exchange. He also saw it in terms of a socialist economy that embraced contemporary industrialization and the productive capacity and potentialities that was creating. Yet Gray's notion of socialism was one that more nearly approximated to that of a centrally planned economy; with the banking system integral to such a planning process. It also lacked any notion of the existing social forces that might be utilized in the construction of a socialist alternative. In that regard it was a vision abstracted from history; one that derived inspiration from the optimistic rationalism of the Enlightenment and which would triumph, therefore, by way of the persuasive and compelling logic of the arguments of *The social system*, rather than the historically rooted struggle of a working class.[30]

These economic arrangements outlined in the *Letters* would allow a number of things. First, as Senex saw it, they would ensure that labor, collectively, would receive its full product with no abstraction of rent and profits. Second, exchanges could, and would, proceed on an equitable basis, both with other unionists and also "*with the industrious and skilful workers of other countries*."[31] Third, it would be a system that would allow labor the freedom to develop and fulfill its creative potentialities. This sense of the need for structures that would permit human fulfilment was a compelling theme in the writings of Senex, and with it went a concomitant sense of the labor alienation that characterized the existing system of production.[32] As he saw it, in their words and in their deeds, organized labor was already telling

> the proud and perverse capitalists that you [are] MEN, and that, instead of them cramming you into their narrow system, in which it [is] impossible for you as human beings to exist, you would have a system of your own, made in every respect conformable to your proper dimensions as men (March 15, 1834, Letter I).

Fourth, production could proceed with reference to the "convenience and comfort . . . of human beings of sensibility and rational faculties," rather than in response to the capricious demands of the rich for "excess and luxury" (June 7, 1834, Letter XI). Finally, like the guild socialists and syndicalists of a later period, Senex and other writers in the *The Pioneer* argued that the system they proposed would end "the folly and insanity" involved "in making their labour a marketable commodity, to be bought and sold by the vicious and crafty."[33]

As to the reward of labor employed in "partnership manufactories," "manufacturing colonies" or collectively organized "trades," various expedients for determining this were suggested. One writer proposed "a grand COURT OF ARBITRATION to establish the price and value of labour of every kind."[34] Another writer suggested that remuneration could be determined by the "trades" themselves, which could both "creat[e] wealth for their mutual benefit and distribut[e] that wealth in just proportions to each member of the fraternity." Such organizations, enjoying autonomy in terms of decision-making, and collectively ordering both the production and equitable distribution of wealth, were seen by this writer as:

> near an approach to perfection as we can make. It is the ultimatum (*sic*) of the progress of society; the beau ideal which we ought at all times to have . . . before us; a stimulant to exertion and a compass to direct our movements.[35]

However, whatever means were used to establish the just wage for labor, the crucial point was that its reward would no longer be determined in the marketplace, where the dice were loaded in favor of the capitalist buyer. The aim should be to "banish the word wages from the language and consign it, with the word slavery, to histories and dictionaries" (June 14, 1834, Letter XII).

Although Senex and others used the language of revolution and although, as we have seen, they emphasized the antagonism of interests which existed between the capitalist class and their employees, the expectation was that the transition to a decentralized socialism could be peacefully accomplished. And there was no suggestion in the *Letters* of strike action as a means of destroying the power of the capitalist class and effecting a transfer of the ownership of existing productive capacity to labor. As will be noted below, such productive capacity was to be acquired by peaceful means. And while some contemporaries advanced the idea of a general strike, or "grand national holiday," and while a "general" strike of trade unionists had occurred in Glasgow in 1820, the idea and this action were linked to the establishment of a "national convention" which would sweep away the existing, corrupt, *political order* by forcing the enfranchisement of "the people."[36] At this historical juncture it was not therefore an idea that was taken up and used by the trade unionists to effect a social transformation and there is no mention of it in the *Letters*; though Senex would certainly have been aware of the concept and the work of William Benbow with whom it was associated.[37]

For Senex, the major obstacle in the way of effecting the changes he sought was that of instilling in the working class the requisite consciousness of their material interests and an understanding of how these interests might best be realized. Here Senex was aware that it was necessary for the working class to transcend the narrow, economistic consciousness of the trade unionist that tended to govern their actions, and to circumscribe their ambitions. He was not opposed to the traditional role that trade unions assumed in defending the interests of their members. "I do not say that Unions for keeping up wages are not highly necessary, but they do not tend to the ultimate view of the unionists. They are temporary preventatives or alleviations of evils" (May 24, 1834, Letter IX). Strikes and other forms of industrial action should be supported but they should not be allowed to obscure what unionists should ultimately be in the business of doing, namely acquiring the productive capacity that would render them independent of existing economic arrangements.

Senex was aware that:

> in the minds of many, a scheme of *general trade unity*, moving in all its various branches as manufacturers, mechanics, agriculturists, and traders to one great end – the general benefit, still appears to be extravagant. The conception, say some, is too much in advance of the present era (April 5, 1834, Letter III).

But as he saw it, contemporary developments were already anticipating the era of "free or associated labour" and a recognition that labor represented the sole source of wealth was proceeding apace. A consciousness of this, he believed, would soon result in the acquisition of productive capacity by the workers; a development that would, inevitably, gather momentum as the surplus that previously went to capitalists and landowners as profits and rents accrued to the trade unions from the productive activity which they had initiated. As for the means of production that remained in private hands, where labor was employed in creating and using its own assets, the owners of land and capital would be powerless to exploit the resources they possessed. In effect that property would be rendered worthless and might, therefore, be more profitably handed over than retained.

It was in this context that Senex suggested that "capitalists, particularly the small ones," would "begin to perceive the wisdom of coalescing with us, and of bringing their funds into partnership with our labour." In this regard he also suggested that by way of an incentive to allow the socialization of their capital, "every 2000 *l.* should be reckoned equivalent to the labour of one man." In effect, therefore, Senex embraced the notion of compensation; those acceding to the public ownership of their capital receiving a return equivalent to that of a fixed-interest security.[28] Moreover, in addition to productive capacity acquired in this way, the laboring class would have that which it already possessed and that which, as noted, trade unions would purchase with the surplus that accrued to them from independent productive activity.

Despite the industrial conflict that characterized the period, Senex's expectation was, therefore, that the transition to the socialist economic arrangements he envisaged could be peacefully made. The compelling logic of the arguments he was propounding, a working class increasingly united and conscious of its interests, a capitalist class progressively demoralized, impoverished and redundant in terms of its contribution to productive activity, the intensifying pressures for it to relinquish its ownership and control of the means of production, increasing awareness of the growing crisis afflicting the existing system of production and distribution, the burgeoning self-confidence of working-class trade unionists in the management of productive activity: all would combine to ensure the ineluctable emergence of a decentralized socialism.

But what of the state? As we have seen, Senex was clear that without social rights and social power, political power was of little significance for the working class. He did not, therefore, "look to political influence as a means to any change in our condition" (June 7, 1834, Letter XI). That said, Senex accepted that the demand of political radicals for "universal suffrage" should be supported.

> We must . . . have universal suffrage; and, in the mean time, we must prepare ourselves to hold it, and enjoy it; but we must not be so weak as to imagine that the possessors of property will grant it as a boon to those who possess nothing but their labour.

Or again,

> We are not free, we cannot be free until we have universal suffrage; but in the spirit and practice of union, we must make it our own, and use it advantageously to ourselves, and to the nation at large . . . we must never lose sight of our want of a political position in this great and powerful country in which we constitute the great productive class (June 14, 1834, Letter XII).

But universal suffrage and its effective utilization would come after the acquisition of economic power. For, at that point, and only at that point, would the House of Commons "be our own."[39] As an editorial in *The Pioneer* of December 28, 1833 (italics in original) saw the causal sequence:

> we are determined that REFORM shall commence from within. We govern within ourselves, and conceive it to be a duty to acquaint ourselves of the principles of government, consisting simply in good internal regulations. *We feel that to regulate trade, or the several branches of labour by which we live, will most speedily regulate government. These are the means we should adopt for the end and we hold them to be more powerful than petitioning. We know that universal suffrage may be obtained by these means.*

The actual mechanics of this progression are unclear, but Senex and others probably envisaged the eventual absorption of governmental authority by an institution such as the Grand National Consolidates Trades' Union (June 7, 1834, Letter XI). Certainly this was what was envisaged by the editor of *The Pioneer* (October 12, 1833) when he wrote of the GNCTU that:

> when it is sufficiently organised . . . it will gradually draw into its vortex all the commercial interest of the country, and, in so doing, it will become, by its own self-acquired importance, a most influential, we might almost say dictatorial, part of the body politic. When this happens we have gained universal suffrage; for if every member of the union be a constituent, and the union itself become a vital and influential member of the state, it instantly erects itself into a House of Trades, which must supply the place of the present House of Commons, and direct the commercial affairs of the country, according to the will of the trades who compose the associations of industry.

Others writing in the *Pioneer* saw things in a similar light.

> See, sir, into what position this mode of pursuing things resolves itself. Every trade has its internal government in every town; a certain number of towns comprise a district, and delegates from the trades in each town form a quarterly district government; delegates from the districts form an Annual Parliament; and the King of England becomes President of the Trades' Unions![40]

The General Union, comprising as it would a multiplicity of unions, each of which would regulate the economic affairs of the trade, industry or sector of industry over which it had secured control, would eventually constitute a true House of *Commons* to replace that which served not the commons but the interests of the capitalist and landowning classes. Or, as one anonymous contributor to the paper put it, such an institution would "supersede all the vacillating, profit-making, unprincipled legislatures, which have hitherto enriched the idle few, and bound in blind ignorance and destitution the industrious many."[41] Instead of political authority resting with the King in Parliament it would rest, in effect, with the King in the GNCTU.

As to the House of Lords this need not be abolished but could become, in effect, a Ministry of Science and Culture composed of:

> the delegates of all of the rest of the community . . . the rich and the noble. . . . The aristocracy have a species of information which is peculiar to themselves . . . they are not acquainted with any particular art, but they are generally conversant with subjects of taste, literature and science, and all the refinements of intellect; an ample and most important field of study, and demanding in a most pre-eminent degree, the paternal regard and superintendence of the legislature (June 7, 1834, Letter XI).

So, while the Commons or House of Trades would wield economic and political power, the rich and the noble could be usefully, and safely, left with the role of enhancing the cultural tone of society.

It is important to stress that, in terms of the socialist economic literature of early-nineteenth-century Britain, the *Letters on Associated Labour* are unique. As mentioned above, they embody a socialist political economy radically different from the dominant contemporary strain of communitarianism socialism. There are parallels with Gray's (1831) *The social system* – particularly in relation to the pivotal role to be played by a public banking system. In terms too of its emphasis upon the socialization of the means of production and the decentralization of economic decision-making, there are some marked similarities with John Francis Bray's *Labour wrongs and labour's remedy*, though this was not published until some five years later in 1839.[42] However, what is distinctive about the *Letters on Associated Labour*, some of *The Pioneer* editorials and some other contributions to the paper is their emphasis on the active role of the working class in its own emancipation through the medium of trade unions. In the final analysis it was the struggle, the class struggle, waged by means of the workers' own organizations, which would be the crucial precipitant of socialist transformation. Such a struggle had the forces of history on its side but Senex is clear that it still had to be waged, and waged too by a politically conscious working class. In this regard papers such as *The Pioneer* were seen as playing a crucial role.

The *Letters*, and other contributions to the paper, also address the question of the relationship between political and economic power; the nature of the existing relationship, and how it might be expected to develop over time in a socialist context. This is not unique in the British anti-capitalist and socialist literature of the period. Such a discussion may be found in the writing of Bronterre O'Brien in the *Poor Man's Guardian*, in the work of Thomas Hodgskin, and in that of J.F. Bray. However, these issues were rarely discussed with the kind of sophistication that is to be found in *The Pioneer*.

How then should we label this political economy? In its critique of the commodification of labor and determination to end the wage system, its emphasis on the transformative agency of trade unions, its prioritization of the winning of economic rather that political power, its embrace of worker ownership and the concomitant articulation of a socialism characterized by decentralized economic decision-making, there is much in the *Letters* and *The Pioneer* which is syndicalist. And the *Letters* have much in common with the subsequent program and position of the IWW.[43] Syndicalist too was their appreciation of a class struggle waged through the trades unions' active engagement with a capitalist class deemed to have material interests opposed to those of labor. And Senex was clear that it was this self-activity of the working class which would usher in a socialist transformation of the economy and society. That said, while Senex used the language of revolution and revolutionary transformation, the *Letters* saw the transference of productive capacity to worker ownership being effected by purchase and compensation. In that respect, and perhaps only in that respect, the *Letters* pointed to the reformist, Fabian shape of things to come. However, for the most part the *Letters on Associated Labour* may legitimately be categorized as a syndicalist political economy in the making.

By the spring of 1834 the strike of the Derby weavers had collapsed and the wave of industrial unrest of which it was a part had subsided, with many employees forced to sign what was termed the "Document" abjuring, for the future, trade union membership. More generally the currents of anti-capitalist and socialist thinking that had flowed with particular force in the late 1820s and early 1830s lost their potency, and the working-class papers which gave them popular currency declined in number and circulation from the mid-1830s. Echoes of the ideas in the *Letters* can be found in the mid-century period in works such as Aristarchus's 1842 *Internal free trade and capitalists trades' unions* and J. Frearson's 1855 *The relative rights and interests of the employer and employed*, a period which also saw a transient interest, in Britain, in producer cooperatives (Thompson 1988: 155–60, 135–54). But it was not really until the turn of the century that a syndicalist political economy was once again articulated in Britain.

It was in that *fin-de-siecle* period too that works such as Anton Menger's 1899 *The right to the whole produce of labour* rescued much of the literature of early nineteenth-century anti-capitalist and socialist political economy from the obscurity into which it had fallen for most of the previous half century. But it was to be another two decades, and the publication of Max Beer's (1921: 326–41) *A history of British socialism* in 1919, before any significant note was taken of Senex's *Letters* and before they were identified with a syndicalist tradition of political economy. Since then they have merited footnotes but rarely more than that in the secondary literature, though Claeys (1989: 194–207) has discussed the "syndicalist" (his quotes) ideas of both Morrison and J.E. "Shepherd" Smith in the context of Owenite socialism and social radicalism.

Yet these pieces are worthy of a significant place in the canon of British socialist political economy; not least because, whether by James Morrison or by J.E. "Shepherd" Smith, they were written by someone actively and self-consciously engaged in a struggle against a capitalist class bent on the destruction of a nascent trade union movement. It is particularly fitting therefore that their place in this canon should be recognized in this the centenary year of the IWW.

Notes

1 On late nineteenth and early twentieth-century British syndicalism see Holton (1976).
2 The *Letters* have been annotated and reprinted and may be found online at http://www.iww.org/culture/senex.
3 On the paper see Harrison, Woolven and Duncan (1977: 414). Newspapers in the period had to carry a government stamp that added 6d (2.5p) to their price and put them beyond the purchasing power of the working classes. In fact *The Pioneer*, like many working-class papers in the early 1830s, was sold illegally without the stamp at 1d (0.5p). An excellent account of the struggle to remove the newspaper stamp tax may be found in Wiener (1969).
4 "The numbers employed in the outwork industries multiplied enormously between 1780–1830. . . . Indeed we may say that large-scale, sweated output was as intrinsic to this revolution as factory production" (Thompson 1963). For a discussion of the difficulties and pressures being experienced by a number of London trades in this period see Goodway (1982) and Bythell (1969, 1978).
5 "This was a decade when all the determinants of the rate of exploitation (the duration, intensity, productivity and price of labour) took a decisive turn for the worse" (Linebaugh 1982: 327).
6 See Clapham (1916). The apprenticeship and wage-fixing clauses of the Statute of Artificers had, in any case, been continually broken by employers and were exceedingly difficult to enforce (Prothero 1979: 32).
7 One of the first such cooperative communities was established at Orbiston, near Motherwell, Scotland, in 1825.
8 On these see, among many other works, Harrison (1969), Claeys (1987), Oliver (1958), Hollis (1969), and Sykes (1988).
9 As one commentator has written of the NAPL: "The NAPL, simply as a general union, was not unprecedented but in size, geographical extent, duration, sophistication, ambitions and class outlook, it did represent much that was new. It was not merely a stage in an unchanging tradition of inter-union co-operation" (Prothero 1979: 185). On this point see also Oliver (1965: 85).
10 On early nineteenth-century, anti-capitalist and socialist political economy, and its popularization in the working-class press of the period, see Thompson (1984).
11 For its cogent articulation see Sever (1963).
12 *The Pioneer*, June 14, 1834, Letter XII.
13 In particular two editorials in *The Pioneer*: May 31 and June 7, 1834.
14 *The Pioneer*, March 28, 1834.
15 The letter written by J.E. Smith is referred to in Smith (1892: 98). I am indebted to Ben Maw for drawing my attention to this reference in Oliver's thesis. For short biographies of James Morrison and J.E. Smith see Rule (2004) and Stunt (2004).
16 *The Pioneer*, May 17, 1834, Letter VIII. There is strong evidence to suggest that "Bronterre" O'Brien's periodization of history in the *Progress and phases of human slavery* was influenced by Senex (Maw 2005: 135).
17 Ibid., April 12, 1834, Letter IV. This view of the realization of profit as an obstacle to the expansion of output was a salient feature of much of the Owenite socialist political economy of the period.

18 Ibid., March 22, 1834, Letter II. There are strong similarities here to the treatment of the issue in Thomas Hodgskin's (1825) *Labour defended against the claims of capital.*
19 April 5, 1834, Letter III; May, 1834, Letter VII.
20 Concord, "To Thomas Attwood," *The Pioneer*, October 5, 1833.
21 Concord, "To the operative builders," *The Pioneer*, September 14, 1833.
22 Editorial, March 22, 1834, p. 257.
23 Concord, "To the operatives," *The Pioneer*, October 12, 1833.
24 Anon., "Address to unionists," *The Pioneer*, June 7, 1834.
25 Concord, "To Thomas Attwood."
26 May 24, 1834, Letter IX; May 17, 1834, Letter VIII.
27 J. Mitchell, "To the Central Committee of London," *The Pioneer*, May 10, 1834, my emphasis.
28 No such institutions were envisaged in communitarian socialism.
29 Concord, "To the operative classes," *The Pioneer*, November 30, 1833.
30 These ideas were to be revised in two further works of a less socialist character: Gray (1842 and 1848).
31 *The Pioneer*, May 24, 1834, Letter IX, my emphasis.
32 As was to be generally the case in the anarchist political economy of the late nineteenth and early twentieth centuries. See Mathew Forstater, "Some notes on anarchist economic thought" (Chapter 3, this volume).
33 Concord, "To Thomas Attwood."
34 Anon., "To the United Lodges of Builders in Leamington," *The Pioneer*, November 23, 1833.
35 Editorial, May 10, 1834.
36 As Prothero (1974: 141) has put it, "the remedy was to restore the independence of the Commons (who controlled supply) by a wide (often manhood) suffrage, annual parliaments and the ballot to make them real representatives of the people." Their ideas paralleled those of William Cobbett, rather than those of contemporary anti-capitalist and socialist writers.
37 The idea was mooted by William Benbow (1832), one of the "ultra" radicals of the period, in a pamphlet, *Grand national holiday and congress of the productive classes*, published in the midst of the agitation over the Reform Bill. On this see Prothero (1974: 132–71).
38 Ibid., June 7, 1834, Letter XI. This was a view more in keeping with guild socialism than revolutionary syndicalism.
39 "Universal suffrage, with all its blessings, must be the immediate result of forcing upon the capitalists incessantly, in one form or another, our demands that wages shall be changed into a fair share of the profits resulting from our labour . . . a fair share of the goods we create" (June 14, 1834, Letter XII).
40 Concord, "To the master builders of England," September 28, 1833.
41 L.R., "Change of government," *The Pioneer*, February 15, 1834.
42 On these writers' conception of the socialist commonwealth see Thompson (1998: 93–110).
43 See Chapter 4.

References

Beer, M. (1921) *A history of British socialism*, London: National Labour Press.

Bythell, D. (1969) *The handloom weavers: A study in the English cotton industry during the Industrial Revolution*, London: Cambridge University Press.

Bythell, D. (1978) *The sweated trades, outwork in nineteenth-century Britain*, London: Batsford.

Claeys, G. (1987) *Machinery, money and the millennium, from moral economy to economic socialism, 1815–60*. London: Polity Press.

—— (1989) *Citizens and saints, politics and anti-politics in early British socialism*, Cambridge: Cambridge University Press.

Clapham, J.H. (1916) "The Spitalfields Acts, 1773–1824," *Economic Journal*, 26(4): 459–71.

Fetter, F. W. (1960) "Economic articles in *Blackwood's Magazine*," *Scottish Journal of Political Economy*, 7: 85–107, 213–31.

Goodway, D. (1982) *London Chartism, 1838–1848*, Cambridge: Cambridge University Press.

Gray, J. (1831) *The social system, a treatise on the principle of exchange*, Edinburgh.

—— (1842) *An efficient remedy for the distress of nations*, Edinburgh.

—— (1848) *A Lecture on the nature and use of money*, Edinburgh.

Harrison, J.F.C. (1969) *Robert Owen and the Owenites in Britain and America, The quest for the New Moral World*, London: Routledge & Kegan Paul.

Harrison, R., Woolven, G. and Duncan, R. (1977) *The Warwick guide to British labour periodicals, 1780–1970*, Hassocks: Harvester Press.

Hollis, P. (1969) *The pauper press: A study in working-class radicalism of the 1830s*, Oxford: Oxford University Press.

Holton, B. (1976) *British syndicalism, 1900–14: Myth and realities*, London: Pluto.

Jones, G. (1983) *Languages of class: Studies in English working-class history*, Cambridge: Cambridge University Press.

Joyce, P. (1990) "Work," in F. M. L. Thompson (ed.) *The Cambridge social history of Britain: People and their environment*, Vol. 2, pp. 131–84, Cambridge: Cambridge University Press.

Linebaugh, P. (1982) "Labour history without the labour process: A note on John Gast and his times," *Social History*, 7: 319–28.

Maw, B. (2005) "Bronterre O'Brien, class and the advent of democratic anti-capitalism: The social and political ideas of Chartism's schoolmaster," unpublished D.Phil. thesis, University of Swansea.

O'Brien, Bronterre (1885) *The rise, progress and phases of human slavery*, London.

Oliver, W.H. (1954) "Organisations and ideas behind the efforts to achieve a general union of the working classes in the early 1830s," unpublished D.Phil. thesis, University of Oxford.

—— (1958) "The labour exchange phase of the co-operative movement," *Oxford Economic Papers*, 10(3): 355–67.

—— (1965) "The Grand National Consolidated Trades' Union of 1834," *Economic History Review*, 17 (1): 77–95.

The Pioneer, or Grand National Consolidated Trades' Union Magazine, 1833–34, London.

Prothero, I. (1974) "William Benbow and the concept of the 'general strike,'" *Past and Present*, 63: 132–71.

—— (1979) *Artisans and politics, John Gast and his times*, Folkstone: Dawson.

Rule, J. (2004) "Morrison, James (1802–1835)," in H. Mathews and B. Harrison (eds) *Oxford Dictionary of National Biography*, Vol. 39, pp. 345–6, Oxford: Oxford University Press.

Samuel, R. (1977) "The workshop of the world," *History Workshop*, 3: 6–72.

Senex (1834) "Letters on associated labour," *Pioneer* (available online at http://www.iww.org/culture/senex).

Sever, J. (1963) "James Morrison and the *Pioneer*," unpublished monograph.

Smith, W.A. (1892) *Shepherd Smith, the Universalist*, London.

Stunt, T. (2004) "Smith, James Elishama [Shepherd Smith] (1801–1857)," in H. Matthews and B. Harrison (eds) *Oxford Dictionary of National Biography*, Vol. 51, pp. 192–3, Oxford: Oxford University Press.

Sykes, R. (1988) "Trade unionism and class consciousness: The 'revolutionary' period of general unionism, 1829–34," in J. Rule (ed.) *British trade unionism, 1750–1850*, pp. 178–99, London: Longman.

Thompson, E.P. (1963) *The making of the English working class*, London: Gollancz.

Thompson, N. (1984) *The people's science, the popular political economy of exploitation and crisis, 1816–34*, Cambridge: Cambridge University Press.

—— (1988) *The market and its critics, socialist political economy in nineteenth century Britain*, London: Routledge.

—— (1998) *The real rights of man, political economies for the working class, 1775–1850*, London: Pluto.

Thompson, W. (1830) *Practical directions for the speedy and economical establishment of communities*. London.

Wiener, J. (1969) *The war of the unstamped. The movement to repeal the British newspaper tax, 1830–36*, Ithaca, NY: Cornell University Press.

Wiener, J.H. (1970) *A descriptive find list of unstamped British periodicals, 1830–36*, London: The Bibliographical Society.

2 Peter Kropotkin's anarchist economics for a new society

Jon Bekken

Working-class movements in the late nineteenth and early twentieth century devoted extensive attention not only to developing a critique of capitalist exploitation but also to outlining their conception of a new society, free from exploitation. But while their critiques of actually existing capitalism shared much in common, their ideas of what a working-class economic system would look like were quite divergent. Many of these prescriptions have fallen by the wayside – no one, today, envisions reviving the Phalanx or the Time Store (even if the latter bears a striking similarity to the local currency movement which fascinates some activists)[1] – while we know most of the other traditions only from the lofty heights of the surviving books and polemics critiquing them written by the leading theoreticians of the day.

Anarchist economic traditions, too, to the extent that they are considered at all by modern-day practitioners of the high church of economics (Knowles 2004), are discussed in terms of Bakunin's collectivism, Proudhon's mutualism, the "individualism" of Josiah Warren or the communism of Peter Kropotkin. But to understand the anarchist economic tradition in these terms is to misunderstand it. Like other theoreticians in the anarchist movement, Kropotkin's economic ideas arose out of an engagement with the workers' movement of his day. They were not abstract principles derived from a lifetime of studying theorems, but rather represented an analysis that was honed in workers' struggles and debates, developed out of their lived experiences and their reflections upon them.

You can see these debates played out in the workers' press of the day, in pamphlets and union congresses that debated economic programs, as well as in the books of theorists like Kropotkin who offered more systematic exposition and support for principles that reflected the emerging consensus of the movement of which he was a part. As a result, Kropotkin's economic works read quite differently than those produced by his contemporaries. Kropotkin addresses questions such as how one might measure each worker's contribution to the creation of value concretely, by examining how one might understand such a question in relation to mining coal or building a house. The result is an economic analysis far more grounded in workers' lived experiences – and, hence, I would argue, far more radical – than may be found in writings by many contemporary radical thinkers.

In this chapter, I argue for the contemporary relevance of Kropotkin's economic analysis and vision, and suggest that contemporary political economists might benefit from following Kropotkin's example, reconnecting their economics to the rich texture of the production process and our diverse and evolving needs, rather than to the abstractions that dominate much of the field and often obscure more than they reveal.

Kropotkin's critique of political economy and capitalism

Kropotkin (1912 [1970]: 180) believed that the purpose of anarchist economics, indeed of any viable economic theory, was to satisfy human needs as efficiently as possible – to promote "the economical and social value of the human being." The task facing the political economist, then, was not the abstract theorizing that, then as now, dominated the field, but rather to study society's needs and the means available (either currently in use, or which could be developed with present knowledge) to meet them:

> It should try to analyze how far the present means are expedient and satisfactory . . . [and] should concern itself with the discovery of means for the satisfaction of these needs with the smallest possible waste of labor and with the greatest benefit to mankind in general.

Unlike most economists, Kropotkin (1912 [1970]: 177–9) insisted on subjecting economic theories to the same rigorous inquiry he would apply to any "scientific" theory:

> When certain economists tell us that "in a perfectly free market the price of commodities is measured by the amount of labor socially necessary for their production," we do not take this assertion on faith. . . . We not only find most of these so-called laws grossly erroneous, but maintain also that those who believe in them will themselves become convinced of their error as soon as they come to see the necessity of verifying the[m] . . . by quantitative investigation.

While there certainly was a relationship between the price of commodities and the amount of labor necessary for their production, Kropotkin argued, they were by no means proportional to one another as the Labor Theory of Value suggests. Nor had socialist economists troubled themselves to investigate whether or not the theory was true by gathering data to test the alleged relationship. Anyone who took the trouble to engage in such an investigation would quickly learn that the theory was false. We need only consider the price of oil or gold to realize that these prices are set not by the amount of labor power required to extract and process them, but rather by external market and social conditions.

Thus, when some Marxists maintain that all commodities – including labor power – are valued under capitalism at the cost of their reproduction under the most-productive available methods, they are reading Marx correctly. There is of course an element of truth to this, which is why the theory was widely accepted by the labor movement. A shirt that takes 60 minutes to make by hand, or five minutes to make by machine, will generally sell for the same price on the world market, although that price can be influenced by other factors such as styling, the prestige attendant to hand tailoring, or the logo affixed to it. However, this theory mistakes an association for a causal relationship. The commodity theory of labor suggests that only by increasing productivity can workers make possible an improved standard of living, and only through socialist revolution can those possible improvements be actually realized (instead of accruing to the capitalists and their hangers-on).[2]

This doctrine readily lends itself to the conclusion that wage struggles are essentially a waste of time and energy (or, at best, a school in which workers learn the futility of struggling for reforms), even though workers through hundreds of years have proved the opposite, and that the only alternative to competing against each other into ever-greater immiseration is a planned economy which can determine labor values and ensure their equitable distribution. But this doctrine is wholly false. I turn to Kropotkin's proof that wage levels have little to do with the cost of reproduction below, but the essential point is that wage levels – like the price of all commodities – are set not by the cost of production of goods or the amount of labor they require, but rather by the relative economic, military and social power held by the respective parties. Monopolies, cartels, police batons, prisons, labor organization, cooperative associations – these and a host of other power relationships skew the relative "value" of commodities, or at least of the price that can be gotten for them. (And it really matters very little whether a cantaloupe has a theoretical, labor-derived value of 25 cents if all the stores charge a dollar.)

Capitalism is not productive

Like most anarchists, Kropotkin initially assumed that an abundance of goods was being produced, and thus that the primary problem was arranging their equitable distribution. But when Errico Malatesta suggested that this could not be true, Kropotkin investigated the matter and found that (quoting Malatesta (1977: 266)) "the bosses normally only allow for the production of what they can sell at a profit. . . . Some countries were continually threatened by shortages." In fact, there was only enough food on hand in most major cities to sustain the population for a few days. However, Kropotkin's (1913 [1985]: 193–9) research established that the shortages, economic crises and general distress endemic to his age (and which continue to this day) did not result, as was widely believed, from overpopulation, poor soil, or other such material causes. Contrary to the view underlying most economic theory, scarcity was not inevitable. Rather, it resulted from a failure to properly utilize the means already at hand to meet society's needs.[3]

Kropotkin (1913 [1985]) presented his findings in *Fields, Factories and Workshops* – an anarchist classic which proved that people using then-existing technologies could meet all of their needs with just a few months of labor per year. With detailed evidence, he demonstrated that the technical means existed to produce abundant and healthful food with relatively little effort or expense (a vision quite distinct from today's factory farms – the precursors of which already existed, but which Kropotkin argued destroyed the soil for generations to come as well as displacing people who might otherwise derive a comfortable living from the land). Although "plenty for all" was no longer merely a dream; to become a reality, the "immense capital" of society – a term Kropotkin used to refer not only to factories, but also to cities, houses, roads, arable lands and education – must be socialized and marshaled to meet the needs of the entire society (Knowles 2004: 234).

Contrary to most economists, Kropotkin argued for decentralizing agriculture and industry, noting that huge industrial establishments were both less common than generally believed, and established less to realize largely dubious economies of scale than to facilitate managerial control. The doctrine of national specialization or comparative advantage – then coming into prominence, and which has since been used as an excuse to ravish "third world" economies – was demonstrably harmful to the interests of the population, as is well known to peasants compelled to grow coffee beans and sugar cane on land that could otherwise feed their families.

If the debilitating influences of capitalist control and social ignorance could be ended, abundance for all was within reach:

> For thousands of years, . . . to grow one's own food was the burden, almost the curse, of mankind. But it need be so no longer. . . . To grow the yearly food of a family, under rational conditions of culture, requires so little labor that it might almost be done as a mere change from other pursuits. . . . And again, you will be struck to see with what facility and in how short a time your needs of dress and of thousands of articles of luxury can be satisfied when production is carried on for satisfying real needs rather than for satisfying shareholders.
>
> (Kropotkin 1913 [1985]: 194–7)[4]

And yet everywhere workers lived in misery. Contrary to the teachings of orthodox economists, Kropotkin argued that overproduction was a problem only in theory – a theory that could not survive confrontation with the actual facts:

> Far from producing more than is needed to assure material riches, we do not produce enough. . . . If certain economists delight in writing treatises on overproduction, and in explaining each industrial crisis by this cause, they would be much at a loss if called upon to name a single article produced by France in greater quantities than are necessary to meet the needs of the whole population. . . . What economists call overproduction is but a production that is above the purchasing power of the worker, who is reduced to poverty by capital and state.
>
> (Kropotkin 1898 [1970]: 126–7)

Only exploiters, he concluded, were in abundant supply. Today, a century later, there may well be overproduction of some goods (nuclear weapons, toxic chemicals, and an avalanche of products that must almost immediately be replaced), but it is just as obscene to talk of, for example, an overproduction crisis in agriculture when millions face immediate starvation. Thus, rather than celebrating capitalism's development of society's productive capacity, Kropotkin demonstrated that capitalism resulted in chronic underproduction and deprivation. Capitalists not only do not equitably distribute the fruits of our production, the entire development of technology and industry is distorted by their short-term profit calculations. Employers faced with the possibility of new labor-saving technologies, for example, often move to drive down labor costs rather than invest in developing the means of production (their historic role, according to Marx), as may be seen most clearly today in a garment industry that travels the world in search of cheaper labor with little regard for technologies that have dramatically reduced the "socially necessary" labor required for production. The social revolution, then, cannot merely expropriate the means of production developed by the capitalists; it will be forced to rapidly develop those means in order to meet even the most basic social needs. Fortunately, the means for doing so have long been in place, and workers are more than capable of meeting the challenge.[5]

Wage slavery

Like all socialists, Kropotkin (1895 [1970]: 162) recognized the self-evident truth that workers work for the employing class because they are forced to – without their weekly wages they and their families must starve:

> Whence come the fortunes of the rich[?] A little thought would suffice to show that these fortunes have their beginnings in the poverty of the poor. When there are no longer any destitute there will no longer be any rich to exploit them.

If workers could meet their daily needs without hiring out their labor power, few would consent to surrender their control over their own labor in order to work for wages that must inevitably be (if the capitalist is to derive any profit) a mere fraction of the goods they produce.

Even an independent artisan, the labor aristocracy of Kropotkin's day, could not hope to do better than support his family and put together an (almost certainly inadequate) pittance for his old age should he rely on his own efforts and diligence:

> Assuredly this is not how great fortunes are made. But suppose our shoemaker . . . takes an apprentice, the child of some poor wretch who thinks himself lucky if in five years' time his son has learned the trade and is able to earn his living. Meanwhile our shoemaker does not lose by him; and if trade is brisk he soon takes a second, and then a third. . . . If he is keen enough and mean enough, his journeymen and apprentices will bring him in nearly a pound a day over and above the product of his own toil. . . . He will gradually become rich. . . . This is what people call "being economical and having frugal temperate habits." At bottom it is nothing more nor less than grinding the face of the poor.
>
> (Kropotkin 1895 [1970]: 166)

After a hundred years of struggle, many workers have succeeded in improving their condition and the apprentice system has all but disappeared. But saving one's earnings is no more the route to real wealth today than it ever was. At best, workers can hope to buy a house, afford some time off from the hated job, and put a little money aside for retirement or hard times. To become wealthy, in economic terms, requires exploitation – either directly from workers' labor, or indirectly by exploiting workers' needs for the necessities of life:

> Under capitalism, "the harder a man works the less he is paid." But the solution to this manifest injustice could not be found in reversing this equation – in payment according to the service each renders to society. For who is to determine the value of another's service?
>
> We know what reply we shall get. . . . The bourgeois economists – and Marx too – will be quoted . . . to prove that the scale of wages has its *raison d'être*, since the "labor power" of the engineer will have cost society more than the "labor power" of the laborer. . . . [But] the employer who pays the engineer twenty times more than the laborer makes the following simple reckoning: if the engineer can save him a hundred thousand francs a year on his production costs, he will pay the engineer twenty thousand. And when he sees a foreman able to drive the workers and save ten thousand francs in wages, he loses no time in offering him two or three thousand. . . . He parts with a thousand francs where he counts on gaining ten thousand, and this in essence is the capitalist system.
>
> So let no one come up with this talk about the production costs of the labor force, and tell us that a student who has cheerfully spent his youth at a university has a "right" to a salary ten times that of a miner's son who has been wasting away down a mine from the age of eleven.
>
> (Kropotkin 1920 [1983]: 101, 99)

Wage differentials, whether under capitalism or in some future "socialist" society, must be condemned as intrinsically unjust. Nor is it possible to determine a "just wage" based on an individual's contribution to production, as so many advocate even today, even if such a system could be tolerated on ethical grounds.[6]

Production is social

Production is nowhere carried out by isolated individuals whose economic contribution can be isolated from that of every other worker so that its value can be determined. To illustrate this, Kropotkin (1920 [1983]: 103–4) turned to coal mining:[7]

> One man controls the lift, continually rushing the cage from level to level so that men and coal may be moved about. If he relaxes his concentration for an instant the apparatus will be destroyed, many men killed, and work brought to a standstill. If he loses as little as three seconds at each movement of the lever, production will be reduced by 20 tons a day or more.

> Well, is it he who renders the greatest service in the mine? Or is it perhaps that boy who from below signals to him when it is time to raise the cage to the surface? Is it instead the miner who is risking his life at every moment of the day? . . . Or again is it the engineer who would miss the coal seam and have the miners dig into stone if he made the smallest error in his calculations? . . .
>
> All the workers engaged in the mine contribute within the limits of their powers, their knowledge . . . and their skill to mine coal. And all we can say is that everybody has the right to *live*, to satisfy their needs, and even their fantasies, once the most pressing needs of all have been satisfied. But how can one estimate their labors?

Obviously one cannot. And yet we have not identified everyone who contributes to the production of that coal. What of the construction workers who built the railways to the pit head, without which the coal would sit useless? What of the farmers who raise the food the coal miners eat? What of those who build the machines that will burn the coal, without which it is rather useless dirt? The list of those whose labor is essential to coal mining is endless.

There was a time, Kropotkin (1891 [1970]: 57) concedes, when a family could support itself through agricultural pursuits, supplemented with a few domestic trades, and consider the corn they raised and the cloth they weaved as products of their own, and no one else's, labor:

> Even then, such a view was not quite correct: there were forests cleared and roads built by common efforts. . . . But now, in the extremely interwoven state of industry of which each branch supports all others, such an individualistic view can be held no more. If the iron trade and the cotton industry of this country have reached so high a degree of development, they have done so owing to the parallel growth of thousands of other industries, great and small; to the extension of the railway system; to an increase of knowledge . . . and, above all, to the world trade which has itself grown up. . . .
>
> The Italians who died from cholera in digging the Suez Canal . . . have contributed as much towards the enrichment of this country as the British girl who is prematurely growing old in serving a machine at Manchester. . . . How can we pretend to estimate the exact part of each of them in the riches accumulated around us?

And if there is no individual production, then how can private ownership be justified? Just as it is impossible to argue that any one person created a lump of coal or a bolt of cloth, so it is impossible to justify private ownership of buildings or land. Homes, after all, are not built by their owners. Their construction is a cooperative endeavor involving innumerable workers in forestry, lumber yards, brick yards, and so on:

> Moreover – and it is here that the enormity of the whole proceeding becomes most glaring – the house owes its actual value to the profit which the owner

> can make out of it. Now, this profit results from the fact that his house is built in a town . . . which the work of twenty or thirty generations has gone to render habitable, healthy, and beautiful.
>
> (Kropotkin 1895 [1970]: 197)

Like the ground they stand upon, buildings are a common heritage:

> Take the town of Paris – a creation of so many centuries. . . . How could one maintain to an inhabitant of that town, who works every day to embellish it, to purify it, to nourish it, to make it a center of thought and art – how could one assert before one who produces this wealth that the palaces adorning the streets of Paris belong in all justice to those who are the legal proprietors today? . . . It is by spoliation that they hold these riches!
>
> (Kropotkin 1898 [1970]: 125)

That this remains so can readily be seen by examining the value of today's office buildings and shopping complexes. Without even the slightest improvements, their value rises so long as the local economy prospers. But no sum of money or quantity of labor invested in maintenance or beautification is sufficient to maintain their value when the local economy fails. For their value is not derived from the money invested, nor from the bricks and mortar (and plastic, steel and cement) of which they are constructed. Not even the labor of the workers who build and maintain these modern temples to capital determine their value. In the final analysis, their value depends almost entirely upon the wealth and prosperity of the greater society. The most luxurious hotel built in a dying city will soon fade with its surroundings, while the meanest hovel increases in value as surrounding properties are developed. We enrich each other – not only spiritually, but materially as well – as we work, contemplate and play together; and without the efforts of society as a whole no one prospers. Private ownership, then, is not merely unjust, it is absurd.

An anarchist economics for a new society

Kropotkin refused to separate his analysis of what was from what could be. He insisted on asking not merely if the present economic order worked on its own terms, but whether it was "really economical,"

> lead[ing] to economy in the expenditure of human forces. Or are [the organization of production] not merely wasteful survivals from a past that was plunged into darkness, ignorance and oppression, and never took into consideration the economical and social value of the human being?
>
> (Kropotkin 1913 [1985]: 193)

The "economic and social value of the human being," for Kropotkin, was the key to anarchist economics – indeed, of any rational economic theory. The anarchist movement devoted much attention in the closing decades of the nineteenth century to the question of how society could best be organized to meet that objective, developing the idea of anarchist communism during the course of the struggle within the First International against Marx's authoritarianism. Although he is its best-known proponent, Kropotkin did not originate the theory. As Caroline Cahm (1989: 40–3, 64) demonstrates, "the ideas themselves evolved spontaneously out of the bakunist collectivism in Italy, Switzerland and Spain, largely independently of each other."[8] But Kropotkin quickly became one of its most prominent advocates and his arguments were influential in convincing the movement to abandon earlier mutualist and collectivist theories in favor of the anarchist communist principles that were supported by most anarchists by the mid-1880s.

Most economists, and even many radicals, Kropotkin (1913 [1972]: 190–2) argued, made a fundamental mistake in beginning their studies from the standpoint of production. Instead, economics should be approached from the standpoint of consumption – of human needs. Needs should govern production; the purpose of economics is not so much to understand the workings of the capitalist economy (to the extent that it may be said to work at all), but rather to study "the needs of mankind, and the means of satisfying them with the least possible waste of human energy." Although human needs are not met at present, there were no technical reasons why every family could not have comfortable homes, sufficient food, and so on. The problem was not simply to increase productivity, however; rather, "production, having lost sight of the needs of man, has strayed in an absolutely wrong direction."

If the goal was the well-being of all, then expropriation (of cities, houses, land, factories) must be the means. "This rich endowment, painfully won, built, fashioned or invented by our ancestors, must become common property, so that the collective interests of men may gain from it the greatest good for all." Society, Kropotkin (1913 [1972]: 55) became convinced, must be reconstituted on a communist basis if humanity was ever to be truly free. "From the first day of the revolution, the worker shall know that a new era is opening . . . that henceforth none need crouch under the bridges while palaces are hard by, none need fast in the midst of plenty."

In his monumental work, *The Conquest of Bread*, Kropotkin (1913 [1972]: 170–4) devoted a lengthy chapter to rebutting such common objections as the notion that nobody would work without compulsion and that overseers were necessary to enforce quality standards. Free association, Kropotkin argued, was the solution to most of these objections. If sluggards and loafers began to proliferate, they should be fed to the extent that available resources permitted, but treated as "ghost[s] of bourgeois society." But few people would in fact refuse to contribute to society, "there will be no need to manufacture a code of laws on their account."[9]

Far from shirking work if they do not receive a wage, when people work cooperatively for the good of all they achieve feats of productivity never realizable through economic or state coercion.

> Well-being – that is to say the satisfaction of physical, artistic and moral needs, has always been the most powerful stimulant to work. . . . A free worker, who sees ease and luxury increasing for him and for others in proportion to his

> efforts spends infinitely far more energy and intelligence, and obtains first-class products in a far greater abundance.
>
> (Kropotkin 1913 [1972]: 161–3)

To the extent possible, all goods and services should be provided free of charge to all. Goods available in abundance should be available without limit; those in short supply should be rationed. Already, Kropotkin noted, many goods were provided based on need. Bridges no longer require tolls for passage; parks and gardens are open to all; railroads offer monthly passes; schools and roads are free; water is supplied to every house; libraries provide information to all without considering ability to pay, and offer assistance to those who do not know how to manage the catalogue. (That many of these services have been eroded in recent years does not invalidate his premise.)

Even under capitalism, anarchist values surface in times of crisis, as we recently saw in New Orleans where people took what they needed from the stores and shared the necessities of life among themselves despite the threats of the police to shoot them down; where thousands of people stepped forward to rescue and assist the survivors in the face of official indifference; and where the government and corporations tallied the costs and the possibilities for profit while ordinary people extended the hand of solidarity and mutual aid:

> Suppose that one of our great cities, so egotistic in ordinary times, were visited tomorrow by some calamity, . . . that same selfish city would decide that the first needs to satisfy were those of the children and the aged. . . . How can we doubt, then, that when the instruments of production are placed at the service of all, when . . . labor, having recovered its place of honor in society, produces much more than is necessary to all – how can we doubt that this force (already so powerful) will enlarge its sphere of action until it becomes the ruling principle of social life?
>
> (Kropotkin 1913 [1972]: 63–5)

Neither corporate nor government control of the economy serves any useful purpose. Already in the nineteenth century, letters could be sent between most countries without any overarching authority. Instead, agreements between scores of autonomous postal systems together made up an integrated postal network. Kropotkin cited many such examples to demonstrate that voluntary and completely non-coercive organizations could provide a complex net of services without the intervention of higher authorities. To this day one can travel across Europe over the lines of a dozen railway systems (capitalist and state-owned alike) on a single pass, coordinated by voluntary agreements. There is no reason to imagine that similar principles could not be realized in this hemisphere, and generalized throughout the society (Dolgoff 1989). As Colin Ward (1982: 54, 58) notes,

> Every kind of human activity should begin from what is local and immediate, linked in networks with no central authority or directing agency, hiving off

new cells as the original ones grow. If there is any human activity that does not appear to fit this pattern our first question should be "Why not?" and our second, "How can we rearrange it so as to provide for local autonomy, local responsibility, and the fulfillment of local needs?"

Shorter hours in the new society

Beginning from the standpoint of actual human needs, Kropotkin (1913 [1985]: 198) examined the means available in his day to satisfy them, concluding that abundance for all was within grasp:

> Modern knowledge . . . tells [thinking men] that in order to be rich they need not take the bread from the mouths of others; but that the more rational outcome would be a society in which men, with the aid of the machinery already invented and to be invented, should themselves create all imaginable riches.

Based upon the technology of his day, Kropotkin (1913 [1972]: 122–3) argued that people would need to put in no more than five hours a day of labor (for 25 years or so of their lives) in order to satisfy their needs for food, clothing, housing, wine transportation and related necessities:

> When we take into account how many, in the so-called civilized nations, produce nothing, how many work at harmful trades doomed to disappear, and lastly, how many are only useless middlemen, we see that in each nation the number of real producers could be doubled.

Kropotkin was writing more than a century ago; the proportion is certainly very much higher today. As a result, "work could be reduced to four or even three hours a day, to produce all the goods that are produced now."

> Such a society could in return guarantee . . . a more substantial well-being than that enjoyed to-day by the middle classes. And, moreover, each worker belonging to this society would have at his disposal at least five hours a day which he could devote to science, art, and individual needs which do not come under the category of *necessities*, but will probably do so later on, when man's productivity will have augmented, and those objects will no longer appear luxurious or inaccessible.

This point was, for Kropotkin, of the greatest importance. It was not enough merely to meet people's material wants – human beings must also be free to pursue their artistic and aesthetic senses. Kropotkin (1913 [1972]: 124) believed that luxury, far from being wasteful, was an absolute necessity. But if these joys, "now reserved to a few . . . to give leisure and the possibility of developing everyone's intellectual capacities," were to be obtained for all, then "the social revolution must guarantee daily bread to all."

Tastes, Kropotkin recognized, varied widely. Some people require telescopes and laboratories to complete their lives, others require dance halls or machine shops. But all of this activity was best removed from the confines of capitalist production and carried out on a voluntary, cooperative basis after participants had completed their few hours of necessary labor. Freed from the drudgery of capitalist production, we would all be free to develop our creative instincts. Kropotkin was certain that the result would be finer art, available to all; dramatic scientific advances (science was, after all, until relatively recently an entirely voluntary endeavor); a society in which humanity's creative potential was for the first time unleashed.

Work need not be painful

Under current conditions, Kropotkin (1891 [1970]: 71) acknowledged, to perform productive labor meant toiling long hours in unhealthy workshops, chained to the same task for 20 or 30 years – maybe for one's entire life. To work meant subsisting on a paltry wage, never sure what tomorrow will bring, with little opportunity to pursue the delights of science and art. But it was overwork, not work itself that was repulsive to human nature:

> Overwork for supplying the few with luxury – not work for the well-being of all. Work is a . . . necessity, which is health and life itself. If so many branches of useful work are so reluctantly done now, it is merely because they mean overwork, or they are improperly organized. . . . As to the childish question, repeated for fifty years: "Who would do disagreeable work?" frankly I regret that none of our savants has ever been brought to do it. . . . If there is still work which is really disagreeable in itself, it is only because our scientific men have never cared to consider the means of rendering it less so. They have always known that there were plenty of starving men who would do it for a few cents a day.

Kropotkin welcomed mechanization, so that "those who are now the beasts of burden of humanity [may] raise their backs . . . to become at last men." But at the same time he recognized that capitalism often introduced machinery in ways destructive both to human life and to the environment. Kropotkin (1913 [1972]: 70, 75–6) was an early critic of factory farming, noting its propensity to exhaust the soil. Machinery, he argued, must be integrated with rational cultivation practices and small-scale production. For Kropotkin, the purpose of agriculture, as of all economic activity, was to meet human needs.

Today, of course, production has little if anything to do with meeting human needs. Studies of famines around the world, for example, have found no correlation between food production and starvation – indeed, food is often exported from areas where people are dying of hunger and hunger-related diseases (Dahrendorf 1988: 9). Even in Kropotkin's day, entire cities produced nothing but shoddy, second-rate goods, while other towns specialized in the manufacture of luxury goods out of reach of the bulk of the population. Today, freighters carrying automobiles made in Japan and the United States pass each other on the high seas, in an endless merry-go-round repeated in almost every realm of human endeavor.

Production must be reorganized on a new basis, and shifted from export and luxury goods to meeting genuine human needs. But it is not simply a matter of producing different goods. The way work is organized and carried out must also be fundamentally transformed. When workers control their own workplaces, they will no longer tolerate poor conditions or allow their energies to be squandered in antisocial production.[10]

Kropotkin saw that it was also necessary to attack the division of labor that both Marxist and capitalist political economists have extolled as a prerequisite of improved productivity (although Marx did argue that ultimately labor must be reintegrated). Kropotkin conceded that it might well be the case that a person who did only one thing, over and over again, would become quite proficient at it. But such a worker "would lose all interest in his work [and] would be entirely at the mercy of his employer with his limited handicraft." Kropotkin (1913 [1972]: 164) found the notion that workers should be confined to a single repetitious activity a "horrible principle, so noxious to society, so brutalizing to the individual." The social revolution must abolish the separation between manual and brain work, give workers control of their workplaces, and abolish wage labor. "Then work will no longer appear a curse of fate; it will become what it should be – the free exercise of all the faculties of man."

Under the rubric of the division of labor, those who actually make things are not supposed to think or make decisions, while owners and "intellectual workers"

> have the privilege of thinking for the others, and . . . think badly because the whole world of those who toil with their hands is unknown to them. . . .
>
> The division of labor means labeling and stamping men for life – some to splice rope in factories, some to be foremen in a business, others to shove huge coal baskets in a particular part of a mine; but none of them to have any idea of machinery as a whole, nor of business, nor of mines. And thereby they destroy the love of work and the capacity for invention.
>
> (Kropotkin 1913 [1972]: 198–9)

It would be far better, Kropotkin (1970: 56) argued, for teachers to share in the duties of washing the floors, sweeping the school yard, and the myriad other tasks essential to school operations than to allow the formation of an intelligentsia, "an aristocracy of skilled labor."

The division of labor was not only incompatible with true freedom; Kropotkin (1913 [1972]: 206) argued that in the long run it was also inefficient – demoralizing and fatiguing workers and stripping them of the knowledge and the means necessary to innovate in their work. Much of the advantage derived from the division of labor is in any event lost through the necessity it creates to cart goods from place to place, and to create enormous bureaucracies to coordinate production of disparate parts that must ultimately be integrated into a single machine.

> It is foolish indeed to export wheat and to import flour, to export wool and import cloth, to export iron and import machinery; not only because transportation is a waste of time and money, but, above all, because . . . the industrial and technical capacities . . . remain undeveloped if they are not exercised in a variety of industries.

Kropotkin believed that work duties should be rotated, agricultural and industrial production integrated, and that towns and regions should, insofar as possible, produce their own food and their own industrial products (Knowles 2004: 239). The division of labor, in industry as in international trade, is ultimately a mechanism for despoiling the great majority. With economic self-reliance and the integration of labor, Kropotkin argued, people could ensure that their needs were met.

The advantages of centralized production are similarly illusory. While it is sometimes convenient for capitalists to bring their operations under centralized control (although even they find it increasingly necessary to encourage local initiative), this is not due to any technical advantages. Industry is centralized to facilitate market domination and control, not because of often non-existent economies of scale (Kropotkin (1913 [1985]: 153–4). To this day, the high-tech, advanced industries so often held up to demonstrate the superiority of centralized control are often carried out in small-scale, dispersed operations. Decentralization is, in fact, more efficient.

Conclusion: abolish the wage system

Kropotkin (1909 [1986]: 180) argued that the coming social revolution's "great[est] service to humanity" would be "to make the wage system in all its forms an impossibility." In Kropotkin's day, most socialists acknowledged the need to abolish the wage system, but argued for its replacement by vouchers representing either the "value" of people's labor or time put in on the job. Kropotkin (1970: 68–9), too, argued for such a system in 1873, but he soon concluded that such schemes were both wildly impractical and thoroughly reformist:

> Once the abolition of private property is proclaimed, and the possession in common of all the means of production is introduced – how can the wages system be maintained in any form? This is, nevertheless, what collectivists are doing when they recommend the use of the 'labor-cheques' as a mode of renumeration for labor.
>
> (Kropotkin 1920 [1983]: 94–6)

Today labor vouchers are out of favor, but most socialists still accept the wage system and money, sometimes disguised as consumption credits, as inevitable. Proponents of such schemes argue that they are needed in order to avoid systematic and massive misallocation of time and resources. The marketplace is, of course, a time-tested mechanism for ascertaining social needs and preferences for goods. The reason why there is periodic mass starvation in Africa and elsewhere is not because the market does not work to meet human needs, but because our fellow workers prefer not to eat.

Such devices make sense only within the framework of a market economy where goods are produced and distributed not on the basis of need, but on the ability to pay. Whether such an economic system maintains wage differentials or proclaims equal wages (or, perhaps, wage differentials favoring those engaged in "disagreeable or unhealthy work"), it nevertheless upholds an organization of production and consumption which originated in private property – and which is realizable only within its constraints.[11]

Kropotkin (1913 [1972]: 179, 189) refuted such arguments 100 years ago, when they were still fresh:

> They say, "No private property," and immediately after strive to maintain private property in its daily manifestations. . . . It can never be. For the day on which old institutions will fall under the proletarian axe, voices will call out "Bread, shelter, ease for all!" And those voices will be listened to; the people will say: "Let us begin by allaying our thirst for life, for happiness, for liberty, that we have never quenched." And when we shall have tasted of this joy, we will set to work to demolish the last vestiges of middle-class rule: its morality drawn from account books, its "debit and credit" philosophy . . . and we shall build in the name of communism and anarchy.

If there was a genuine shortage of necessities, Kropotkin argued that it was more just to ration goods than to maintain mechanisms for exchange. The wage system, in all its forms, should be rejected in favor of communist principles; for if wages are to be maintained (whether based on labor, or any other measure), a state apparatus is perforce necessary as well in order to enforce the attendant property rights.

But the fundamental point for Kropotkin (1913 [1972]: 229) was that people must seize control of their economic destiny – must be prepared to experiment with new processes and new methods of organization while taking advantage of the existing methods to meet immediate needs. The technical means of satisfying human needs were at hand:

> The only thing that may be wanting to the revolution is the boldness of initiative. . . . Ceasing to produce for unknown buyers, and looking in its midst for needs and tastes to be satisfied, society will liberally assure the life and ease of each of its members, as well as that moral satisfaction which work gives when freely chosen and freely accomplished.

The new society would be built by the people themselves, through their solidarity and direct action. Kropotkin noted that social revolution could not be imposed from above, but rather must result from popular struggles. Although he had originally been critical of strikes and unions, arguing that they could not substantially improve workers' conditions, he came to recognize the importance of

> taking an active part in those workers' organizations which carry on the *direct* struggle of labor against capital and its protector – the state. Such a struggle . . . permits the worker to obtain some temporary improvements in the present conditions of work, while it opens his eyes to the evil that is done by capitalism and the state that supports it, and wakes up his thoughts concerning the possibility of organizing consumption, production and exchange without the intervention of the capitalist and the state.
>
> (Kropotkin 1912 [1970]: 171)

Elsewhere, Kropotkin noted that strikes and other forms of industrial action were not only a manifestation of human solidarity, but also offered workers an opportunity to prepare themselves to make the revolution:

> Resistance and the strike are excellent methods of organization for doing this. . . . They do not take the movement off course, but keep it continually at grips with the principal enemy, the capitalist. . . . Far from developing egoistical instincts, the strike develops the sentiment of solidarity.
>
> (Cahm 1989: 25–6)

In this, we can see the basis for the later fusion of anarchist communism and anarcho-syndicalism that inspired the Spanish anarcho-syndicalist movement – a vision which recognized that the social revolution must begin upon the basis of the existing industries, transforming these into the building blocks from which to construct a free society:

> We must take possession . . . of the granaries, the shops full of clothing and the dwelling houses. Nothing must be wasted. We must organize without delay a way to feed the hungry, to satisfy all wants, to meet all needs, to produce not for the special benefit of this one or that one, but so as to ensure to society as a whole its life and further development.
>
> (Kropotkin 1913 [1972]: 55, 59)

While it is neither possible nor desirable to spell out in every detail how such an economy might operate, Kropotkin argued that it is in fact essential to think about its general outlines in advance, so that we might build with a purpose. Expropriation, direct action, federalism and self-management are, for Kropotkin, the means. A society not built upon communist principles would inevitably succumb to the central power it established to oversee production and distribution. Only the free distribution of necessities, in all their variety, on the basis not of position or productivity but of need, is compatible with a free society.

In all of this, Kropotkin was careful to test his theories against the real world. As Knowles (2004: 241–3) notes, *Fields, Factories and Workshops*, in particular, demonstrates his wide-ranging research and his rigorous application of the data to support his arguments. Had more economists – radical or otherwise – followed Kropotkin's suggestion that they rely less on formulas and theories and instead analyze concrete economic developments, we might have fewer "economic laws" and theories which are often demonstrably absurd and more understanding of the actual challenges that we face in organizing an economy, and a society, geared to meeting human needs.[12]

Notes

1 For discussion of local currency schemes, see Sculthorpe (1995); Carson (2004) attempts to update the mutualist tradition, of which the time store was a part, but does not suggest reviving that particular experiment – instead looking to local currency schemes and other attempts to carve out spheres of economic activity largely outside the larger capitalist economy and the state.

2 The Socialist Labor Party (1940 [1958]: 53, 54, 57), for example, while "applaud[ing] the spirit which prompts the workers to strike against the inhuman wage slavery under which they suffer," "such efforts . . . must prove futile," as will "all attempts made by them to better their conditions under capitalism." This argument, that it is impossible for workers to ameliorate their conditions so long as capitalism persists, at least in the present era, is quite common among left-wing Marxists of various stripes.

3 Malatesta argued that Kropotkin's revised view remained wildly optimistic in its assessment of what could be accomplished. History, however, has confirmed that agriculture can indeed produce much greater yields than was generally believed at the time – yields that far exceed those Kropotkin discussed.

4 This is an abridged and annotated version of Kropotkin's second edition, eliminating entire chapters of statistical data eclipsed in the years since this work first saw print.

5 See, e.g., Kroptkin's (1909 [1986]: 594) *The Great French Revolution*. Freed from the landlords, peasants dramatically increased production. "A new France was born. . . . For the first time in centuries the peasant ate his fill" and the country was immeasurably strengthened. Similar results were found in the Spanish Revolution in 1936 (Leval 1975).

6 Many Marxists, and even some who consider themselves anarcho-syndicalists, continue to argue for maintaining the wage system in such a guise. Most prominent in this regard are the advocates of "Participatory Economics," which, in the Orwellian style, they refer to as Parecon. See, e.g., Albert and Hahnel (1991a, 1991b) and Albert (2003).

7 At the time, miners worked either individually or in gangs at the coal face and were paid by the ton. In today's coal mines, of course, the issue of individual production would never arise.

8 Indeed, Kropotkin argued initially for a collectivist vision, adopting the anarchist communism for which he became famous only in the process of the debates within the Swiss and French anarchist movements – and between them and an increasingly reformist socialist movement – that led to agreement on an anarchist communist program by 1880. Elsewhere, Kropotkin noted that he had learned much from simple workers who could barely write, and argued that "great thinkers" at bottom "have only (in their best work) expressed the ideas, aspirations and ideals which existed in a vague way among the people" (Cahm 1989: 285).

9 Published in French in 1892, *The Conquest of Bread* actually pre-dates *Fields, Factories and Workshops* (both of which were issued in revised English-language editions in 1913). My references are from the 1972 edition; *Conquest* is available in several editions including a 1995 Cambridge University Press edition introduced by Marshall Shartz, and recent popular editions by AK Press and Black Cat Press.

10 In Spain, the anarcho-syndicalist CNT union, which had a long history of working to articulate its own economic approach, launched a practical experiment in anarchist economics while they battled the fascists (De Santillan 1937; Leval 1975). More recently, in Australia, militant construction workers refused to allow several projects they determined were ecologically or socially unacceptable to proceed (Burgmann and

Burgmann 1998; Mallory 2005). Transport workers around the world have in several instances refused to handle war material and other cargo on political grounds. The record is clear that workers will consider the broader ramifications of their work when they have the power to take decisions regarding it.

11 For one such approach see Michael Albert and Robin Hahnel's (1991b) *Looking Forward: Participatory Economics for the Twenty-first Century*. They expand upon these arguments in other works including Albert's (2003) *Parecon: Life After Capitalism*, and at their website www.zmag.org/parecon/indexnew.htm (which includes the text of several of their books and articles). Similarly, syndicalist Richard Laubach argues, in the *Discussion Bulletin* (#25, September 1987, pp. 17–22), for "giving all workers a set of votes on what to produce . . . 'consumption credits'" used "to acquire goods and services [and thereby] provide information about the community's cumulative preferences." (Laubach does not mean that we would inform central planners of our consumption plans, as Parecon envisions – an unwieldy system, though not a market economy. Instead, consumers would be provided with an equal number of "consumption credits" which they would use to buy products and services.) We are clearly talking about money here, and an economic system that must quickly revert to a full-fledged market economy or to central planning – in either case a system that has little if anything to do with meeting human needs and promoting human freedom. A similar inability to break cleanly with the market undermines much radical thinking about the shape of a future economy. However, unlike most economists, Albert and Hahnel (1991a, 1991b) do address the problem of the stultifying effects of the division of labor, even if their approach is rather mechanistic and ultimately unworkable.

12 Frank Ackerman and Lisa Heinzerling (2004) mercilessly dissect one school of economics resulting from this sterile theorizing.

Bibliography

Ackerman, F. and Heinzerling, L. (2004) *Priceless: On Knowing the Price of Everything and the Value of Nothing*, New York: New Press.

Albert, M. (2003) *Parecon: Life After Capitalism*, New York: Verso.

Albert, M. and Hahnel, R. (1991a) *The Political Economy of Participatory Economics*, Princeton, NJ: Princeton University Press.

Albert, M. and Hahnel, R. (1991b) *Looking Forward: Participatory Economics for the Twenty-first Century*, Boston: South End Press.

Burgmann, M. and Burgmann, V. (1998) *Green Bans, Red Union: Environmental Activism and the New South Wales Builders Labourers Federation*, Sydney: University of New South Wales Press.

Cahm, C. (1989) *Kropotkin and the Rise of Revolutionary Anarchism 1872–1886*, Cambridge: Cambridge University Press.

Carson, K. (2004) *Studies in Mutualist Political Economy*, Fayetteville AR, http://mutualist.org/id47.html (accessed June 12, 2008).

Dahrendorf, R. (1988) *The Modern Social Conflict*, Berkeley: University of California Press.

De Santillan, D.A. (1937) *After the Revolution: Economic Reconstruction in Spain Today*, New York: Greenberg. Reprinted 1996, Petersham, NSW: Jura Media.

Dolgoff, S. (1989) *The Relevance of Anarchism to Modern Society* (3rd edn), Chicago, IL: Charles H. Kerr.

Knowles, R. (2004) *Political Economy from Below*, London: Routledge.

Kropotkin, P. (1891 [1970]) *Anarchist Communism: Its Basis and Principles*, London: Freedom Press. Collected in R. Baldwin (ed.) (1970) *Kropotkin's Revolutionary Pamphlets*, Mineola, NY: Dover Publications (facsimile reprint of the 1927 Vanguard

Press edition, the text of which is online at http://dwardmac.pitzer.edu/ANARCHIST_ARCHIVES/kropotkin/revpamphlets/toc.html).

—— (1895 [1970]) *Expropriation*, London: Freedom Press. Reprinted in M. Miller (ed.) (1970) *Selected Writings on Anarchism and Revolution*, Cambridge, MA: MIT Press.

—— (1898 [1970]) *Anarchism: Its Philosophy and Idea*, San Francisco, CA: Free Society. Collected in R. Baldwin (ed.) (1970) *Kropotkin's Revolutionary Pamphlets*, Mineola, NY: Dover Publications.

—— (1909 [1986]) *The Great French Revolution*, Reprinted London: Elephant Editions.

—— (1912 [1970]) *Modern Science and Anarchism*, London: Freedom Press. Collected in R. Baldwin (ed.) (1970) *Kropotkin's Revolutionary Pamphlets*, Mineola, NY: Dover Publications.

—— (1913 [1972]) *The Conquest of Bread*, New York: G.P. Putnam's Sons. Reprinted 1972 with an introduction, notes and related articles by M. Shatz, New York University Press.

—— (1913 [1985]) *Fields, Factories and Workshops* (expanded edn), London: Nelson. Reprinted 1985 in abridged and annotated form as *Fields, Factories and Workshops Tomorrow*, ed. C. Ward, London: Freedom Press.

—— (1920 [1983]) *The Wage System*, London: Freedom Press. Collected in V. Richards (ed.) (1983) *Why Work? Arguments for the Leisure Society*, London: Freedom Press.

—— (1970) "Must We Occupy Ourselves with an Examination of the Ideal of a Future System?" in M. Miller (ed.) *Selected Writings on Anarchism and Revolution*, Cambridge, MA: MIT Press.

Leval, G. (1975) *Collectives in the Spanish Revolution*, London: Freedom Press.

Malatesta, E. (1977) "Peter Kropotkin – Recollections and Criticisms," in V. Richards (ed.) *Malatesta: Life & Ideas*, London: Freedom Press.

Mallory, G. (2005) *Uncharted Waters: Social Responsibility in Australian Trade Unions*, Brisbane: Boolarong Press.

Miller, M.A. (1976) *Kropotkin*, Chicago, IL: University of Chicago Press.

Richards, V. (ed.) (1983) *Why Work? Arguments for the Leisure Society*, London: Freedom Press.

Sculthorpe, H. (1995) "LETS: Local Exchange and Trading Schemes," *The Raven*, 31: 234–46.

Socialist Labor Party (1940 [1958]) "Resolution on Strikes," in N. Karp (1958) *Unionism: Fraudulent or Genuine?*, New York: New York Labor News.

Ward, C. (1982) *Anarchy in Action*, London: Freedom Press.

3 Some notes on anarchist economic thought

Mathew Forstater

> anarchism assimilates to itself that hostility to law which naturally results from evil doing. The antipathy of the rogue for the halter reinforces this movement. It gathers to itself disreputable elements, and by its outbreaks moves society to resistance. It is a self-terminating movement.
>
> (John Bates Clark 1910? [2002]: 451)

Anarchism, when taken seriously at all, is usually analyzed as a political philosophy, and few attempts have been made to address the question of whether there is a distinctive anarchist *economics*. Anarchist economics, like many other schools of economic thought, makes both "positive" and negative" contributions: the negative contributions focus primarily on the critique of capitalism and state socialism, while the positive ones outline the main features of an alternative economic organization of society based on anarchist principles.[1] While very little attention is paid to anarchism in history of economic thought texts, there is a rich history of anarchist economic thought, both "classical" and contemporary. Anarchist economics also links up in interesting ways to other contemporary schools, including, but not limited to, ecological, feminist, institutionalist, and Marxist.

One preliminary order of business is to define what we mean by anarchist, since the word "anarchism" has been used in many different contexts. We exclude those "free market" usages of the term, sometimes associated with "anarcho-capitalism," which should more properly be called *libertarian* (see Prychitko 1997). Libertarian thought includes its own economics, including a variety of Austrian, Public Choice, and other approaches, all of which generally defend a "capitalist" (some representatives of these schools reject this term) market organization against the State, whether Keynesian, socialist, or otherwise. They also tend to reject the kinds of anarchism this chapter is concerned with, which are limited here to "left" anarcho-communism, syndicalism, and social anarchism.[2]

The critique of capitalism

Anarchism in this sense is not only opposed to the State, but also to capitalism. As Kropotkin (1910: 914) put it in his *Encyclopedia Britannica* entry:

> As to their economical conceptions, the anarchists, in common with all socialists, of whom they constitute the left wing, maintain that the now prevailing system of private ownership in land, and our capitalist production for the sake of profits, represent a monopoly which runs against both the principles of justice and the dictates of utility. They are the main obstacle which prevents the successes of modern technics from being brought into the service of all, so as to produce general well-being. The anarchists consider the wage-system and capitalist production altogether as an obstacle to progress.

On this, as Kropotkin indicates, anarchists may be seen as part of a larger, broad conception of socialism. Thus anarchists share many of the traditional socialist positions opposing capitalism:

> Anarchism is synonymous with the term "free socialism" or "social anarchism." As the term "social" itself implies, anarchism is the free association of people living together and cooperating in free communities. The abolition of capitalism and the state; workers' self-management of industry; distribution according to needs; free association; are principles which, for all socialist tendencies, constitute the essence of socialism.
>
> (Dolgoff 1986: 187)

Yet anarchists part from socialists on a number of accounts, and not only with regard to their vision of a post-capitalist society. One of the hallmarks of anarchism is its critique of political and economic centralization and the scale of political-economic activity, whether capitalist or socialist. It is to these issues that we now turn.

Decentralization, bioregionalism, and municipal confederalism

Anarchist economic views large, centralized political and economic activity as problematic in and of itself. Anarchists therefore promote decentralization and to a certain extent adopt Schumacher's notion of "small is beautiful" (Schumacher 1973). Of course, many have often noted that small is not *always* beautiful, and so some clarification will be in order. First, though, it is fair to say that for the most part, anarchists adopt the policy that to the extent possible, consumption should be primarily from local production and production should be primarily for local consumption. This reduces many environmental and other social costs.

This says nothing about the scale of productive activity, though, except that it need not be at a scale beyond the needs of the local population. Anarchists see that there might be situations where economies of scale may be beneficial, but they also see many diseconomies involved in over-centralized industrialization. Anarchists view most present political units as too large, and even those that are not oversized often have boundaries that make no economic or ecological sense. In this they are guided by bioregionalism, which sees the natural political and economic unit as an ecological one (Milani 2000; for a sympathetic critique, see Kovel 2002: 173–6).

While localized, self-sustaining production and distribution is the norm, there are of course a number of issues that require some coordination between local communities, and in this anarchists have developed the notion of municipal confederalism or confederal municipalism (see Bookchin 1993). This recognizes that interdependence remains crucial, even among otherwise self-sustaining bioregions.

Anarchists use municipal confederalism (MC) as the basis for alternative economic planning. MC makes an important distinction between policy making and execution of policies. Policy making is based on the local community assemblies practicing participatory democracy, but administration and coordination are the responsibility of confederal councils. There is a significant literature on the details of the political aspects of this form of social organization (see, for example, references in Hawkins 1993), but since the present focus is on the economics of anarchism, we turn instead to the local economic organization.

Division of labor and work

Anarchists have paid particular attention to issues regarding the division of labor. They oppose the division between manual and intellectual labor, claiming that all society's members need the opportunity to engage in both physical and mental work. In addition, anarchists oppose the division between the "field" and the "workshop," again proposing that all individuals require the chance to operate in both settings (Kropotkin 1913 [1974]). They claim that communities can enjoy the benefits of increased productivity from specialization without the negative effects on workers by employing a division of tasks while permitting individuals to alternate between the various assignments. Anarchists would also accept Braverman's (1974) distinction between the social division of labor and the detail worker, as well as his conclusion that essentially all the productivity-increasing benefits can be had with the former without the breaking up of crafts, de-skilling, and alienation associated with the latter.

Anarchists pay close attention to the role of work in human development. In this they take something of an anthropological view of work as an integral part of human existence. As Schumacher – whose work Roszak (1973: 3) states "belongs to that subterranean tradition of organic and decentralist economics whose major spokesmen include Prince Kropotkin" – argues, work is not only not a "disutility" (as neoclassical economics views it), and not only brings "forth the goods and services needed for a becoming existence," but also importantly gives people the opportunity to develop their faculties and enables them to overcome their ego-centeredness "by joining with other people in a common task" (Schumacher 1973: 51).

Appropriate technology

For anarchists, any loss in productivity due to smaller scale production with a looser division of labor will be offset by increases in productivity. People who hate their jobs are less productive, those who feel alienated or hate their bosses or managers will be less productive, low job security means low job satisfaction means low productivity. A stronger sense of community, commitment to the larger project of building an alternative society, and the feeling of having a stake in one's productive activity may all increase productivity. In addition, anarchists reject the traditional notion of "efficiency" and adopt a broader notion of social efficiency that goes beyond minimizing costs and maximum output. Alexander Berkman (1929 [2000]: 96–7) also emphasized the benefits an anarchist form of economic organization gains from doing away with things such as advertising, sales, marketing, speculation, and concerns with profits, wage scales, and the like. Corporations often have entire departments devoted to such activities that will no longer be necessary, simplifying production and releasing laborers to join in the productive activities that remain.

Anarchists embrace the notion of appropriate (or intermediate) technology, that is, utilizing organizational and technological means that are ecologically, politically, socially, and economically appropriate, rather than the private cost-minimizing, profit-maximizing (and usually capital-intensive) method of production (Schumacher 1973). So a labor-intensive method may be used even when a more capital-intensive method is available, or methods that are ecologically harmful or dangerous to human health will be abandoned. Longer time horizons will also be employed in planning, so that pesticides and fertilizers that are now used to maximize short-run profits will be replaced by organic and other greener methods that maintain the long-term fertility of the soil and water, as well as human health. Europeans who upon arriving in West Africa observed farmers using the simple hoe scoffed at them as "primitive" and "backward," but we now know that the very delicate, thin topsoil characteristic of West Africa rapidly deteriorated after introduction of the plough, and the hoe was in fact more "appropriate" a technology. The same for shifting cultivation – colonial plantation owners thought it "inefficient" to leave land untilled and ceased the practice, to the detriment of long-term sustainability and therefore long-run productivity.

Reciprocity and mutualism: consumption, production, and property

Social organization in an anarchist society will be based on reciprocity and mutualism: institutionalized sharing and cooperation as the basis of social and economic organization. This explains the anarchist interest in pre-capitalist modes of production, as examples of both what is desirable and what is to be avoided. Egalitarian societies based on communalistic principles demonstrate that social relations need not be hierarchical or exploitative, and that satisfactory provisioning is possible without either markets or command. In addition, anarchists reject the standard treatment of property as either "private" in the modern, Western, legal sense, or "open-access," in the sense of "anything goes." This view is exemplified in Garrett Hardin's (1968) infamous "The Tragedy of the Commons," in which the author fails to make the important distinction between "commons" and "open-access." "Commons" refers to property that is neither individually owned nor possessed, but for which there are specific rules governing use that prevent misuse. Social institutions mediate the management of resources and thereby prevent its degradation (see Forstater 2002). Anarchists distinguish between various types of property, including individual possession without ownership, and with specific rules regarding use.

In general, as Malatesta (1995) put it, property becomes "property of all." Berkman (1929 [2000]) also called for personal possession for use, collective property of all. In terms of consumption, Berkman indicates that initially rationing would be necessary (but without the Bolshevik mistake of discriminatory rationing), until production was sufficiently reorganized; thereafter, consumption would be "to each according to their needs," with special consideration to the sick, elderly, children, and women during and following pregnancy. With no buying and selling, exchange is free, so money becomes useless.

In terms of production, the community would initially live on supplies and inventories, then return to work with new energy to keep goods flowing and produce enough to bring all out of poverty. Workers manage the firms, but there is no ownership. No capitalistic businesses, no compulsory labor (Berkman 1929 [2000]). Berkman does finally admit, though, that although "free communism, a life of voluntary cooperation and equal sharing" is the primary guide to all social organization, some small experiments in limited forms of markets and collectivist organization may be tried in some circumstances. Characteristic of the anti-dogmatism of many anarchists, various methods and practical experiments would be permitted.

Malatesta (1995) makes similar arguments. Communism, collectivism, and individualism will all be tried. Communism means production is managed by producers' associations and free consumption for all; under collectivism, all production is commonly owned and run, and distribution is determined by contribution; individualism means to each the individual means of production and for each the product of their own labor. Malatesta prefers total communism in the long run, but (and one also gets this from Berkman and others), "the important thing is the spirit which moves these organizations . . . that they are guided by the spirit of justice and desire for the good of all, and that they are always created freely and on a voluntary basis" (Malatesta 1995: 115). Collectivism is an intermediate system which brings together the merits and defects of the other two; individualism is economically unviable and impossible; total communism, perhaps in the future, but at the start would also be impossible and anti-libertarian.

Anarchism and heterodox economics

Anarchist economics has a number of potential links to other heterodox economic paradigms, including feminist, ecological, institutionalist, and Marxist. L. Susan Brown has written on feminism and anarchism. Her argument is that feminism has to make a critique of power and domination per se, and that anarchist theory provides that critique. There can be feminism without anarchism, but there cannot be anarchism without feminism. She cautions, however, that "classical" anarchist thought suffers from its out-of-date and unacceptable conception of "natural" law and "nature." This needs to be replaced by an historical approach, and she proposes existentialist epistemological groundings for anarchism. One could extend this sort of argument to Black Political Economy as well – that a true anarchist critique of power and domination should imply racial equality.

As should be clear from the above, there are obvious links between anarchism and ecological economics. In fact, the social ecology approach of Bookchin and others, and the appropriate technology and "small is beautiful" approach of Schumacher, are both a combination of the two (see also Ekins 1986; Foutopoulos 1993; Heller 1999; Milani 2000). The alternative planning approaches of Mumford and Patrick Geddes also point to connections between the two paradigms (see, for example, Luccarelli 1995). An anarchist environmental ethic may also be found via Brown's argument above concerning feminism; that is, the anarchist critique of domination can be the basis of a "green" economics.

A number of authors have explored the relation of anarchism and institutionalist economics (Dugger 1984; Edgell and Tilman 1989; Knowles 2004). Dugger explores the relation between Kropotkin's ideas and Veblenian political economy. Edgell and Tilman view anarchism as one of the "intellectual antecedents" of Veblen's thought. Knowles sees more recent work by institutionalist authors such as Hodgson and others as fitting well with anarchist economic thought. In particular, in the areas of economic anthropology, evolutionary economics, and the analysis of institutions, the two have much to complement one another.

While Marxists and anarchists have engaged in a long history of debates – sometimes acrimonious – the two approaches clearly share much in their critique of capitalism and broad general views on socialism. In fact, even their ultimate goals, such as pure communism without a state, are in some instances virtually identical. In any case, even with some strong disagreements, the two may benefit from dialogue. If they were already the same there would be little point in constructive engagement. The Marxist approach may offer help in the area identified by Brown – that of discarding the conception of a "natural" for an historical approach.

Conclusion

Anarchism, both "classical" and contemporary, has a rich literature filled with distinctive and provocative ideas concerning economics. With a few exceptions, there is very little consideration in economics of anarchism as a distinct paradigm worthy of analytical investigation. Even within heterodox economics, there are almost no discussions of anarchism. This chapter has argued that anarchist thought is full of economic insights and that there are important links between anarchism and other heterodox schools, especially ecological, feminist, institutionalist, and Marxian. It is the intention here to call for more research into anarchist thinking on economic issues.

The insights of anarchism discussed in this chapter, from decentralization and bioregionalism to reciprocity and mutualism, are just some examples of what anarchist economic thought has to offer. Throughout the voluminous anarchist literature, both classical and contemporary, there are many more unique perspectives and approaches that may both complement and supplement heterodox political economy. This is not simply an exercise in the history of ideas, however, as anarchism may also contribute to envisioning post-capitalist possibilities for the twenty-first century.

Notes

1 Anarchism has also made substantial contributions to economic anthropology, or the analysis of pre-capitalist modes of production, as well as comparative systems.
2 Little attention is also paid here to what has been called "life-style anarchism," where concerns may be addressed in a more individualistic way, such as in consumption decisions (e.g., eating natural foods) and where there tends to be a more romanticized view of nature (Bookchin 1995).
3 The bibliography contains some works not cited in this chapter, to introduce the reader to additional texts in and around anarchist economics.

Bibliography

Albert, M., Cagan, L., Chomsky, N., Hahnel, R., King, M., Sargent, L., and Sklar, H. (1986) *Liberating Theory*, Boston, MA: South End Press.
Avrich, P. (ed.) (1995) *Anarchist Voices: An Oral History of Anarchism in America*, Princeton, NJ: Princeton University Press.
Berkman, A. (1929 [2000]) *ABC of Anarchism*, London: Freedom Press.
Bookchin, M. (1971) *Post-scarcity Anarchism*, Montréal: Black Rose Books.
—— (1991) *The Ecology of Freedom*, Montréal: Black Rose Books.
—— (1993) "The Meaning of Confederalism," *Society and Nature*, 1(3): 41–54.
—— (1995) *Social Anarchism or Lifestyle Anarchism*, San Francisco, CA: AK Press.
—— (1999) *Anarchism, Marxism, and the Future of the Left*, San Francisco, CA: AK Press.
Braverman, H. (1974) *Labor and Monopoly Capital*, New York: Monthly Review Press.
Brown, L.S. (1993) "Anarchism, Existentialism, Feminism," *Society and Nature*, 2(1): 117–36.
Chomsky, N. (1973) "Notes on Anarchism," in *For Reasons of State* (pp. 370–86), New York: Vintage.
Christie, S. and Meltzer, A. (1970) *The Floodgates of Anarchy*, London: Sphere Books.
Claessen, H.J.M. and van de Velde, P. (eds) (1991) *Early State Economics*, New Brunswick, NJ: Transaction.
Clark, J.B. (1910? [2002]) "Anarchism, Socialism, and Social Reform," *Journal of the History of Economic Thought*, 24(4): 451–62.
Clastres, P. (1977) *Society Against the State*, New York: Urizen.
Cutler, R.M. (ed.) (1992) *The Basic Bakunin*, Buffalo, NY: Prometheus.
Dickson, D. (1975) *The Politics of Alternative Technology*, New York: Universe.
Dolgoff, S. (ed.) (1974) *The Anarchist Collectives*, Québec: Black Rose Books.
—— (1986) *Fragments: A Memoir*, Cambridge: Refract Publications.
Dugger, W.M. (1984) "Veblen and Kropotkin on Human Evolution," *Journal of Economic Issues*, 18(4): 971–85.
Edgell, S. and Tilman, R. (1989) "The Intellectual Antecedents of Thorstein Veblen," *Journal of Economic Issues*, 23(4): 1003–26.

Ehrlich, H.J. (ed.) (1996) *Reinventing Anarchy, Again*, San Francisco, CA: AK Press.
Ekins, P. (ed.) (1986) *The Living Economy*, London: Routledge & Kegan Paul.
Fernández, F. (2001) *Cuban Anarchism*, Tucson, Ariz: See Sharp Press.
Forstater, M. (2002) "Bones for Sale: 'Development,' Environment, and Food Security in East Africa," *Review of Political Economy*, 14(1): 47–67.
Foutopoulos, T. (1993) "The Economic Foundations of an Ecological Society," *Society and Nature*, 1(3): 1–40.
George, D.A.R. (1997) "Self-management and Ideology," *Review of Political Economy*, 9(1): 51–62.
Glassgold, P. (ed.) (2001) *Anarchy! An Anthology of Emma Goldman's Mother Earth*, Washington, DC: Counterpoint.
Goldman, E. (1917 [1969]) *Anarchism and Other Essays*, New York: Dover Press.
Gowan, S., Lakey, G., Moyer, W. and Taylor, R. (1976) *Moving Toward a New Society*, Philadelphia, PA: New Society Press.
Guérin, D. (ed.) (1998) *No Gods No Masters*, San Francisco, CA: AK Press.
Guillen, A. (1988) *Economia Libertaria*, Bilbao: Fundacion de Estudios Libertarios.
Hardin, G. (1968) "The Tragedy of the Commons," *Science*, 162(3859): 1243–8.
Hawkins, H. (1993) "Community Control, Workers Control, and the Cooperative Commonwealth," *Society and Nature*, 1(3): 55–85.
Heller, C. (1999) *Ecology of Everyday Life*, Montréal: Black Rose Books.
Hewitt, M. and Roussopoulos, D.I. (eds) *1984 and After*, Montréal: Black Rose Books.
Knowles, R. (2000) "Political Economy from Below: Communitarian Anarchism as a Neglected Discourse in the Histories of Economic Thought," *History of Economics Review*, 31: 30–47.
—— (2004) *Political Economy from Below: Economic Thought in Communitarian Anarchism, 1840–1914*, New York: Routledge.
Kovel, J. (2002) *The Enemy of Nature: The End of Capitalism or the End of the World?*, London: Zed Books.
Kropotkin, P. (1899 [1968]) *Memoirs of a Revolutionist*, New York: Grove Press.
—— (1910) "Anarchism," *Encyclopaedia Britannica*, vol. 1, pp. 914–19, New York: The Encyclopaedia Britannica Company.
—— (1913 [1974]) *Fields, Factories, and Workshops Tomorrow*, London: Allen & Unwin.
Leval, G. (1975) *Collectives in the Spanish Revolution*, London: Freedom Press.
Luccarelli, M. (1995) *Lewis Mumford and the Ecological Region*, New York: Guilford Press.
Makhno, N. (1996) *The Struggle Against the State and Other Essays*, San Francisco, CA: AK Press.
Malatesta, E. (1995) *The Anarchist Revolution*, London: Freedom Press.
Mason, E.S. (1928) "Fourier and Anarchism," *Quarterly Journal of Economics*, 42(2): 228–62.
Mbah, S. and Igariwey, I.E. (1997) *African Anarchism*, Tucson, Ariz: See Sharp Press.
McKercher, W.R. (1989) *Freedom and Authority*, Montréal: Black Rose Books.
Milani, B. (2000) *Designing the Green Economy*, Oxford: Rowman & Littlefield.
Morrison, R. (1995) *Ecological Democracy*, Boston, MA: South End Press.
Nettlau, M. (1996) *A Short History of Anarchism*, London: Freedom Press.
Prychitko, D.L. (1997) "Expanding the Anarchist Range: A Critical Reappraisal of Rothbard's Contribution to the Contemporary Theory of Anarchism," *Review of Political Economy*, 9(4): 433–55.
Richards, V. (ed.) (1965) *Errico Malatesta: His Life and Ideas*, London: Freedom Press.
Roszak, T. (1973) "Introduction," in E.F. Schumacher, *Small is Beautiful* (pp. 1–9), New York: Harper & Row.

Roussopoulos, D.I. (ed.) (1990) *The Anarchist Papers 3*, Montréal: Black Rose Books.
Schumacher, E.F. (1973) *Small is Beautiful*, New York: Harper & Row.
Skalnik, P. (ed.) (1989) *Outwitting the State*, New Brunswick, NJ: Transaction.
Thomas, P. (1980) *Karl Marx and the Anarchists*, London: Routledge & Kegan Paul.
Ward, C. (1973) *Anarchy in Action*, New York: Harper & Row.
Wolff, R.P. (1970) *In Defense of Anarchism*, New York: Harper & Row.
Woodcock, G. (1962) *Anarchism*, Cleveland: Meridian Books.
Woodcock, G. (1987) "Anarchism," in J. Eatwell, M. Milgate and P. Newman (eds) *The New Palgrave* (pp. 90–3), London: Macmillan.

4 The economics of the Industrial Workers of the World

Job control and revolution

Frederic S. Lee

Introduction

The Industrial Workers of the World (IWW) understanding and critique of capitalism drew largely upon "classical" Marxian arguments. These arguments, at least in the minds of Wobblies, justified their tactical positions of direct action and the general strike, their ethical-theoretical position that workers not the bosses should control their jobs and hence their working lives, and their theoretical-revolutionary position of taking possession of the earth and the machinery of production and abolishing the wage system. However, the core of Marxian economic theory is not as sound as the Wobblies believed one hundred years ago, which means that robust arguments supporting job control and revolution may not exist. The aim of this chapter is to examine this predicament and offer an alternative set of arguments. Thus the second section of the chapter briefly covers the IWW's Marxian critique of capitalism and its justification of direct action for increasing wages and job control and of the general strike for abolishing capitalism and the wage system. The third section outlines an alternative heterodox economics framework for the examination of capitalism, while the fourth section examines its theoretical relationship to job control and revolution. The final section concludes the chapter.

IWW's critique of capitalism

As a revolutionary trade union devoted to the day-to-day struggle of workers against the bosses, the IWW devoted little energy to articulating their own particular critique of capitalism and a theoretical justification for direct action, the general strike, job control, and the abolition of the wage system. Given the prevalence of Marxian and anarcho-syndicalist arguments against capitalism and for workers' action, it was expedient for hard-pressed working Wobblies to borrow judiciously from the existing arguments of the day when writing propaganda qua informative pamphlets or engaging in discussions with workers.[1] Thus, the early pamphlets generally accepted Marxian economic theory and its critique of capitalism and the Marxian-anarcho-syndicalist arguments for direct action; and the views expressed in them are broadly held within the IWW today.[2]

Marx's labor theory of value was accepted by Wobblies not just for its explanation of relative prices but more so because of its account of the workers' role in capitalism. That is, the Marxian argument of labor power as a commodity was accepted because of its characterization of capitalism as a class relationship between bosses and workers that resulted in workers being wage-slaves. This is captured in the preamble to the Constitution of the IWW:

> The working class and the employing class have nothing in common. . . . Between these two classes a struggle must go on until the workers of the world organize as a class, take possession of the earth and the machinery of production, and abolish the wage system.

With capitalism characterized as a system of social relationships that enslave workers and make their livelihood and existence dependent upon the decisions of bosses, other components of Marxian economics were accepted because they capture the social relationships in production and distribution so visible to Wobblies and advanced possible ways to escape from wage slavery. First, since all produced goods required interdependent laboring activity, it was not possible for a particular worker or industry to produce any output by themselves:

> Production of any article is impossible to any worker under the capitalist arrangement of industry; the simplest article as well as the most complicated machine is the product of the entire working class. From the sulphur match to the aggregate of the world's commodities there cannot be eliminated any classification of labor, and have the match, or the world's wealth.
>
> (IWW 1922: 3)

With production a social, differentiated, interdependent whole, the IWW advanced the argument that the organizing of industry requires the establishment of One Big Union – one working class, one union. Second, it was accepted that the value of all commodities was based on the quantitative amount of social labor power embodied in them and that the origin of profits was derived from the exploitation of labor. In short, the labor theory of value was accepted because of its embodiment of the social relationship between workers engaged in production and between workers and bosses.[3] And the labor theory of value was also accepted because it suggested the solution to being a wage-slave:

> The chief demand of revolutionary industrial unionism [is] that workingmen and women cease selling themselves, or their strength, as commodities. We propose to *own* the commodities we produce *ourselves* and to exchange commodities containing a certain quantity of necessary social labor, for other commodities representing an equal quantity of necessary social labor. . . . When you and I and our fellow workers *own* the factories in which we work, or the land we cultivate, we will no longer need to turn over to anybody the commodities we have produced. We shall be joint owners of the things we have made socially. We shall demand labor for labor in the exchange of commodities. This is the kernel of the I.W.W. It proposes to make men and

women of us instead of sellers of a *commodity* to be bought and sold upon the cheapest market as men buy shoes or cows.

(Marcy 1911: 17–18)

With the labor theory of value accepted, it was then applied to a range of economic issues, most specifically prices and the wage-profit nexus. There was and is a recurring argument advocated by reformers of capitalism that workers' standard of living could improve if the prices of subsistence goods declined and, conversely, if the price of subsistence goods increased (say, due to monopoly) living standards would decline. The IWW rejected this argument in the following manner. It first argued that the prices of theoretical interest were *prices of production* toward which market prices gravitate; hence while variations in supply and demand cause market prices to deviate from prices of production, these deviations are not permanent. The IWW then argued (almost assumed) that prices of production were equal to labor values, which enabled the analysis to use values and prices interchangeably. Finally, it assumed that whatever conditions exist, the capitalists could ultimately drive workers' wages to subsistence level. Hence for a given weekly subsistence bundle of goods to sustain a worker, the weekly wage (w) was equal to that bundle of goods times their prices:

(1) $w = c_1p_1 + \ldots. + c_ip_i + \ldots + c_np_n$ or
$w = \mathbf{cp}$

where c_i is the amount of good i needed by the worker;
$\mathbf{c} = c_1. \ldots c_n$ a row vector of the weekly subsistence bundle of goods;
p_i is the price of production of good i; and
$\mathbf{p} = p_1. \ldots p_n$ a column vector of prices of production for the subsistence goods.

Since the subsistence bundle of goods was assumed more or less fixed, a decline in any one or more of their prices (p_i) resulted in the decline in the wage (w); while an increase in prices increased the wage. So irrespective of the movement of prices, the workers' subsistence standard of living would not change.[4] Consequently, concern about high or low prices, the IWW argued, was of little interest to workers; rather their concern should be directed at the wage-profit nexus that represents the social relationship between workers and capitalists.[5]

The above argument implied that prices were essentially unimportant when it came to understanding wage slavery and the operations of the capitalist system, clearly one of the major theoretical points made by the labor theory of value. This was conceded by the IWW through its acceptance of Marx's argument that the increase of wages and the consequent fall in profits and the rate of profit did not lead to a permanent change in the prices of production: "A general rise in the rate of wages would result in a fall of the general rate of profit, but, broadly speaking, not affect the prices of commodities" (Marx 1976: 62, cited in Marcy 1911: 32).

Hence it is necessary to directly face the wage-profit nexus and determine how to increase the wage so as to improve the workers' subsistence standard of living while simultaneously reducing the rate of profit, and how to increase workers' control over their jobs and working conditions to free them from the authoritarian control of the bosses and also at the same time reduce the rate of profit. Both actions therefore contribute to the downfall of capitalism and the ushering in of socialism.[6] However, with regard to increasing wages, because the causal direction goes from the value of the subsistence goods to the wage, $\mathbf{cp} \rightarrow w$, and since prices are invariant with respect to changes in wages and the rate of profit, the only option is to directly increase the components of **c** (which reduces the rate of profit). On the other hand, increasing job control and better working conditions directly reduces the rate of profit through reducing the surplus (although it may increase some of the components of the consumption vector **c**).[7] And most significantly, both of these actions require direct action by workers at the point of production if they are to come about:

> The struggle between the capitalist class and the working class take place in production and *nowhere else*; that it is over surplus value and over nothing else; that the interest of the capitalist is to retain and to increase the amount of surplus value, and the interest of the worker lies in diminishing surplus value until finally no surplus value remains. In other words, the struggle on the side of the capital is to continue labor power as a commodity, and on the side of the workers to destroy the commodity character of labor power. The capitalist wants to continue the wage system, and the worker must abolish it.
>
> (IWW 1922: 58)

Direct action for the IWW is that workers directly engage in affecting the production process at the point of production so that the bundle of subsistence goods, **c**, increases, job control increases and working conditions improve, and the surplus for profits decline:[8] "Only when 'direct actions' are applied in efforts to undermine the economic power of the employing class, are they essentially and socially useful and beneficial" (William Trautman, in Salerno 1997: 27).

One way the IWW attempted to increase **c** was to argue that a specific amount of work corresponded to a specific bundle of subsistence goods; hence if the amount of work expected was more than the corresponding amount of subsistence goods, then the direct action needed was to reduce the amount of work – through working slowly or less effectively – to correspond with the amount of subsistence goods; and the outcome would be a fall in the rate of profit. Another direct action demand that the IWW advocated was shorter hours/work week – the four-hour day. This would reduce the surplus for profits without reducing the subsistence bundle of goods; so while the workers' material standard of living would not increase, control over their working and non-working lives would, and this, for the IWW, was a significant step toward achieving socialism.[9] The question was how to achieve this and one tactic advocated by the IWW was that workers should just walk off the job after, say, eight hours. Finally, the most important direct action demand that the IWW advocated was more control by workers over the work process, which included better and safer working conditions at the point of production – that is, more control over the job since it reduced the degree to which a worker was a wage-slave and thus advanced the cause of socialism. The general tactic used in this regard was the explicit withdrawal of their efficiency in the work process, such as working slower or ineffectually, refusing to work in unsafe conditions, working to rule, random short-term work stoppages, sit-down strikes, and even walk-out strikes as a last resort (Bekken 1986; IWW 1922, 1934, 1938, 1982, 2001; Marcy 1911; Miller 2002; Salerno 1997).[10]

Being limited to dealing with "immediate" workplace issues, the direct action tactics noted above generated only a piecemeal advance toward socialism. Moreover, the IWW does not believe that socialism will arrive on its own due to some kind of historical law; workers' direct action is absolutely necessary. However, the capitalist class and its accomplice the capitalist state will oppose the coming of socialism with armed force.[11] But armed insurrection is uncertain in its outcome as well as producing loss of lives and the destruction of the stocks of goods and services that are essential for the material well-being of the working class. Thus, the IWW supports the ultimate direct action, the general strike. In this case, workers refuse to work for the bosses and take over the means of production and distribution for the benefit of the working class. Consequently, capitalist relationships, most particularly wage-slavery, are dissolved, while at the same time employment increases, production expands, and workers' standard of living rises (IWW 1982). The general strike targets the capitalists not the working class:

> According to the modern idea of the General Strike . . . the effort would be made to get workers into the industries instead of out of them in order to keep the wheels of production going. . . . The wheels of industry would operate in their customary manner only for the purpose of supplying human needs instead of the enrichment of the profit-greedy Kept Class. The General Strike there would simply mean that the army of production under competent technical and managerial direction, would continue to man and remain in the industries, producing and transporting goods for consumption but refusing any longer to yield up surplus value to the parasite class. The General Strike would be a General Lockout against these idle drones who now hold as their "private property" the machinery upon which the human race depends for life.
>
> (IWW 1982: 41)

Heterodox economics model of capitalism

The roots of heterodox economics are located in the heterodox traditions that emphasize the wealth of nations, accumulation, social relationships, full employment, and economic and social reproduction. Therefore the discipline of economics is, from the heterodox perspective, defined as being concerned with explaining the process that provides the flow of goods and services required by society to meet the needs of those who participate in its activities. That is, for heterodox economists, economics is the science of the social provisioning process. Using empirically grounded concepts, the heterodox explanation involves human agency in a cultural context and social processes in historical time affecting resources, consumption patterns, production and reproduction, and the meaning (or ideology) of economic activities engaged in social provisioning. Thus *heterodox economics* has two interdependent parts: theory and policy. *Heterodox economic theory* is a theoretical explanation of the historical process of social provisioning within the context of a capitalist economy. Therefore it is concerned with explaining those factors that are part of the process of social provisioning, including the structure and use of resources, the structure and change of social wants, the structure of production and the reproduction of the business enterprise and other relevant institutions, and distribution.

In addition, heterodox economists extend their theory to examining issues associated with the process of social provisioning, such as racism, gender, and ideologies and myths. Because heterodox economics involves issues that are inseparable from ethical values, social philosophy, and the historical aspects of human existence, heterodox economists feel that it is also their duty to make *heterodox economic policy* recommendations to improve human dignity; that is, recommending ameliorative and/or radical, social, and economic policies to improve the social provisioning for all members of society and especially the disadvantage members. Moreover, they adopt the view that their economic policy recommendations must be based on an accurate historical and theoretical picture of how the economy actually works – a picture that includes class and hierarchical domination, inequalities, and social-economic discontent. In this section, the basic framework of heterodox theory will be delineated and then in the following section it will be used to examine job control and revolution (Dugger 1996; Lee 2008; Lutz 1999; O'Boyle 1996; Power 2004).

Micro-macro structural organization of economic activity

Structure of production

The social provisioning process is founded on the social and interdependent production of goods and services; thus the core framework of economic activity of a capitalist economy consists of its schema of production and the income flows relative to goods and services for social provisioning. The schema of production of the economy may be represented as a circular production input-output matrix of material goods combined with different types of labor power skills to produce an array of goods and services as outputs. Many of the outputs replace the goods and services used up in production and the rest constitute a surplus to be used for consumption, private investment, and government usage. More specifically, the production schema of the economy is empirically represented in terms of a product-by-product input-output table (or matrix). The table shows that m goods and services are produced, and that n goods and services and z labor power skills are used in their production, where the former constitute the *intermediate inputs* where $m > n$

and the latter constitute the *labor power skills inputs* where $z \geq m$. Thus, letting q_{ij} represent the amount of the jth product (good or service) and L_{iz} represent the amount of the zth labor power skill to produce Q_i amount of the ith product, the production of the ith good or service may be represented by the following:

$$\text{(2)}\quad [q_{i1}, \ldots, q_{in}, L_{i1}, \ldots, L_{iz}] \rightarrow Q_i \text{ or}$$
$$[G_i, L_i] \rightarrow Q_i$$
$$\text{where } G_i = (q_{i1}, \ldots, q_{in}) \text{ and}$$
$$L_i = (L_{i1}, \ldots, L_{iz}).$$

Hence, the input-output table of the economy takes the following form:

$$[G_1, L_1] \rightarrow Q_1$$
$$\text{(3)}\quad \ldots\ldots\ldots\ldots\ldots\ldots$$
$$[G_m, L_m] \rightarrow Q_m.$$

Representing the array of $(G_1, \ldots, G_m)$ as G a product-by-product input-output table, the array of $(L_1, \ldots, L_m)$ as L a labor power skills-by-product table, and the total quantity produced of each product as Q_d, the input-output table of (3) can be depicted as follows:

$$\text{(4)}\quad G + L \rightarrow Q_d \text{ or}$$

$$\text{(5)}\quad \begin{bmatrix} G_{11} \\ G_{21} \end{bmatrix} + \begin{bmatrix} L_{11} \\ L_{21} \end{bmatrix} \rightarrow \begin{bmatrix} Q_{d1} & 0 \\ 0 & Q_{d2} \end{bmatrix}$$

where G is a *m* x *n* flow matrix of intermediate inputs of goods and services;
L is a *m* x *z* flow matrix of labor power skills;
Q_d is a diagonal *m* x *m* matrix of output;
G_{11} is a square *n* x *n* matrix of intermediate inputs used in the production of Q_{d1}, a *n* x *n* diagonal matrix of intermediate inputs of goods and services;
G_{21} is a *m-n* x *n* matrix of intermediate inputs used in the production of Q_{d2}, a *m-n x m-n* diagonal matrix of final goods and services for consumption, investment, and government;
L_{11} is a *n* x *z* matrix of labor power skills used in the production of Q_{d1}; and
L_{21} is a *m-n* x *z* matrix of labor power skills used in the production of Q_{d2}.

One feature of circular production is that in the case of $G_{11} \rightarrow Q_{d1}$, all the outputs also appear as inputs (either directly or indirectly) in their own production.[12] This implies that both inputs and outputs are tied to technically specified, differentiated uses, production is a circular flow, and all intermediate capital goods and services are produced inputs. Consequently, the production of intermediate inputs is a differentiated, indecomposable and hence emergent schema or system of production that cannot be segmented, aggregated, disaggregated, reduced or increased. Building on circular production, a second feature is that there are no scarce resources, which means that intermediate inputs are not scarce factors of production and the surplus does not consist of "relatively scarce" goods and services (Aspromourgos 2004; De Gregori 1987; Eichner 1987; Kurz and Salvadori 1995, 2005; Lee 1998; Lowe 1976; Sraffa 1960; and Zimmermann 1951).

Monetary structure of the economy and the linkage between incomes and the surplus

The second component of the framework is the relation between the money wages of workers, profits of enterprises, and government "money income" and expenditures on consumption, investment, and government goods and services, and on financial assets. That is, the social surplus of the economy, which consists of the goods and services not used directly in production, has to be distributed across three classes of claimants – workers, capitalists and business enterprises, and the state: $\mathbf{Q_2} = (Q_{n+1}, \ldots, Q_m)$ is a column vector of goods and services not used directly in production and hence may be used for (that is, purchased for) consumption, investment, and/or government purposes. And the distribution has to be done in money terms. Hence letting $\mathbf{p} = (p_1, \ldots, p_m)$ be a column vector of money prices of all *m* goods produced in the economy, $\mathbf{p_1} = (p_1, \ldots, p_n)$ be a column vector of money prices of intermediate inputs, $\mathbf{p_2} = (p_{n+1}, \ldots, p_m)$ be a column vector of all surplus goods and services, $\mathbf{w} = (w_1, \ldots, w_z)$ be a column vector of money wage rates, $\mathbf{Q} = (Q_1, \ldots, Q_m)$ be a column vector of output, and **e** is a unit row vector, then:

(6a) $W = \mathbf{e}\,(\mathbf{Lw})$ which is scalar and is the total wage bill;
(6b) $\Pi = (\mathbf{Q^T p}) - \mathbf{e}\,[\mathbf{Gp_1} + \mathbf{Lw}]$ which is a scalar and is total profits;
(6c) $VS = (\mathbf{Q^T{}_2 p_2})$ which is a scalar and is the total monetary value of the surplus.

While the wage bill and profits are directly connected to economic activity, government money income is not. That is, following the Chartalist argument, the government creates its own money income for spending by crediting bank accounts. So while taxation hence taxes can exist, they are not relevant with regard to expenditure decisions by the government. The point of taxes is first, to create demand for money (government IOUs), and second, to drain reserves out of the system thereby affecting the expenditure decisions of enterprises and households. Complementing and reinforcing the Chartalist tax argument is the argument that the demand for government money arises through state and class power coupled with access to the social provisioning process. In this case, the state acquires the goods and services it needs by paying for them with government money which is backed by state power of simply acquiring them without any compensation. By accepting the money the capitalists in turn make access to the social provisioning process dependent on having it. Thus, capitalists demand money to obtain access to social provisioning and they use their class power over workers to impose on them the acquisition of it as their only way to gain access to the social provisioning process. Hence workers have to sell their labor power for government money to be able to purchase goods and services necessary for their survival. But irrespective of the particular argument used, both imply that government money income is not associated with or derived in some sense from economic activity.

To simplify the following analysis, taxes will be ignored and the second argument is utilized to underpin the acceptance and demand for government money; and it will be assumed that government money income (GOV_m) is only spent on goods and services. Since the state does not actually produce the goods but the capitalists do, government income qua expenditures is transferred to the capitalists and shows up as an indistinguishable component of their profits. Therefore the national income (NI) directly associated with economic activity is equal to the sum of the wage bill and profits (which includes GOV_m):

(6d) $NI = W + \Pi$.

Together, the production and monetary structures generate a monetary input-output structure of the economy:

(4) $G + L \rightarrow Q_d$ is the productive structure of the economy;
(5′) $(eG)^T + \mathbf{Q_2} = \mathbf{Q}$ which is the structure of the total output of the economy that equals the material inputs used in production plus the surplus;
(6b′) $G\mathbf{p_1} + L\mathbf{w} + \mathbf{\Pi} = Q_d\mathbf{p}$ is the monetary structure of the economy where $\mathbf{\Pi} = (\Pi_1, \ldots, \Pi_m)$ is a column vector of the profits in each market;
(6c′) $Q_{d2}\mathbf{P_2} = Q_{d2C}\mathbf{P_2} + Q_{d2I}\mathbf{P_2} + Q_{d2G}\mathbf{P_2}$ which is the monetary structure of the surplus of goods and services in terms of consumption, investment, and government purchases.

Since workers spend all their wage income only on consumption goods, capitalists spend part of their profit income on consumption goods and the remaining part on investment goods and services and financial assets, and government income is spent on government goods and services, then:

(6e) $\mathbf{Q_{2C}}^T\mathbf{p_2} = \mathbf{e}(L\mathbf{w}) + \mathbf{c_c}\mathbf{\Pi}$ which is that consumption is equal to the wage bill and the capitalist consumption out of profits where $\mathbf{Q_{2C}}$ is a column vector of consumption goods and $\mathbf{c_c} = (c_{c1}, \ldots, c_{cm})$ is a row vector of capitalist propensities to consume out of profits;
(6f) $\mathbf{Q_{2I}}^T\mathbf{p_2} + Q_F = \mathbf{re}\mathbf{\Pi}$ which is investment plus financial assets (Q_F) are equal to retained earnings where $\mathbf{Q_{2I}}$ is a column vector of investment goods and $\mathbf{re} = (1 - c_{c1}, \ldots, 1 - c_{cm})$ is a row vector of capitalist propensities to retain earnings out of profits;

(6g) $\mathbf{Q_{2G}}^{T}\mathbf{p_2} = Q_F = GOV_m$ which is the value of government goods purchased is equal to the value of the financial assets purchased by business enterprises which is equal to government expenditures where $\mathbf{Q_{2G}}$ is a column vector of government goods.

Therefore,

(7) $\mathbf{e}\,(Q_{d2}\,\mathbf{p_2}) = \mathbf{e}\,(\mathbf{Lw}) + \mathbf{c_c\Pi} + \mathbf{re\Pi}$ or the value of the goods and services surplus equals national income (Bortis 1997, 2003; Kregel 1975; Lee 1998; Wray 1998).

Social framework of the social provisioning process

Complementing the structure of the economy is the social framework of the social provisioning process in a capitalist economy. It consists of the organizations that generate and direct the social provisioning process; that is, the business enterprise and the state, and the social relationships that permit them to direct the process. Starting with the latter, there are two broad social classes with respect to economic activity: those who do not own or control the means of production and hence do not have privileged access to incomes, and those who do own and do control the means of production and hence have privileged access to incomes. Hence the former have no choice but to work for the latter while the latter are able to control and direct the working lives of the workers for their own benefits and hence are the bosses or the capitalists. The latter's benefits include not only a superior material standard of living but also the social power to maintain ownership and control so as to continue directing the social provisioning process for their benefit. Whether the two broad classes have anything in common is a complex question; however, what they do not have in common is who owns, controls, and directs the economic activity underpinning the social provisioning process. In particular the capitalist class wants to retain the power associated with ownership, control, and direction so as to make workers dependent upon them and therefore be able to direct workers' lives for their own benefit.

Business enterprise and prices

The organization through which the capitalist class directs the social provisioning process is the business enterprise and the state. The business enterprise is a specific social organization for coordinating and carrying out economic activities in a manner that mirrors the social relationships in capitalist society and, most importantly, reproduces the capitalist class itself. It consists of an organizational component, a production and cost component, a series of routines that transmit information (such as costs, sales, and prices) to enable workers and managers to coordinate and carry out their activities, and a management team that makes strategic decisions about prices and investment. The organization of the business enterprise is essentially a particular social technique for the production of goods and services. Hierarchical in structure and authoritarian in terms of social control, the organization of the enterprise enables senior management to make decisions that in turn are carried out by lower management and workers. The enterprise has three tools by which to effect economic activity and hence the social provisioning process for its own interest: setting prices, undertaking investment, and making production and employment decisions. When making decisions, management of an enterprise is motivated by different goals, the most fundamental being the survival and continuation of the enterprise, followed by various strategic goals, such as growth of sales, developing new products, entering new geographical regions or markets, generating dividends for shareholders, and/or attaining political power. Given that the enterprise has an unknown but potentially very long life span, the time period to achieve each of the goals is likely to differ, and management cannot be sure that they can achieve them. Thus the goals are not ends in themselves but are established so as to direct the activities of the enterprise in a radically uncertain environment. As a result, profits are not an end goal for management, but rather an intermediate objective that facilitates the directing of its desired activities (Campbell *et al.* 1991; Downward 1999; Dunn 2001; Eichner 1976, 1987; Fligstein 1990, 2001; Lavoie 1992; Lee 1998).

Pricing and the price model

Management views price setting, the choosing of investment projects, and production and employment targets as strategic decisions designed to meet their goals. With regard to the former, management utilizes cost-plus pricing procedures that involve first calculating the costs of producing the product at normal output and then adding a profit mark-up to set the price. The resulting price remains fixed for a period of time (and many transactions) and does not change when sales increase or decrease. Its two most important properties are its potential, depending on the state of demand (sales), to generate a cash flow for the enterprise that will cover its costs producing the product and to generate profits and its strategic capabilities, such as penetrating markets and altering market shares. Once set the price is then administered to the market as the enterprise's market price. However, the business enterprise sells its goods and services in markets that include products from other competing enterprises; thus there needs to be a market arrangement by which the market price is set. For simplicity's sake, it will be assumed that the market price is set by a price leader or a cartel. Hence the *price equation for a single market* is not significantly different from the enterprise pricing equation:

(8) $[\mathbf{m}_i\mathbf{p}_1 + \boldsymbol{l}_i^*\mathbf{w}][1 + r_i] = p_i$

where $\mathbf{m}_i = (m_{i1}, \ldots, m_{in})$ is a row vector of average material pricing coefficients at normal output or capacity utilization;
$\boldsymbol{l}_i^* = (l_{i1}^*, \ldots, l_{iz}^*)$ is a row vector of average labor pricing coefficients at normal output or capacity utilization;
r_i is the profit mark up;
p_i is the market price for the ith good.

Since market refers to all the transactions of a specific product, the economy consists of as many markets as there are products. Thus there are m markets that may be classified as consumer, investment, intermediate capital, or government goods markets.[13] Common to all the markets is that the relationship between the market price and market sales is non-existent; thus a reduction in the market price by itself will generate little if any increase in market sales. Finally, the *price model of the economy* is:

(9) $[R_d][M\mathbf{p}_1 + l^*\mathbf{w}] = \mathbf{p}$

where R_d is a m x m matrix of profit mark ups and the ith element is $(1 + r_i)$;
M is a m x n matrix of normal average material pricing coefficients that are invariant with respect to short-term variations in output and the ith row in $\mathbf{m}_i$; and
l^* is a n x z of normal average labor pricing coefficients that are invariant with respect to short-term variations in output and the ith row is $\boldsymbol{l}_i^*$.

Business enterprise, the state, investment and the quantity model

Management of the business enterprise distinguishes between investment projects that are designed to replace broken equipment or maintain the operations of an existing plant, to meet state-mandated environmental and safety standards, and to expand capacity, create new products, and expand the enterprise's marketing capabilities. Management generally funds all the investment projects in the first two categories on the grounds that, if they were not supported, the enterprise's capacity for current production would be severely reduced. Investment projects in the third category, on the other hand, are justified either in terms of their contribution to meeting the future demand of the enterprise's existing products or in terms of producing new products for current and novel future demands. In addition, such investments have to meet a range of financial guidelines ranging from generating a flow of profits that would cover their costs in a given number of years to a minimal rate of return (that is greater than the market interest rate). Given management's goals, however, the financial guidelines play a secondary role in investment decisions. Once the investment decision is made, management then determines whether it can be internally financed from profits or that external funds will have to be obtained from financial institutions. From the above discussion we find that investment is a demand for goods and services that are not used up in production and hence are part of the surplus. Therefore for the economy as a whole, the total investment or total demand for the surplus in the form of investment goods and services can be represented by Q_{2I}.

Both workers and capitalists demand consumer goods, but they do not command the direct production of those goods. That is, capitalists and workers do not receive a predetermined inventory of goods derived from the surplus in the previous time period; nor do they directly order the production of the goods they consume. Rather, workers and capitalists partake in the surplus, but not of their own choosing. Drawing upon past consumption patterns, enterprises make production and employment decisions that result in consumption goods (Q_{2C}) being produced ahead of payments for them while the consumers simply choose from among the already produced goods for them. Finally, the state also demands goods not used up in production; that is, it demands surplus goods (Q_{2G}). Thus the output of the economy may be represented as:

(5′) $(eG)^T + \mathbf{Q_{2I}} + \mathbf{Q_{2C}} + \mathbf{Q_{2G}} = \mathbf{Q}$.

Letting $Q^{-1}{}_dG = \begin{bmatrix} Q^{-1}{}_{d1}G_{11} \\ Q^{-1}{}_{d2}G_{21} \end{bmatrix} = A = \begin{bmatrix} A_{11} \\ A_{21} \end{bmatrix}$ a *m* x *n* matrix of material

production coefficients that vary with output and $Q^{-1}{}_dL = \begin{bmatrix} Q^{-1}{}_dL_{11} \\ Q^{-1}{}_dL_{21} \end{bmatrix} = l$ a *m* x z

matrix of labor production coefficients that vary with output, the *output-labor quantity model of the economy* is:

(10) $A^TQ + \mathbf{Q_{2I}} + \mathbf{Q_{2C}} + \mathbf{Q_{2G}} = \mathbf{Q}$
$(Q_d\, l)^T\mathbf{e}^T = \mathbf{L}$ where $\mathbf{L} = (L_1, \ldots L_z)$ a column vector of labor power skills.

Micro-macro model of a capitalist monetary production economy

The micro-macro model of the economy may be represented as follows:

(4′)	$Q_dA + Q_d\, l \rightarrow Q_d$	productive structure of the economy;
(10)	$A^TQ + \mathbf{Q_{2I}} + \mathbf{Q_{2C}} + \mathbf{Q_{2G}} = \mathbf{Q}$	quantity model of the economy – output;
	$(Q_d\, l)^T\mathbf{e}^T = \mathbf{L}$	quantity model of the economy – labor;
(9)	$[R_d][M\mathbf{p_1} + l^*\mathbf{w}] = \mathbf{p}$	price model of the economy;
(11)	$Q_dA\mathbf{p_1} + Q_{d2}\mathbf{p_2} = Q_d\mathbf{p}$ $(Q_d\, l)^T\mathbf{w} = \mathbf{Lw}$	price-output model of the economy as a whole;
(7’)	$\mathbf{e}\,(\mathbf{Lw}) + \mathbf{c_c\Pi} + \mathbf{re\Pi} = \mathbf{e}\,(Q_{d2}\mathbf{p_2})$ $GOV_M = Q_F$	national income equals the value of the goods and services surplus and government expenditures equals the value of the financial assets purchased by the business enterprise.

As the model stands, the economy operates in terms of the decisions concerning prices and the production of the surplus of goods and services; these decisions are made by the business enterprise and the state.[14] What this means for workers, job control, and revolution will be discussed in the next section.

Heterodox economics, job control, and revolution

Price determination, price changes, and the labor theory of value

Given the price model, $[\mathrm{Rd}][\mathbf{Mp_1} + l^*\mathbf{w}] = \mathbf{p}$, in a monetary production economy, for any given values of the profit mark-up and money wage rates, prices are determined without recourse to labor values.[15] Moreover, since L is a irreducible matrix of labor power skills, it is not possible to reduce it to a single homogeneous amount of labor power, which implies that prices cannot be "reduced" to a homogeneous quantity of labor power and, consequently are not proportional to embodied homogeneous quantities of labor power. In short, labor values are not needed to determine prices, labor values are not calculable, and the labor theory of value is not capable of explaining the determination of prices. Rather, because prices can exist as long as the profit mark-ups and the wage rates are positive, then it is the price system as a whole that determines prices. However, since the price system reflects and is embedded in the social system of production, it is the latter that "determines" prices or more accurately provides the material and social basis for their existence.

This argument has two implications. The first is that price changes can only occur when enterprises decide to vary money wage rates or profit mark-ups, or by altering the pricing coefficients (which is predicated on changing the underlying technology or an alteration in the capital-labor relationship within the enterprise). Thus, prices in the economy reflect agency, the costing-pricing structures of the business enterprise, and the structures of the social system of production. The second implication is that since the price model and prices are embedded in a monetary production economy where government money is the *numeraire* and wages are denoted in terms of it, wage rates and profit mark-ups can vary independently of each other, which means that the Marxian wage-profit nexus accepted by Wobblies no longer holds. Thus an increase in wage rates does not require a "structural" reduction in profit mark-ups and vice versa. Consequently an equal percentage increase in money wage rates will not alter the price-wage ratio whereas an equal percentage increase in the profit mark-up will do so. This asymmetrical outcome is due to the fact that that money wages do not equal real wages whereas the profit mark-up appropriates real goods and services and thus is equivalent to the real wage but for capitalists; that is, they are different types of variables – one is "nominal" and the other is "real."[16] Hence, as will be argued below in the context of distribution, the profit mark-up has a more significant impact on the economy relative to the money wage rate.

Output determination, production of profits, and exploitation

The decisions concerning the production of the surplus determine output and employment. This may be seen in the following way:

$$(10') \quad (\mathrm{I} - \mathrm{A}^{\mathrm{T}})^{-1} [\mathbf{Q}_{2\mathbf{I}} + \mathbf{Q}_{2\mathbf{C}} + \mathbf{Q}_{2\mathbf{G}}] = \mathbf{Q}$$

Hence, enterprise investment and production decisions and government purchases decisions determine the composition and amount of the surplus ($\mathbf{Q}_2$); and given $\mathbf{Q}_2$ (or $\mathbf{Q}_{2I} + \mathbf{Q}_{2C} + \mathbf{Q}_{2G}$), the composition and the amount of output (**Q**) and employment (**L**) is determined. Thus, the material basis of the social provisioning process is determined by one class or segment of society – the capitalist class and the dependent capitalist state – for society as a whole. Since the composition and amount of the surplus is determined by the capitalist class and by the state, they have the dominant influence qua control over the economy and society. In other words, since workers as a class cannot directly command the production of their consumption goods, they cannot control their own social provisioning process.[17] This argument has four implications. The first is that while workers must be employed to have access to the social provisioning process in a capitalist economy, the employment process is controlled by the capitalists and by the state. Therefore the composition of and the number of workers employed are determined by the capitalists and the state. While workers may choose the particular jobs they do, they cannot, as Marx argued, as a class choose not to work or not to be employed by capitalists. In short, workers are government money wage-slaves. Second, workers as a whole are employed to produce what the capitalists and the state wants and in the process, as a by-product, produce their own material reproduction; that is, the goods and services they buy with their wages: Wage bill = $\mathbf{e}\,(\mathbf{Lw}) = (\mathbf{Q}_{2C})^{\mathrm{T}}\mathbf{p}_2 - \mathbf{c}_c\mathbf{\Pi}$. On the other hand, by being employed to produce consumption, investment, and government goods and services for capitalists and the state, workers have also produced the profits for the capitalists: Profits = $(\mathbf{Q}_{2I})^{\mathrm{T}}\mathbf{p2} + [(\mathbf{Q}_{2C})^{\mathrm{T}}\mathbf{p}_2 - \mathbf{e}\,(\mathbf{Lw})] + (\mathbf{Q}_{2G})^{\mathrm{T}}\mathbf{p}_2$ since $Q_F = (\mathbf{Q}_{2G})^{\mathrm{T}}\mathbf{p}_2$. Thus, the origins of profits is found in the possibility and capability of capitalists and the state to "force" workers to produce surplus goods and services for them; and since profits consist of reproducible goods, they are not "technologically" constrained. Hence the only limit to profits is how many goods and services the capitalists and the state want.

Third, since workers are compelled to work to get government money as a way to gain access to the social provisioning process, the state can also employ (or command) workers to produce state goods and services; however in this case, workers do not produce state income as the state can "create" its own "income." Rather, by producing state goods, workers are "producing" profits for capitalists as a form of transfer payment. In any case, the state is in a powerful position to direct the economy through commanding labor power to produce its goods and services. In spite of its role in generating capitalist profits, the capitalist state is constrained by the capitalist class in its ability to command labor and direct the economy, but that should not obscure the fact that capitalists and the state are able, in the same way, to command labor power in pursuit of their own objectives. Stated in this way, capitalism and the capitalist state is not very different from a feudal economy except that the former has rejected any "social" responsibility for ensuring that all workers have a right to a place in the social provisioning process; that enough workers' consumption goods are produced to reproduce the working class as a whole; or that particular workers and their families have sufficient access to the social provisioning process to socially reproduce themselves. Finally, since the capitalist and the state command workers to produce surplus goods and services, workers are not made to provide surplus labor; rather it is the command for "surplus labor" to produce surplus goods for capitalists and the state that has as its by-product the production of wage goods for workers. Thus, the causal structure runs from surplus goods to surplus labor to wage goods; or more bluntly it is the production of profits that produces wage goods. This inverts the traditional Marxian argument that underpins its theory of exploitation and the origin of profits. Yet, while the use of surplus labor as an entry point into the analysis of exploitation and profits is misleading, the outcome is more or less the same: capitalists and the state direct the economy and hence the social provisioning process for their own interests, with the material reproduction of workers as a nagging afterthought. This suggests that full employment (that is, access to the social provisioning process for all members of society) is not an inherent component of capitalism and hence not a real concern of capitalists or the capitalist state.

Price system and distribution

Bringing the quantity and price models together produces a price-quantity model of the economy as a whole:

$$(11) \quad \begin{aligned} Q_d A\mathbf{p}_1 + Q_{d2}\mathbf{p}_2 &= Q_d\mathbf{p} \\ (Q_d l)^T\mathbf{w} &= L\mathbf{w} \end{aligned}$$

with the principle characteristic that output and prices are determined independently of each other. Hence the "coordination of economic activity" and the "allocation of scarce resources" is not done via prices. Rather it is the variations in the desire for surplus goods and services by the capitalist class and the state and not variations in prices and money wage rates that generate variations in output, market transactions, and employment of workers. If prices are not required for the "coordination of economic activity" or the allocation of scarce resources, then what does the price system do? The answer rests not so much with prices per se but with their two principal determinants: the profit mark-up and the money wage rate. As noted above, wages and profits are spent on consumption and investment goods and services and on financial assets: $\mathbf{e}\,(L\mathbf{w}) + \mathbf{c}_c\boldsymbol{\Pi} + \mathbf{re}\boldsymbol{\Pi} = (\mathbf{Q}_{2C})^T\mathbf{p}_2 + (\mathbf{Q}_{2I})^T\mathbf{p}_2 + Q_F$. Since consumption goods are for the reproduction of workers and their households, money wage rates is the agency qua institutional qua distributional mechanism through which this is achieved. However, variations in money wage rates among workers mean that there are variations in workers' participation in the social provisioning process. In particular, under capitalism with its ethos of individualism and a capitalist class strategy of preventing the emergence of a unified working class, a hierarchy of money wage rates is established through the interaction of capitalists, "business" trade unions, and workers that results in some workers having not just more goods and services than others but also having different ones, while others and their dependants have less than what is needed for survival. The profit mark-up is designed to capture a portion of the global surplus of consumption and investment goods and services and financial assets to enable the enterprise and the capitalists to reproduce themselves and to have financial claims on future goods and services. That is, like wage rates, profit mark-ups are the agency qua institutional qua distributional mechanism that enable capitalists to have current and future access to the social provisioning process and enterprises are able to reproduce themselves. Therefore, as with wage rates, variations in profit mark-ups generate among capitalists differential access to social provisioning and differential capabilities among enterprises to reproduce and grow.

Considering the relationship between wage rates and profit mark-ups, as noted above, increasing money wage rates cannot encroach upon the portion of consumption goods that is acquired by the capitalist class. However, increasing profit mark-ups reduces the "purchasing power" of wage rates, which results in changing the composition of the production of consumption goods so that fewer are produced for workers and more for capitalists are produced. Thus, the profit mark-up and the "wage share" of the value of consumption goods $[(\mathbf{Q}_{2C}{}^{T})\,\mathbf{p}_2]$ are inversely related.[18] While the profit mark-up is independent of the wage rate, it is quite different for the capitalist propensity to consume (or the capitalist wage rate). That is, if the latter increases, the profit mark-ups must increase in order to obtain the amount of profits to purchase the same amount of investment goods while at the same time driving down the "wage share." Thus the answer to what does the price system do is that under the existing capitalist social relationships it "ensures" the reproduction of capitalists, business enterprises, and but not necessarily all of the workers, which is important in understanding some of the operations of a capitalist economy. However, it provides no understanding of wage slavery.

Job control and revolution

The heterodox model of capitalism makes it clear that the decisions that determine the production of consumption, investment, and state goods and services, $\mathbf{Q}_2$, and the profit mark-ups, R_d, govern the real direction of a capitalist economy, control the volume of and access to the social provisioning process, and maintain the dominate-subordinate-dependent social relationships necessary for capitalism to exist. These decisions and variables are controlled directly by capitalists and the state, and the state provides legal sanctions for the control and armed forces to protect the control. In particular, while consumption is equal to the wage bill and capitalist consumption out of profits – $(\mathbf{Q}_{2C})^T\mathbf{p}_2 = \mathbf{e}\,(\mathbf{Lw}) + \mathbf{c}_c\mathbf{\Pi}$, variations in the wage rate do not vary the overall "real wage" of the working class (although it can alter consumption patterns within the working class) since any change will produce offsetting changes in $\mathbf{p}_2$ and $\mathbf{\Pi}$. Moreover, capitalists decide the quantities of $\mathbf{Q}_{2C}$ that are directed toward workers' consumption and wage rates are adjusted accordingly. Consequently, direct action designed to affect the "real wage" for the working class by altering the money wage is not possible, although direct action to make wage rates more equitable among the working class is possible. But adjusting money wage rates is not a movement toward socialism.

Even if direct action could increase the goods and services consumed by workers, the goods and services produced for capitalist consumption and investment would not necessarily decline and nor would the amount of goods and services procured by the state decline. To reduce capitalist-state control of the economy and capitalist consumption of goods and services requires reduction in the production of investment goods, capitalist consumption goods, and state purchases of goods and services. This in turn would result in fewer workers being employed and hence having access to the social provisioning process. Thus, any attempt to bring about the demise of capitalism through a reduction of profits via the curtailment of the production of capitalist consumption goods, $\mathbf{Q}_{2I}$, and $\mathbf{Q}_{2G}$ without first altering the social relationships underpinning capitalism and reducing the decision-making power of the capitalists and the state will impoverish the lives of many workers.

To move toward socialism, direct action for increasing job control is necessary. That is, direct action to establish and increase workers' control over the laboring process weakens the social dominance that capitalists and its state have over them. Direct action to control the length of the working day, to regulate the speed of machinery and the amount of work to be done, to increase job safety and health benefits, to improve working conditions and eliminate abusive, authoritarian behavior by management, and to ensure that workers actually get paid for both regular and overtime work on a regular basis, creates a work environment in which workers have increased control over their working lives. Since struggle over job control affects the laboring-production process, it has only an indirect impact on the decisions that determine $\mathbf{Q}_2$ and R_d. Consequently, job control issues have little if any impact on profits, on capitalist consumption, or on the state's ability to obtain the goods and services it desires; thus they are most likely to be attainable by piecemeal direct action and hence promote the movement toward socialism, but in a halting manner.

As noted above, the key decisions that determine $\mathbf{Q}_2$ and R_d are controlled by the capitalists and the state. While Wobblies would use direct action in an attempt to affect the decisions, both law and tradition have removed them from the labor-management bargaining arena. Hence workers do not have a job-place bargaining mechanism internal to the capitalist system to affect the decisions and gain control of the variables. Consequently, the only workplace direct action tactic available is the general strike that simultaneously eliminates capitalist social relationships and directly takes control of the decisions and determines $\mathbf{Q}_2$ and R_d in the interest of the working class. Thus, while the composition of $\mathbf{Q}_2$ and the magnitudes of R_d (and $\mathbf{c}_e$) will change in response to the needs and interests of the working class, no worker would be unemployed and without access to the social provisioning process. In addition to taking over the key decisions regarding $\mathbf{Q}_2$ and R_d, workers through the general strike also eliminate the capitalist social relationships: no more authoritarian-hierarchical relationships inside the business enterprise and the state, and no more regulation of access to the social provisioning process via wage slavery. In short, the general strike produces a "peaceful" revolution that ushers in socialism.

Conclusion

Marxian theory and its labor theory of value and heterodox theory and its micro-macro model of the economy identify the social relationships that underpin capitalism and the key decisions and variables that control and direct the economy. In addition, both support the tactic of direct action to increase job control and to bring about a general strike that would usher in socialism. However, because the theoretical weaknesses of the labor theory of value are well established, it appears that direct action tactics of job control and the general strike might be inappropriate for bringing about socialism. Thus, a different theoretical approach, heterodox theory, is introduced and delineated. It shows that the theory and its micro-macro model of the economy is capable of providing a radical understanding of wage slavery similar to Marxism (but without the contradictions) and supporting job control and revolution to bring about socialism. In particular, heterodox theory and its model identifies job control and the key decisions and their variables that workers must take control of before socialism can be achieved. So with a heterodox theory underpinning, the IWW can continue to advocate direction action for job control and the general strike to bring about the demise of capitalism and the flowering of socialism.

Notes

1 Since virtually all Wobblies had to work for a living, they rarely had time to engage in theorizing. This was certainly the case during the first 50 years of the IWW. Moreover, most Wobblies in the first 50 years did not have university education, although many were well read and idiosyncratically learned.
2 Marxian and anarchist economic theory and critiques of capitalism draw largely on the same body of ideas. Thus, their analysis is similar if not identical in many respects. Yet some anarchists argue that their economic theory of capitalism is different from if not superior to Marxian theory. While small differences exist, their arguments are unconvincing largely due to an inadequate grasp of classical political economy in general and Marxian theory in particular. Moreover, at times they argue, rather strangely, that the utilization of neoclassical economic theory is an advance over Marxism (for example, see Stein 1994). However, their economic theory of the new society differs in important ways (see Knowles 2004).
3 When explaining this, reference was frequently made to Marx's two pamphlets, *Wage-Labor and Capital* and *Value, Price and Profit.*
4 One consequence of this position was that the IWW argued that, while monopolies might raise prices above values, this had no impact on workers' subsistence standard of living since wages would adjust accordingly. Rather, when a monopolist raised prices, it was redividing the surplus in its favor: "Monopoly generally means that the monopolist is strong enough to force other employers to *divide* with him a portion of the value of our products formerly appropriated by them" (Marcy 1911: 29). Hence, from the IWW's perspective, the issue of monopoly should be of no special interest to workers. This

perhaps accounts for the absence of special critiques of big business by the IWW. See Galambos (1975) for some interesting comments on this position.

5 In fact, the concepts of high and low prices have no substantive meaning in this context, except as temporary deviations from values or prices of production.

6 Socialism for the IWW means that "industry [is] run by those who do the work using democratic procedures on a daily basis for the equal benefit of all" (IWW 2001: 8). To achieve this it is necessary for workers to have control of their jobs; thus for the IWW any action that gives workers more control over their jobs is a movement toward socialism.

7 The IWW never really signed on to Marx's claim that the profit rate tends to fall due to rising organic composition of capital, in that they never really thought that this outcome would occur independently of workers' actions. That is, the IWW always thought that the end of capitalism would come about through the direct action of workers rather than through some working out of a "natural law." This reflects the anarchist-syndicalist influence in the IWW.

8 Indirect action is seen as political activities and boycotts. The IWW rejects the view that an increase in workers' standard of living and the coming of socialism can be achieved via politics without any need of revolutionary industrial unionism. However, there is much disagreement over whether any political activity is needed to achieve these outcomes.

9 The IWW also argued that shorter hours would permit more workers to have jobs since productivity gains reduced capitalists' need for workers. However, the argument assumed that there would be no reduction in the subsistence bundle of commodities, so in effect the surplus for the capitalists would be reduced. However, the issue of shorter hours, more workers employed, and the standard of living is more complex than the IWW realized – so their arguments in this regard are somewhat less convincing. In particular, the IWW does not address the issue of effective demand and employment. At times it seems to assume that the aggregate amount of goods needed is fixed or somehow the demand for goods grows more slowly than increases in productive capabilities – that is, there is the problem of underconsumption. The view was widely held among radicals, including Wobblies and Marxists, during the first 50 years of the IWW. And the mechanism by which it was overcome was the existence of non-capitalistic societies that were ripe for economic conquest:

> It follows that capitalism can exist only as long as it has open markets and regions undeveloped capitalistically in which to expand, for the condition of profit-taking requires that the worker who produces the values shall always produce more for the capitalist than he receives in wages or purchasing power. A stabilizing exchange between the producers or workers and their exploiters is, therefore, impossible. Machinery and technology are the means through which surplus value is increase at the expense of the workers and thereby hasten the ultimate collapse of the capitalist system.
> (IWW 1934: 31)

10 These actions are sometimes call sabotage. The IWW has never advocated the destruction of the means of production, agricultural produce, or products; has never willfully idled machinery; nor has adulterated food or products. But capitalists have done so in the name of profit. For examples of capitalist sabotage of this sort, see Salerno (1997) and Veblen (1921).

11 The history of the IWW is replete with capitalists and the state using armed forces – police, private militia, vigilante groups, and the national guard – as well as laws and the legal system to kill Wobblies, break their strikes, prevent peaceful assembly, and attempt to suppress the union: Frank Little, Wesley Everest, Bisbee deportation, Everett massacre, free speech fights, Lawrence textile strike, Wheatland, Colorado coal strike, espionage trials, and criminal syndicalism are the names, places, events, and political

actions that illustrate this. Such actions were not limited to the IWW, but were and are directed at any activities where workers wanted to take more control over their working lives (Conlin 1981; Dubofsky 1969; Kornbluh 1988; Preston 1963; Thompson and Murfin 1976).

12 In Sraffian nomenclature, all intermediate capital goods and services are *basics*.

13 Financial markets also exist but for simplicity's sake they are not dealt with in this chapter.

14 The purchase of financial assets by business enterprises as a whole is simply a necessary by-product of government expenditures.

15 Specifically, we have the following:

$$(I - R_{d1}M_{11})^{-1}R_{d1}\, l^*{}_1\mathbf{w} = \mathbf{p}_1 \text{ and } R_{d2}M_{21}\,[(I - R_{d1}M_{11})^{-1}R_{d1}\, l^*{}_1\mathbf{w}] + R_{d2}l^*{}_2\mathbf{w} = \mathbf{p}_2$$

Thus, as long as the structures and agency are given, then p_1 and p_2 exist as solutions, which means that the price model is "internally" coherent.

16 From note 15, we find that each price is equal to a row vector of non-price coefficients (which include profit mark-ups) times the wage rates. Hence an equal percentage increase in wage rates will generate the same percentage increase in prices, leaving the coefficients unchanged. On the other hand, if profit mark-ups increase, the coefficients, hence prices, increase, resulting in an increase of the price-wage rate ratio.

17 Of course they may indirectly through the state affect a command of the goods they consume and hence affect their own social provisioning process. However, the capitalist state limits this possibility so the only question is whether the actual "government" goods made available are those actually wanted by workers as opposed to those "imposed" upon them by capitalists.

18 It is possible to explore the same issue through varying the capitalist propensity to consume out of profits, but since this propensity is tied to the reproduction of the capitalist class, the analysis will be more complex.

References

Aspromourgos, T. (2004) "Sraffian Research Programmes and Unorthodox Economics," *Review of Political Economy*, 16(2): 179–206.

Bekken, J. (1986) "Fight for the Four-hour Day," *Libertarian Labor Review*, 1: 28–36.

Bortis, H. (1997) *Institutions, Behaviour and Economic Theory: A Contribution to Classical-Keynesian Political Economy*, Cambridge: Cambridge University Press.

—— (2003) "Keynes and the Classics: Notes on the Monetary Theory of Production," in L-P. Rochon and S. Rossi (eds) *Modern Theories of Money* (pp. 411–74), Cheltenham: Edward Elgar.

Campbell, J., Hollingsworth, J., and Lindberg, L. (eds) (1991) *Governance of the American Economy*, Cambridge: Cambridge University Press.

Conlin, J.R. (ed.) (1981) *At the Point of Production: The Local History of the I.W.W.*, Westport, CT: Greenwood Press.

De Gregori, T.R. (1987) "Resources Are Not: They Become: An Institutional Theory," *Journal of Economic Issues*, 21(3): 1241–63.

Downward, P. (1999) *Pricing Theory in Post Keynesian Economics: A Realist Approach*, Cheltenham: Edward Elgar.

Dubofsky, M. (1969) *We Shall Be All: A History of the Industrial Workers of the World*, Chicago, IL: Quadrangle.

Dugger, W.M. (1996) "Redefining Economics: From Market Allocation to Social Provisioning," in C. Whalen (ed.) *Political Economy for the 21st Century* (pp. 31–43), Armonk: M. E. Sharpe.

Dunn, S.P. (2001) "An Investigation into a Post Keynesian Contribution to the Theory of the Firm," unpublished Ph.D. dissertation, University of Leeds.

Eichner, A.S. (1976) *The Megacorp and Oligopoly: Micro Foundations of Macro Dynamics*, Cambridge: Cambridge University Press.

—— (1987) *The Macrodynamics of Advanced Market Economies*, Armonk: M. E. Sharpe.

Fligstein, N. (1990) *The Transformation of Corporate Control*, Cambridge, MA: Harvard University Press.

—— (2001) *The Architecture of Markets: An Economic Sociology of Twenty-first-Century Capitalist Societies*, Princeton, NJ: Princeton University Press.

Galambos, L. (1975) *The Public Image of Big Business in America, 1880–1940: A Quantitative Study in Social Change*, Baltimore, MD: The Johns Hopkins University Press.

Industrial Workers of the World (1922) *An Economic Interpretation of the Job*, Chicago, IL: Industrial Workers of the World.

—— (1934) *Unemployment and the Machine*, Chicago, IL: Industrial Workers of the World.

—— (1938) *The I.W.W. in Theory and Practice*, Chicago, IL: Industrial Workers of the World.

—— (1982) *The General Strike*, Chicago, IL: Industrial Workers of the World.

—— (2001) *One Big Union* (8th edn), Philadelphia, PA: Industrial Workers of the World.

Knowles, R. (2004) *Political Economy From Below: Economic Thought in Communitarian Anarchism, 1840–1914*, New York: Routledge.

Kornbluh, J. L. (ed.) (1988) *Rebel Voices: An IWW Anthology*, Chicago, IL: Charles H. Kerr Publishing.

Kregel, J. A. (1975) *The Reconstruction of Political Economy* (2nd edn), London: Macmillan.

Kurz, H.D. and Salvadori, N. (1995) *Theory of Production: A Long-period Analysis*, Cambridge: Cambridge University Press.

—— (2005) "Representing the Production and Circulation of Commodities in Material Terms: On Sraffa's Objectivism," *Review of Political Economy*, 17(3): 413–42.

Lavoie, M. (1992) *Foundations of Post-Keynesian Economic Analysis*, Aldershot: Edward Elgar.

Lee, F.S. (1998) *Post Keynesian Price Theory*, Cambridge: Cambridge University Press.

—— (2008) "Heterodox Economics," in L.E. Blume and S. Durlauf (eds) *New Palgrave Dictionary of Economics*, New York: Palgrave Macmillan.

Lowe, A. (1976) *The Path of Economic Growth*, Cambridge: Cambridge University Press.

Lutz, M.A. (1999) *Economics for the Common Good: Two Centuries of Social Economic Thought in the Humanistic Tradition*, London: Routledge.

Marcy, M.E. (1911) *Shop Talks on Economics*, Chicago, IL: Industrial Workers of the World.

Marx, K. (1976) *Wage-labour and Capital and Value, Price and Profit*, New York: International Publishers.

Miller, A.J. (2002) *Whatever Happened to the Eight-Hour Day?*, Tacoma: Working People's Library.

O'Boyle, E.J. (ed.) (1996) *Social Economics: Premises, Findings and Policies*, London: Routledge.

Power, M. (2004) "Social Provisioning as a Starting Point for Feminist Economics," *Feminist Economics*, 10(3): 3–19.

Preston, W. (1963) *Aliens and Dissenters: Federal Suppression of Radicals, 1903–1933*, New York: Harper & Row.

Salerno, S. (ed.) (1997) *Direct Action and Sabotage: Three Classic IWW Pamphlets From the 1910s*, Chicago, IL: Charles H. Kerr Publishing.

Sraffa, P. (1960) *Production of Commodities by Means of Commodities*, Cambridge: Cambridge University Press.

Stein, J. (1994) "Marxism: The Negation of Communism," *Libertarian Labor Review*, 17: 20–6.

Thompson, F.W. and Murfin, P. (1976) *The I.W.W.: Its First Seventy Years, 1905–1975*, Chicago, IL: Industrial Workers of the World.

Veblen, T. (1921) *The Engineers and the Price System*, New York: The Viking Press.

Wray, L.R. (1998) *Understanding Modern Money*, Cheltenham: Edward Elgar.

Zimmermann, E.W. (1951) *World Resources and Industries: A Functional Appraisal of the Availability of Agricultural and Industrial Materials* (Revised edn), New York: Harper & Brothers.

5 Economic science and the Left

Thoughts on Sraffa's equations and the efficacy of organized labor

Tony Aspromourgos

In all the intellectual ferment surrounding economics during the middle half of the twentieth century – controversy which looks extraordinarily refreshing in comparison with the mind-numbing dullness that has settled upon the discipline since – "Cambridge" was of course a central element. Among the strands of thought which arose during those years, the contribution of Piero Sraffa seems to have suffered the greatest incomprehension. This pertains most particularly to his constructive contribution – rather than his early critique of Marshall, his edition of Ricardo's *Works and Correspondence*, and the destructive implications of his constructive work (Sraffa 1960) for marginalist capital theory (and thereby, it should be said, for the whole marginalist edifice). This is so much so that some have thought that *Production of Commodities* had *only* a critical or negative purpose. In fact, it seems to me that the most vital significance of Sraffa's intellectual efforts is as a positive contribution to the theory of prices under alternative possible distributions of the net product of a society, in the framework particularly of a capitalist social economy – taking also into account the possibility of multiple methods of production for the various commodities produced (or processes in use), joint production, fixed capital and scarce natural resources.

Beyond this scientific level, it is quite well known that Sraffa was, in some sense, a man of the Left – even if the sense is not precisely clear from just the public record of his life. It seems to me further that Sraffa's system of price equations was intended to convey a strong substantive supposition about the possibilities for social forces, beyond "mere" competition, to impact upon the distribution of the net product or social surplus in a capitalist society. This aspect is outlined in the following section. By implication, such a conception of how capitalism functions provides "space" for organized labor to have impact as an element of those social forces. The third and penultimate section considers the question of the capacities for organized labor (most notably, labor unions) to influence outcomes in such societies.[1] All this raises the question of the relationship between economic "science" and political belief. To go to the heart of the matter, are economic theories just a façade for ideologies of one sort or another? I do not think so, notwithstanding that there is a great deal of ideological junk in evidence in contemporary economics. The second section below addresses this issue, partly by reference to what we are learning from the archive of Sraffa's papers, about his conceptions concerning these sorts of issues.[2]

The concluding section raises the related but wider issue of science, postmodernism and the Left.

Feasible income distributions in a capitalist economy

Sraffa's approach to production and distribution may be illustrated as follows. Suppose a society in which there are n distinct production activities, employing k distinct commodities as inputs (together with homogeneous labor, L), and producing quantities of the same k commodities. The n activities may be represented by the following array of given quantities (parameters), where LHS subscripted terms refer to inputs and RHS superscripted terms refer to outputs.

$$A_1, B_1, \ldots, K_1, L_1 \rightarrow A^1, B^1, \ldots, K^1$$
$$A_2, B_2, \ldots, K_2, L_2 \rightarrow A^2, B^2, \ldots, K^2$$
$$\ldots$$
$$A_n, B_n, \ldots, K_n, L_n \rightarrow A^n, B^n, \ldots, K^n$$

The commodity inputs may be construed as including the subsistence consumption of the labor employed in each activity. Then, the commodity surplus is constituted by the sum of the total gross output of each of the k commodities, net of the total input of each commodity, across the n activities. The production of a social surplus requires:

$$A_1+A_2+\ldots+A_n \leq A^1+A^2+\ldots+A^n$$
$$B_1+B_2+\ldots+B_n \leq B^1+B^2+\ldots+B^n$$
$$\ldots$$
$$K_1+K_2+\ldots+K_n \leq K^1+K^2+\ldots+K^n$$

with at least one of these satisfied as a strict inequality.[3] Sraffa's equations, representing a coherent specification of Smithian "natural prices" or Marxian "prices of production," are then given by:

$$(p_aA_1+p_bB_1+\ldots+p_kK_1)(1+r)+wL_1 = p_aA^1+p_bB^1+\ldots+p_kK^1$$
$$(p_aA_2+p_bB_2+\ldots+p_kK_2)(1+r)+wL_2 = p_aA^2+p_bB^2+\ldots+p_kK^2$$
$$\ldots$$
$$(p_aA_n+p_bB_n+\ldots+p_kK_n)(1+r)+wL_n = p_aA^n+p_bB^n+\ldots+p_kK^n$$

where $p_a, p_b, \ldots, p_k$ are the nominal commodity prices, r is the uniform rate of profit on capital (thereby abstracting from any economically relevant differential characteristics of capital in each industry), and w is the surplus wage per worker (an excess of worker nominal remuneration, above that required to meet subsistence), or per any other unit of labor measurement. These k+2 magnitudes are the unknowns in the equations.

This quite general characterization of what may be called "normal prices" under conditions of free competition (freedom of entry and exit of capital) is a system of very considerable complexity as to the behavior of prices and distribution: the behavior of such price systems has been the object of considerable intellectual work since 1960.[4] For our merely general conceptual purposes here, we may consider instead a very simplified, two-commodity version of such "circular"[5] production systems:

$$p_K a_{KK} Q_K (1+r) + w l_K Q_K = p_K Q_K$$
$$p_K a_{KC} Q_C (1+r) + w l_C Q_C = p_C Q_C$$

where commodity K is the only (circulating) capital good (the only commodity input required in the production of itself, and of the consumption good, C – and entirely used up in the production cycle); commodity C is the only consumption good; a_{KJ} (J = K, C) is the given input of capital per unit of output of commodity J (constant-returns-to-scale production methods are assumed); and similarly for labor input, l_K, l_C. The joint production possibilities allowed for in the previous system of equations have been eliminated: each of the two activities produces a single commodity. The social surplus or net product is the output of the consumption-good industry (Q_C) plus the output of the capital-good industry net of capital used up in the production processes (Q_K net of $a_{KK}Q_K$ and $a_{KC}Q_C$).[6]

From these price equations one may derive the inverse relation between the real wage per worker ($w_C = w/p_C$) and r:

$$w_C = [1-(1+r)a_{KK}]/\{l_C + l_C l_K (1+r)[(a_{KC}/l_C)-(a_{KK}/l_K)]\}$$

where the denominator is necessarily positive, so long as the set of production methods in use is capable of producing a surplus, and r does not exceed $(1-a_{KK})/a_{KK}$. In this simple model, the capacity of the system to produce a surplus is equivalent to requiring that $a_{KK}<1$: the capital-goods industry uses up in a production cycle less capital than it produces. A positive real wage requires in addition that $r<(1-a_{KK})/a_{KK}$: profits do not eat up the entire net product of the capital-goods industry. An intuition of the inverse relation between rates of real wages and profit can be gained by supposing uniform capital-labor ratios in the two industries: then the denominator becomes just l_C; and the real wage is equal to the wage share per unit of gross output produced (a negative function of r), divided by labor input per unit of gross consumption output produced.[7] Relative prices ($p_{CK} = p_C/p_K$) in general vary with distribution, as part of the process bringing about a change in the (w_C, r) outcome:

$$p_{CK} = \{l_C + (1+r) l_C l_K [(a_{KC}/l_C)-(a_{KK}/l_K)]\}/l_K$$

where the restriction on r to ensure a positive real wage ensures also that this relative price is positive. Multiple methods of production may be allowed for also, with a distinct (w_C, r) function for each possible technique of production ("technique" being a combination of methods for producing both commodities). It was the exploration of the behavior of systems like this, incorporating profit-maximizing choice of technique, which was at the center of the critique of the orthodox marginalist theory of distribution in the decades following publication of Sraffa's 1960 book – the so-called "capital debates" (see Kurz and Salvadori (1995: 427–67) and Aspromourgos (2004a) for a listing of the relevant literature).

The striking feature of a system of price equations along these lines is that they preserve a "degree of freedom" in the determination of income distribution and prices. Unlike the now dominant marginalist theories which originated in the late nineteenth century, competitive equilibrium does not fully or uniquely determine functional income distribution: competition establishes a set of relative commodity prices, together with either the real wage or rate of profit, once either the rate of profit or real wage is given from *outside* the system of price equations. In short, the division of the surplus between labor and capital is open to contest by wider forces, by social forces – even within the confines of a competitive capitalist economy. Insofar as Sraffa's equations are intended as a coherent representation of the approach of the classical economists and Marx (see Garegnani 1984 or 1987), his thought from this point of departure involves a kind of inversion of classicism: instead of the real wage being directly determined by the balance of social forces (bargaining power) in the labor contract, it is the general rate of profit which is the independently determined distributive variable – by reference to rates of interest determined in money markets (Sraffa 1960: 33). Competition brings yields on capital assets into a kind of parity, net of economically relevant differential characteristics of those assets (for example, risk and illiquidity differences); so that if the yields on interest-bearing securities are independently determined, then the profitability of capital in production must come into line with those interest rates.[8] Here, there is an important point of connection between the views of Sraffa and Keynes. The latter is led to the conclusion that, since interest is not uniquely determined by the process of investment/saving equilibration, the level of the (riskless) rate of interest is conventional or arbitrary.[9] This then provides the basis for the possibility of abolishing pure property income, even within the confines of a mixed capitalist economy, outlined in the final chapter of the *General Theory*.[10] It seems to be precisely this also that Sraffa points to by the degree of freedom in his equations: the functional distribution of income is arbitrary – though within certain limits clarified by Sraffa, limits to which Keynes is apparently oblivious.

Of course, any theory of distribution for a capitalist economy offers multiple feasible distributional outcomes: insofar as a theory endogenously determines a unique outcome for certain income distribution magnitudes, by reference to some set of exogenous variables or parameters, there will be as many feasible distributional outcomes as there are feasible values of those parameters. The marginalist theory of distribution has as its fundamental parameters, technology, individual preferences and the level and distribution of resource endowments among the individuals constituting the economy. Technology is a parameter it shares with Sraffa's system. The presumed individualistic arbitrariness of preferences suggests that variation in preferences is incapable of systematic significance. However, for every conceivable distribution of resource endowments, even of given *aggregate* levels of resource endowments, a different set of "factor" prices is implied. That is to say, the equilibrium set of factor prices is as arbitrary as the distribution of the "initial endowment" of resources. However, such arbitrariness is of a very different character to the degree of freedom in distribution in Sraffa's equations. Note that in the marginalist approach a positive return *as such* on capital – howsoever arbitrary the distribution of property rights over the initial "endowment" of non-labor resources or "capital" – is founded upon "scarcity" of savings. On the other hand, Sraffa's approach, by allowing a role for social forces in the "bargain" over the distribution of the surplus, seems to make clear enough his belief that a multiplicity of functional income distribution outcomes is consistent with a *given* set of ownership relations. That is to say, a particular set of property rights with regard to productive resources does not uniquely foreclose the distribution of the net product of a social economy. Not only is the *personal* distribution of income arbitrary – a very evident fact – but also the *functional* distribution, even given the scale and the distribution of resource "endowments." To put the point bluntly, capitalism in and of itself does not require a unique outcome for the wage share and associated profitability of capital.

Economic science and politics

It may be emphasized that all that has been said so far is independent of political values. That is to say, it is scientific in a straightforward sense – Sraffa's equations are a purely descriptive account of the outcome for an abstract object (normal prices and distribution), of hypothesized forces of competition. This is important because it is not the case that all of economics is, and can only be, nothing more than a kind of intellectual decoration for partisan socio-economic or political viewpoints. There is a social economy "out there," and systematic elements of its structure and behavior can be understood correctly – empirically and rationally. Such objectivism was evidently a temper to which Sraffa was deeply committed. How he acquired it, I do not know. It is certainly now clear that in part he was consciously seeking to emulate successful contemporaneous natural science research programs. He also much approved of the empiricism of William Petty at the advent of classical economics, though whether this actually influenced his methodological temper is not clear (to me at least). Petty's formula for an objective social science – in the form of his invention, "political arithmetic" – to consider only "*Number*, *Weight*, or *Measure*," is well known (Petty 1690: 244; Aspromourgos 1996: 46–9, 57–60). A perhaps more engaging expression of that deeply felt empiricism and commitment to modernity and to science – also capturing something of Petty's personality – is provided by an anecdote of John Aubrey:

> I remember one St Andrewe's day (which is the day of the Generall Meeting of the Royall Society for Annuall Elections) I sayd, Methought 'twas not so well that we should pitch upon the Patron of Scotland's day, we should rather have taken St George or St Isidore (a Philosopher canonized). No, said Sir William, I would rather have had it on St Thomas day, for he would not beleeve

> till he had seen and putt his fingers into the Holes, according to the Motto *Nullius in verba* [not bound to swear obedience to any man's dogma].
>
> (Dick 1972: 402)

Thus it would be a great mistake to think that Sraffa's theoretical work in economics was driven by a political or ideological purpose, or had a political or ideological goal – and equally a mistake whether one regards this as an indictment or commendation of him. In particular, the Sraffa archive does not provide support for the view that Marx's economics played a significant role in the formulation of Sraffa's equations, notwithstanding his evidently sharing somewhat similar political views to Marx (Garegnani 2005: 475–6, 485 and note 30 at 487–8). It was only after the outlines of Sraffa's own constructive work clarifying the classical, "surplus approach" became clear in his own mind – probably mainly inspired by Physiocracy (if by anyone at all) – that he better appreciated Marx's scientific significance. It may be added that the irrelevance of ideological purposes is also supported by an important piece of circumstantial evidence: the strong element of kinship between Sraffa's system and the growth model of von Neumann (1937), whose politics, to put it mildly, were very different to those of Sraffa (see Kurz and Salvadori 1993). The thoroughgoing objectivism of Sraffa's methodological temper is an expression of his vigorous scientific intention. The idea, popular in some heterodox circles, that a plurality of "visions" in economics is an inevitable even acceptable situation, reflecting the diversity of political beliefs or ideologies – as if selecting theories were like choosing courses from a restaurant menu – I do not think would be congenial to Sraffa. It is one thing to say that actually existing economics is littered with ideological rubbish, or even deeply ideologically compromised; it is another to say that scientific work is impossible in that domain.

Nevertheless, economics by its very nature is always and everywhere vulnerable to ideological corruption or capture. It is too much forgotten that there are qualitative differences between the social sciences and (much of) the natural sciences which no amount of intellectual progress will ever eliminate. With respect to economics, almost uniquely – and certainly unlike natural science – it is subject to a kind of pincer movement which is a continual threat to its integrity: on the one hand, it deals with the distribution of material resources among humans, a subject close to the (greedy) hearts of vested material interests; on the other, its doctrines are generally not subject, in any straightforward manner, to the discipline of *compellingly evident* facts. This combination makes economics, on the one hand, extremely attractive for, and on the other, very vulnerable to, ideological capture – a vulnerability to which it often succumbs. If we observe two chemists, one of whom we know to be a democratic socialist (or otherwise progressive), and one of whom we know to be a cringing lackey of the ruling classes (or otherwise reactionary), we do not really think that this information about them is pertinent to the scientific status of the intellectual work each of them does – though it may influence the problems to which each chooses to devote his or her efforts. But if we now observe two economists with the same two sets of views, we are far more likely to expect this to be relevant to the scientific status of their intellectual work.

One might say that almost by definition, scientists and academics belong to the middle or upper classes, and therefore might naturally be more inclined to conservatism. On the other hand, one could retort that as people committed by the nature of their working lives to seeking rational solutions to problems, they might naturally be inclined to progressive politics of some kind or other. In fact, the point to be emphasized is that (in the main) the socio-political beliefs of natural scientists do not matter to their work – they do to the work of economists.

Does the intrinsic proneness of economics to ideology make a mockery of Sraffa's objectivist scientific temper? I think, on the contrary, that it could even be treated as a *justification* for that temper. One could say that Sraffa's "minimalist" theory is precisely the expression of his endeavor to see how far one could get in economics, proceeding on a strictly objective basis, and with very austere recourse to behavioral postulates which would be specific to particular cultures, mores, ethics, psychologies, and so on. Documents in the archive seem to support this interpretation. In a certain sense, this line of thought actually leads back to the concept of the "surplus." The production of the social surplus is an expression, in large measure, of objective natural laws: the specification of the technology available – the spectrum of techniques of production – describes how the using up or destruction of a set of commodities can lead to the production of another set of commodities. Of course, while natural laws bind that process of transformation of inputs into outputs in production, there are also conventional elements involved, particular to specific societal settings – as to what constitutes socially acceptable minimum human "subsistence," and as to the socially acceptable ways in which work may be performed (both of which, themselves will partly evolve in response to technological change over time). In this sense one can say that, in particular forms of social economy, the human outcomes are bound not only by immutable natural laws, but also by contingent social laws (using *law* here advisedly), which are alterable, and add further constraints so to speak – not only further constraints to the spectrum of distribution and consumption outcomes, taking technology as given, but also constraints to the set of feasible ("socially feasible," one may say) methods of production which may be employed. The notion of surplus is an expression of the potential of technology to enable the outputs of the system to exceed the inputs used up in their production. This is the objective basis for the analysis of distribution, even allowing that both the minimum or subsistence consumption of workers, and aspects of the input-output technical relationships, will be specific to particular socio-economies – or conventional and contingent if one prefers.[11]

Hence, when considering the composition and distribution of the surplus of commodities produced in the specific form of social economy, liberal capitalism, one necessarily partly moves to the level of contingent *social* laws, in three respects in particular. (1) The minimum or subsistence consumption per worker or per capita is in part, but only in part (humans, as such, must consume to survive), a social datum, the historical evolution of which has been shaped by social forces – of which organized labor has been by no means the least element. This contingent subsistence per capita enters into the determination of the upper bound on the profitability of capital (see the next section). (2) Similarly, the feasible in the sense of *permissible* methods of production available – the ways in which labor, machines and so on can and may be combined to produce outputs – are also in part (but again, only in part: inputs are necessarily used up or destroyed, in the making of outputs) a social datum, historically shaped by social forces – again, importantly including organized labor. (These partly contingent production conditions of course also enter into the set of (w_C, r) functions which govern possible distributional outcomes, referring to the simple illustrative model of the previous section.) In this regard the almost universal practice in economics of taking technology as given relegates to oblivion (or some area of intellectual inquiry other than economics) an important subject matter of economic life: the set of feasible production methods is inseparable from the ways in which societies are willing to have workers treated. (3) Finally, Sraffa's price equations of course express conditions that are specific to a decentralized economy with division of labor, free competition, capital, wage-labor and so on. The results associated with them are therefore an expression of specific "social laws" of liberal capitalism – represented in the roles of wages, prices and profits in distributing the social surplus. At the abstract level of Sraffa's theoretical system, the contingency of subsistence consumption and of production methods are of no qualitative significance: with subsistence expressed as a set of abstract quantities of commodities, and production methods expressed as abstract ratios of inputs to outputs, the mathematical structure of the price equations is unaffected by any consideration of the forces governing those two sets of data. But with regard to the third, if we were to examine the distribution of the social surplus in a non-capitalist economy of some kind, different social rules for that process of distribution would imply replacement of the price equations themselves with some other analysis, abstractly capturing those alternative rules of distribution.[12]

What can organized labor do?

What then do Sraffa's equations imply for the possibility of organized labor's efficacy in the pursuit of its objectives? My focus has been on income distribution within the confines of a capitalist economy, and I will largely limit myself to that domain (including in this the role of organized labor with respect to technical change).

For the purposes of this question, the central result from Sraffa's equations is that for a given technology, there is a spectrum of feasible functional income distribution outcomes – and this provides "space" for organized labor to influence, and influence persistently (not merely temporarily), the distribution between wage and non-wage income. For a given technology, the inverse relation between the rate of profit and the real wage implies that the maximum level of the real wage per worker depends upon the minimum feasible rate of profit. What is the magnitude of the latter? Conceived of in terms of the pure or riskless rate of return, this in principle, it seems to me, can be reduced to zero in a capitalist social economy. Indeed, this is just the point of Keynes's "euthanasia of the rentier" proposals in the last chapter of the *General Theory*. Organized labor therefore should favor – and it is achievable as a matter of principle – a policy of central banks pushing the interest rate on riskless government securities toward zero: a positive riskless interest rate is income for doing nothing. In practice there are a number of difficulties which need to be taken into account – three in particular. First, is there an instrument available to public policy, for the purposes of inflation control, which would enable interest rate variations to be relieved of this responsibility? Second, in a regime of permanent "cheap money," there is probably a need for regulatory mechanisms which would constrain (thereby cheap) financing of speculative activities. Third, a transition to permanent zero riskless yields should probably be gradual: in the transition, it would be unfortunate if those who have paid positive interest rates early in their life cycle (as net liability holders) should then find themselves earning significantly lower rates as net asset holders.[13]

It is important to add that the "space" for social forces to persistently influence distribution, which the surplus approach demonstrates, is a two-edged sword: the inverse relation plus degree of freedom is the objective basis for a persistent tendency to conflict because it provides *as well the employing classes*, or their agents, with a rational basis to pursue class struggle – reduction in labor income, working conditions, industrial and employment rights of workers, and so on. Hence we have witnessed the rise in recent decades of labor-market deregulation and all that. In light of this, it is a pity that now so many who depend upon wage income delude themselves that their conditions and rights are in some sense natural or irreducible – that even if those conditions are the product of past union campaigns and heroism (if that is at all widely understood), their preservation no longer requires the buttress of strong, deep and wide industrial unionism.[14]

Turning from the maximum real wage to the opposite end of the spectrum, the *minimum* real wage depends upon the conventional notion as to what is the minimum subsistence consumption acceptable to society, in any particular socio-economic setting. Insofar as labor input is necessary for production, and some minimum consumption is necessary for labor, the equations of the simple, illustrative model in the first section above do not properly account for the fact that the production of consumption goods (not just capital goods) must be necessary to the system. This inescapable fact may be reintroduced here, by way of adding a constraint on the lower bound of the real wage: $w_C \geq c$ (a quantity of the consumption good representing the understanding of what is subsistence, in a particular socio-historical setting). This also has the effect of reducing the spectrum of possible r values:

$$0 \leq r \leq \{(1-cl_C)-[a_{KK}(1-cl_C)+cl_K a_{KC}]\}/[a_{KK}(1-cl_C)+cl_K a_{KC}]$$

where a positive maximum profit rate now requires

$$[(1-cl_C)(1-a_{KK})-cl_K a_{KC}] > 0$$

The production methods in use now must be capable of producing a surplus of outputs over and above both the capital goods used up and the consumption goods required for the subsistence of the workforce.[15] This leads to a second inference, that organized labor should vigorously support a high level of public or social welfare provision for non-working persons or households. The point here is that this is not just a matter of moral decency, or of solidarity with the unemployed (though both decency and solidarity are worthy of strong endorsement): the socially acceptable subsistence consumption of those unable to work, or able and willing to work but unable to find work, sets the effective lower bound for the wages of those working – so that even those who face no plausible prospect of not having work have a quite direct interest in the standard of living implied by the public or welfare safety net, since this sets *the minimum* below which they cannot be pushed. The public sector acting as employer-of-last-resort and guaranteed minimum income (or basic income) policies are means toward this objective.

There is also a danger worth noting here. Sectional labor union activity in advancing the wages of one group in the workforce can be at the expense of other workers, rather than non-wage (or in particular, property) income. Consider a situation in which monetary policy, (successfully) aimed at a particular inflation target, is able to more or less continuously, on average, enforce a particular value of the trend real rate of interest on a riskless government security. So long as this yield regulates the general profitability of capital, it will fix real wage rates – for a given set of production methods and given wage relativities for heterogeneous labor. Under these conditions, success by a particular element of the workforce in increasing its real wages may occur at the expense of the real wages of other workers, via change in wage relativities. (With productivity growth over time, the same kind of process would manifest itself in differential growth rates of wages.) In effect, in this scenario, roughly speaking, a redistribution of purchasing power *among* wage-earners occurs. Rather than "socialism in one country," this is at best socialism in one class, and may be of a kind which increases inequality. This points to the importance of a unionism which is widely organized and as comprehensive as possible in its reach (particularly at the lower end of the wages dispersion) – a conclusion which resonates with the Wobblies' aspiration to "One Big Union."[15] In the limit, one may say, there is a need for unionism with a global perspective, parallel with global capitalism, and with a view to global conventions with respect to the labor contract.

Within the confines of a mixed capitalist economy, it is also open to organized labor to vigorously support political parties that project policies which preserve and advance the interests of the great bulk of working people and ordinary citizens (without necessarily "marrying" those political parties[17]). Such policies would include the following. Fiscal policy can serve progressive redistributive purposes, both on the expenditure and the revenue sides, though this of course is not the only purpose of the public sector. While this may seem an unfashionable idea at the moment, in fact virtually *all* elements of political opinion support a redistributional role for the public sector – the differences are only over the direction and degree of such redistribution.[18] In particular, a tax system which serves to break, or at least meliorate, the intergenerational inheritance of inequality – which, apart from its material inequity, corrupts democratic politics insofar as it encourages plutocracy – is extremely important. On the expenditure side, the conditions for equality of opportunity[19] and meritocracy (that is, economic mobility, upward and downward) vitally include public provision of free education and health services of relatively high minimum quality (that is to say, relative to the services available to the wealthy), severing the dependence of health and educational outcomes upon private income. It has already been mentioned that the content of minimum consumption (and hence minimum real wages) can be influenced by improvements in the standard of living associated with the social security or welfare safety net (which has implications for policies toward transfer payments), and organized labor can also play a role in campaigns around that objective. More directly, unions can influence the production methods which enter into determination of rates of wages and profits – occupational health and safety measures, maximum shifts, manning levels of machines (partly linked to occupational safety), penalty rates and so on. This is partly about establishing strong general conventions constraining the outcomes of particular labor contracts. Furthermore, it should not be overlooked that an increased labor share of the social surplus can be realized in the form of increased leisure: a reduction in labor-time worked, at an unchanged commodity real wage, rather than higher purchasing power. In general, once one steps out of the straitjacket of marginalist theory, the focus of economic policy naturally becomes growth with a view to full employment – since there is no automatic tendency for a competitive capitalist economy to generate full utilization of potential productive capacity, including labor capacity – and the distribution of the resulting surplus or net product, since distribution is not foreclosed by competition (Garegnani, in Foley *et al.* 2004: 36–8). As well, fiscal policy may offer the only alternative to monetary policy as an anti-inflationary device – if a sufficiently flexible fiscal instrument exists or can be devised.[20]

Conclusion: economics, modernity and the Left

We may conclude by standing back from the fairly narrowly economic-theoretic focus pursued above, and considering a further and wider issue of Left and Right in relation to modernity and postmodernism. It is disquieting that the intellectual Left has tended to become so commonly identified with postmodernism (hence the subtitle of Gross and Levitt 1998). It is obvious enough that socialism and the Left, from at least the nineteenth century forward, were historically wedded to Enlightenment and modernity. Those elements of the Left who have turned on modernity, in some sense or other, are free to do so. But a *logical* point needs to be kept firmly in mind: the traditional economic values of the Left – that the arbitrarily inequitable distribution of material resources among human beings, and the intergenerational inheritance of inequality, can be reformed or overturned (in one way or another), via the agency of collective action – in no way entail the beliefs associated with the more recent turn toward relativism, subjectivism and nihilism, and other aspects of postmodernism. If the latter were completely false, those traditional economic values would be untouched; on the other hand, it may be that postmodern beliefs are inimical to those values.[21] In short, both the Left and the Right have their anti-modern elements; and modernity is not a political party of uniform beliefs. It does not belong to Left or Right.

One could say that there is an argument (and long has been) *within* modernity, between Left moderns and Right moderns, over the distribution of the material and other benefits of modernity. That argument will not go away. In this regard the valuable study of Gross and Levitt (1998), repudiating the postmodern attack on science, is very largely deserving of endorsement, even if their use of the phrase "academic Left" to describe their target is ill-conceived.[22] There is nothing *essentially* Leftist about postmodernism; that is to say, one can be Left – in terms of economic values, as defined above – and repudiate all of it. The status of economics in particular as a science – commonly (if rather too generously) viewed as situated somewhere between the standing of the natural sciences and the standing of the other social sciences – is nevertheless still an open question. The proneness of economics to ideological capture, discussed in the second section above, is encouraged by the isolation of academic economics from other, more authentic sciences: the intellectual division of labor, whatever other benefits it may bring, enables economics to proceed in isolation from genuine empirical sciences, reproducing itself self-referentially, without any external yardstick of scientific significance intruding. This facilitates a certain infantile disposition, given the lack of discipline by compelling facts – though it must be said that there is a significant minority of serious people in the discipline too. The average academic economist finds it all too easy to ignore the example of the natural sciences, which can offer compelling (technological) evidence that they work – and instead to look toward (and down their noses at) the other social sciences.[23]

It was emphasized above that there will always remain a qualitative difference between the natural and social sciences. This is so for a number of reasons. One proceeds from the important truth that human values are partly shaped by our beliefs about the objective structure of the world; that is to say, the "relevant world" – in particular, in this context, the structure of society, economy, polity, and so on. Our beliefs as to what is *desirable* can hardly be independent of our beliefs as to what are *feasible or possible* states of the world. This perhaps apparently rather abstract characterization of human belief is not merely idle academic chatter. To take an immediately pertinent example, what is possible and desirable *vis-à-vis* the distribution of income between wages and non-wage income can hardly be independent of our beliefs about what are the feasible distributional outcomes in a capitalist economy. We could hardly have the same values about what distributional outcomes to desire, and perhaps pursue, in a capitalist framework – if, on the one hand, we believe there is a unique competitive equilibrium outcome under those social conditions (the conventional view); or if, on the other hand, we believe that a considerable spectrum of distributions is feasible.[24]

With the latter, we return to Sraffa's degree of freedom in the determination of competitive distribution and prices, which is indeed an analytical expression of the capacity of social forces – of which the labor movement is one – to exercise a measure of autonomy *vis-à-vis* competitive forces, in the working out of the distribution of the social net product or surplus.[25] That "degree of freedom" – the openness of distribution to social forces (arbitrariness, within certain limits) – is the objective basis for class antagonism (in the realm of *action*, not mere sentiment).

It leaves open – so long as distribution is not at one of its limiting positions (the maximum profit rate or maximum wage) – the possibility of *either* side making gains at the expense of the other. It therefore suggests the possibility of an endless cycle of conflict, as the balance of social and institutional forces shifts power to one side and then to the other, with the balance in recent decades happening to shift back in favor of the employing class. Marx thought that such conflict must ultimately be resolved or overcome by a shift to a different kind of socio-economic order. But *must it* be overcome? Perhaps not.[26]

Acknowledgments

I am indebted to G. Argyrous and G. Mongiovi for comments and advice, without thereby implicating them in the final product.

Notes

1 There is also a (quite useful) short answer to this question: if unions were so impotent to affect outcomes, the Right would not be so determined to curtail and otherwise impede their existence and operation. In this regard there has commonly been a distinct tension in the arguments of labor-market deregulation advocates of recent decades – as to whether labor unions are impotent and therefore irrelevant, or injurious and therefore worthy of more or less severe restraint if not proscription.

2 A clearer picture of Sraffa's self-understanding concerning his intellectual program is emerging from examination of his archive, in the Wren Library, Trinity College, Cambridge. My knowledge of the documents and what they reveal is derived from discussions with a number of people closely studying them, particularly Heinz Kurz, who has written a number of papers based on the archive (see especially Kurz and Salvadori 2005; Kurz 2006). See also the important paper by Garegnani (2005). An edition of selected manuscripts from Sraffa's archive is in preparation, projected at approximately 2,000 pages, under the general editorship of Professor Kurz, to be published by Cambridge University Press.

3 Actually, for the purpose of the price equations which follow, the production of a non-negative surplus of every commodity is not strictly necessary: only a weaker viability condition is required – that the production system is *capable*, in principle, of at least self-replacement of its inputs (Sraffa 1960: 5n). The use of particular commodities can decline over time, even disappear. In such circumstances the aggregate, system-wide input quantities of some commodities can exceed the same commodities' outputs, for some time periods, in entirely viable systems.

4 See Kurz and Salvadori (1995) for a rigorous formal treatment of the issues, and Aspromourgos (2004a) for detail of the relevant literature.

5 By this term I mean any system which specifies the technology of production such that at least one produced commodity is required directly or indirectly for the production of all produced commodities. That is to say, in Sraffa's language, there is at least one "basic" commodity (see Sraffa 1960: 8). The capital good fulfills that role here.

6 Workers' subsistence consumption requirements are being ignored, for the moment, so that w is now the *total* wage per worker, and with no necessary consumption component here included in it.

7 The wage share in the numerator of our real wage equation is the wage share in the capital goods industry; but with uniform capital-labor ratios across the two industries, distributional shares will also be uniform:

$$wl_C/p_C = [1-(1+r)a_{KC}p_{KC}]$$

where $p_{KC} = p_K/p_C = l_K/l_C = a_{KK}/a_{KC}$. The equation for the inverse relation between w_C and r may be derived by dividing through the two price equations by p_C, then rearranging each equation as an expression for p_{KC}, and equating the two expressions. This generates

$$w_C l_K a_{KC}(1+r) = (1-w_C l_C)[1-a_{KK}(1+r)]$$

which can be rearranged to give:

$$w_C = [1-a_{KK}(1+r)]/\{l_C+(1+r)[l_K a_{KC}-l_C a_{KK}]\}$$

The two restrictions on a_{KK} indicated in the text ensure that both the numerator and the denominator are positive. The somewhat more complex expression for w_C given in the text (derived by multiplying and dividing the square-bracketed term in the w_C equation here, by $l_C l_K$) is designed to render more transparent the role of capital-labor ratios.

8 Here again, see Aspromourgos (2004a) for the literature since 1960 which has followed up this suggestion of Sraffa. The most significant is Pivetti (1991).

9 See Keynes (1936: 202–4; 1937: 212–13) and Aspromourgos (2004b). Viewed from this standpoint, the standard interpretation of Keynes's theory of interest, in terms only of "liquidity preference," does not do justice to his understanding of interest – though Keynes is himself partly to blame for the misunderstanding.

10 Recall the opening sentences of that chapter (Keynes 1936: 372):

> The outstanding faults of the economic society in which we live are its failure to provide for full employment and its arbitrary and inequitable distribution of wealth and incomes. The bearing of the foregoing theory on the first of these is obvious. But there are also . . . important respects in which it is relevant to the second.

11 But note, in relation to Sraffa's objectivism, that even though in any particular social setting there are non-natural or conventional elements embedded in the level and content of necessary consumption, and the feasible methods of production, these data remain observable, empirical phenomena – unlike, for example, "preferences" or "disutility".

12 Perhaps Marx's most fundamental and persistent criticism of the classical economists was that they presented historically specific social laws as if they were ineluctable natural laws.

13 The possible retort, that we are "all" now recipients of non-wage income – via pension, superannuation and other retirement-type funds – so that abolishing pure property income is in no one's interest, is too trite. The net impact of a permanent shift to zero pure property income, on individuals or households of particular economic profiles, has to be considered in terms of *the entire life cycle* of such household profiles – for example, the net effect upon real income for a particular life cycle profile, taking into account reduced expenditure obligations during periods of net liabilities, and reduced income receipts during periods of net assets.

14 The inverse relation between the rate of wages (or wage share) and the rate of profits is *necessary* to the persistent tendency to conflict, but it is not sufficient. If competition determined a unique distributional outcome (in the manner of orthodox marginalist theory, or at least in the manner *hoped for* by that theory), so that there was no space – no degree of freedom – for bargaining power to play a role in distribution of the net product or surplus, then any scope for either side to press for a larger share would evaporate. (The capital debates, mentioned in the first section above, demonstrated that even with profit-maximizing choice from among multiple available production methods, competition cannot plausibly be construed as leading to a determinate and unique real wage and rate of profits – precisely because in general orthodox demand functions for factors of production, with respect to those rates of remuneration, cannot be derived.) An end to this basis of persistent conflict would seem to require either: (1) a distribution of income-earning property more or less in proportion to wage income; or (2) an even more different kind of society – if the former possibility cannot be achieved within the

framework of capitalist society. (This leaves aside the question of how satisfactory is the distribution of wage and salary income itself.)

15 This entails also (symmetric with the restriction $a_{KK} < 1$ in the first section above) that $cl_C < 1$: the consumption-goods industry uses up in a production cycle less consumption goods (in the form of necessary labor consumption) than it produces. Notice that as c tends toward zero, the maximum value of r here tends toward $(1-a_{KK})/a_{KK}$ – the value of r associated with a zero real wage in the first section above.

16 See Kornbluh (1964: 1–34, esp. 2, 6, 9). The "Manifesto" of January 1905 is reprinted at pp. 7–9: "A movement . . . of one great industrial union embracing all industries,—providing for craft autonomy locally, industrial autonomy internationally, and working class unity generally" (9). Note also the statement earlier in the Manifesto (8):

> Craft unions may be and have been used to assist employers in the establishment of monopolies and the raising of prices. One set of workers are thus used to make harder the conditions of life of another body of laborers.

In this context the point about monetary policy and union wage behavior may be elaborated a little further: if, in the contemporary situation, inflation-targeting monetary policy is effective in its objective – fixing the overall growth rate of money-wages (relative to productivity growth) – then successful money-wage claims in excess of this growth rate will be at the expense of other groups of workers. Along similar lines, and following somewhat more closely the above Wobbly formulation, even public sector enterprises (typically, monopolies) have been used to raise wages and prices at the expense of consumers, including working-class consumers.

17 In Australia, a traditional conservative line of attack upon the Labor Party – historically the main (slightly) left-of-center political party – has been that it is controlled by the unions. One Labor figure, in a moment of engaging frankness, pointed out that the *real* problem was that the Labor Party controlled the unions.

18 That the differences between Right and Left with regard to distribution are better regarded as differences of degree, rather than qualitative differences, may be compared with Keynes's important letter of June 28, 1944 to F.A. von Hayek, in response to his *Road to Serfdom* (1944), concerning planning versus non-planning:

> You admit here and there that it is a question of knowing where to draw the line. You agree that the line has to be drawn somewhere, and that the logical extreme is not possible. But you give us no guidance whatever as to where to draw it. In a sense this is shirking the practical issue. It is true that you and I would probably draw it in different places. I should guess that according to my ideas you greatly under-estimate the practicability of the middle course. But as soon as you admit that the extreme is not possible, and that a line has to be drawn, you are, on your own argument, done for, since you are trying to persuade us that so soon as one moves an inch in the planned direction you are necessarily launched on the slippery path which will lead you in due course over the precipice.
>
> (Moggridge 1980: 386–7)

19 Though the extent to which that species of equality ensures social justice depends upon how "opportunities" are configured. On this, see the valuable analysis by Barry (2005, esp. 37–94).

20 All this is concerned with policy within the confines of a mixed capitalist social economy (and a closed system). When the closed system is actually a closed *global* system – of multiple interacting currency areas and legal jurisdictions – the tasks confronting both unions and governments of course are rendered much more difficult. On the other hand, I discount any currently foreseeable possibility of transcending the mixed capitalist economy as such. For a diagnosis of the politico-economic situation which has developed (in the U.S.) since the 1970s – consistent with our analysis above – see Chapter 6 below.

21 It also should not go unnoticed that, in a real sense, it is the success of thoroughly modern science since the advent of modernity which provides the objective precondition for postmodernists to pursue their purposes: the resulting scale of the per capita social surplus enables the "luxury" of funding such socially unnecessary activities. Or is postmodernism just a post-Christian manifestation of an enduring human phenomenon, which in pre-modern times was largely the preserve of religious activity?

22 They themselves more than once in the course of the argument admit to discomfort with that phrase, fully realizing that postmodern humanities and social sciences academics, even if Left in some sense (this is contestable too), are certainly not "the" Left:

> When we use the phrase *academic left* we do *not* refer merely to academics with left-wing political views. There are plenty of such people with whom we have no quarrel. There are countless academics who do excellent and penetrating work . . . from a left-wing viewpoint. There are countless left-wing scientists – although we are stodgy enough to insist that there is no such thing as left-wing science.
>
> (Gross and Levitt 1998: 9; also 2–3, 27–37, 252; see also Wolin 2004)

23 Here, a general university opinion reported by Gross and Levitt (1998: 12) is instructive. (They do not exactly say they share this view, but it is implied.)

> For decades certain assumptions about the epistemological ranking of various fields have prevailed, though rarely explicitly, among academic intellectuals. The rule of thumb has been that the hard scientists produce reliable knowledge, assembled into coherent theories. Historians, it is conceded, generate reliable factual knowledge (as long as they keep their methodological noses clean); but this is often contaminated by unprovable and bootless speculation. Economics has rigor of method; but its assumptions are serious, often fatal, oversimplifications of the real world. In the other social sciences impressionistic description and subjective hermeneutics rule, though they may come dressed in elaborate statistical costumes. The more theoretical the social scientists are, the less respect they get. Literary criticism, finally, has been looked upon as a species of highly elaborated connoisseurship, interesting and valuable, perhaps, but subjective beyond hope of redemption, and thus out of the running in the epistemological sweepstakes.

Notice the ambivalence about economics; but the very fact that Gross and Levitt are willing to epistemologically rank economics between the natural sciences and the other social sciences suggests that economics is nevertheless being overrated.

24 And beyond consideration of the confines of a capitalist society, one sees similarly how facts – or more precisely, people's *understanding* of what the facts are – shape values, in a traditional two-step conservative attack on the Left: the socialism which is possible, we are told, is bad; and the socialism which is good . . . is impossible.

25 Is there a difference between the concepts of net product and surplus? Two points may be made. First, the classical concept of surplus differs from more modern notions of net product, in netting out of the gross product, the necessary consumption of labor. Second, the net product (at least once conceived of as net also of necessary labor consumption) becomes a "surplus" *when it can be thought of as available for "free disposal"* – rather than distribution being uniquely determined by the functional requirements of system equilibrium (as marginalist theory at least hopes or attempts).

26 Indeed, what we have witnessed in recent U.S. elections, and in somewhat different forms, elsewhere in the developed world, is a willingness of working-class people to vote for traditional (or is it radical?) social conservatism, at the apparent expense of their own economic interests (except that the left-of-center parties which wage-workers

traditionally supported have considerably abandoned avowal of their economic interests at the same time – surely not a mere coincidence). There thus arises the possibility of the upper classes preserving their economic interests by pandering to the social-cum-religious conservatism of the lower classes. (No doubt many of the U.S. neo-conservative leadership, among themselves, conceive of American religiosity as the contemporary equivalent of the Platonic "noble lie" – particularly those who claim a connection to the thought of Leo Strauss.) This I take to be the central conundrum of Frank (2004), which by happy coincidence, focuses on the region of the U.S. in which this conference is being held, that region being treated as an exemplar of the wider U.S. political shifts which have occurred since the late 1960s – Kansas as America "writ small," so to speak. (In the U.S. the book was published under the title, *What's the Matter with Kansas? How Conservatives Won the Heart of America*, New York: Metropolitan Books.)

References

Aspromourgos, T. (1996) *On the Origins of Classical Economics: Distribution and value from William Petty to Adam Smith*, London: Routledge.

—— (2004a) "Sraffian Research Programmes and Unorthodox Economics," *Review of Political Economy*, 16: 179–206.

—— (2004b) "'The Functionless Investor': Keynes's euthanasia of the rentier revisited," in T. Aspromourgos and J. Lodewijks (eds) *History and Political Economy: Essays in honour of P.D. Groenewegen*, London: Routledge.

Barry, B. (2005) *Why Social Justice Matters*, Cambridge: Polity Press.

Dick, O.L. (ed.) (1972) *Aubrey's Brief Lives*, Harmondsworth: Penguin.

Foley, D.K., Garegnani, P., Pivetti, M. and Vianello, F. (2004) "Classical Theory and Policy Analysis: A round table," Centro di Ricerche e Documentazione "Piero Sraffa," Università degli Studi Roma Tre, *Materiali di Discussione n. 1*.

Frank, T. (2004) *What's the Matter with America? The resistible rise of the American Right*, London: Secker & Warburg.

Garegnani, P. (1984) "Value and Distribution in the Classical Economists and Marx," *Oxford Economic Papers*, 36: 291–325.

—— (1987) "Surplus Approach to Value and Distribution," in J. Eatwell, M. Milgate and P. Newman (eds) *The New Palgrave: A dictionary of economics*, vol. 4, London: Macmillan.

—— (2005) "On a Turning Point in Sraffa's Theoretical and Interpretive Position in the Late 1920s," *European Journal of the History of Economic Thought*, 12: 453–92.

Gross, P.R. and Levitt, N. (1998) *Higher Superstition: The academic Left and its quarrel with science* (2nd edn), Baltimore, MD: Johns Hopkins University Press.

Keynes, J.M. (1936) *The General Theory of Employment, Interest and Money*, London: Macmillan.

—— (1937) "Alternative Theories of the Rate of Interest," Economic Journal, 47; as reprinted in D. Moggridge (ed.) (1973) *The General Theory and After Part II. Defence and development* (The Collected Writings of John Maynard Keynes, vol. XIV), London: Macmillan (for the Royal Economic Society).

Kornbluh, J.L. (ed.) (1964) *Rebel Voices: An I.W.W. anthology*, Ann Arbor, MI: University of Michigan Press.

Kurz, H.D. (2006) "The Agents of Production are the Commodities Themselves: On the classical theory of production, distribution and value," *Structural Change and Economic Dynamics*, 17: 1–26.

Kurz, H.D. and Salvadori, N. (1993) "Von Neumann's Growth Model and the 'Classical' Tradition," *European Journal of the History of Economic Thought*, 1: 129–60.

—— (1995) *Theory of Production: A long-period analysis*, Cambridge: Cambridge University Press.

—— (2005) "Representing the Production and Circulation of Commodities in Material Terms: On Sraffa's objectivism," *Review of Political Economy*, 17: 413–41.

Moggridge, D. (ed.) (1980) *Activities 1940–1946. Shaping the Post-War World: Employment and commodities* (The Collected Writings of John Maynard Keynes, vol. XXVII), London: Macmillan (for the Royal Economic Society).

Neumann, J. von (1937) "Über ein Ökonomisches Gleichungssystem und eine Verallgemeinerung des Brouwerschen Fixpunktsatzes," *Ergebnisse eines Mathematischen Kolloquiums*, 8: 73–83 [translated as "A Model of General Economic Equilibrium," *Review of Economic Studies*, 1945–46, 13: 1–9].

Petty, W. (1690) *Political Arithmetick . . .*, London; as reprinted in C.H. Hull (ed.) (1899) *The Economic Writings of Sir William Petty . . .*, 2 vols, Cambridge: Cambridge University Press.

Pivetti, M. (1991) *An Essay on Money and Distribution*, New York: St. Martin's Press.

Sraffa, P. (1960) *Production of Commodities by Means of Commodities: Prelude to a critique of economic theory*, Cambridge: Cambridge University Press.

Wolin, R. (2004) *The Seduction of Unreason: The intellectual romance with fascism from Nietzsche to postmodernism*, Princeton, NJ: Princeton University Press.

6 John Kenneth Galbraith's new industrial state 40 years later

A radical perspective

Spencer J. Pack

Introduction

In the middle years of the twentieth century, John Kenneth Galbraith[1] developed a profound vision of the U.S. economy: both how it worked in practice and how he hoped it would be in the future. I will consider this Galbraithian vision of U.S. capitalism, which he termed "the new industrial state," in his book of that title published in 1967. I will also outline key aspects of this vision which were developed in two earlier major, popular, influential works: *American Capitalism: The Concept of Countervailing Power*, first published in 1952; and *The Affluent Society*, first published in 1958. Taken together,[2] these three books present a view of the dynamic, important parts of U.S. society being dominated by big business, big government, and to a slightly lesser extent, big labor. These three large sectors, big business, big government, and big labor, could to some extent balance, control, and countervail the power of the other two. They had helped guide the U.S. economy through the relatively prosperous post World War II years with rising standards of living for the average U.S. worker. Galbraith hoped/expected to see continuously rising living standards for the average worker. He felt that limitations of the system, such as its neglect of environmental and aesthetic values, could be overcome through appropriate reforms. In a sense, the industrial state could conceivably be transcended, or put in its place, as a technical aspect to society, but subservient to broader non-economic goals, needs, and purposes.[3]

Some 40 years later, the living standards of the average U.S. worker have largely stagnated or grown only slowly. Big labor is no longer so big. Those parts of the government which are not under the sway of the military industrial complex are either not so big now or under attack (for example, social security). The ability of government to act as a countervailing power to business is weakened. So, contrary to Galbraith's hopes, only one part of the big three sectors is today functioning as a big, independent sector; and that is big business, which appears to be bigger and more powerful than ever. What went wrong? I think from a general radical perspective,[4] there were two major shortcomings to Professor Galbraith's analysis and hopes for the future.[5] First, Galbraith insufficiently stressed and was insufficiently cognizant of the class struggle, and the potential power of capital and its representatives to warp the industrial system to their own sectarian interests. Second,

Galbraith paid insufficient attention to the fact that capitalism is a global, international system. Galbraith's vision of big business potentially checked by the countervailing powers of big labor and a large welfare-oriented government was undermined by the international mobility of capital. Using what the finance-type people call taxation, regulatory, and wage arbitrage,[6] capital was able to move to those parts of the world where taxes were lower, government regulations fewer or more easily avoided, and labor power available at lower wages than in the U.S. This led to the stagnation of U.S. living standards, and facilitated the brutal attack on labor unions, as well as the weakening of the liberal welfare state.

The second section of the chapter discusses Galbraith's book *American Capitalism*. It describes Galbraith's concept of countervailing power and the positive role big unions can play in society. The third section discusses Galbraith's *The Affluent Society*. It stresses that for Galbraith we now live in a relatively affluent society in terms of private goods. However, the public sector is impoverished and there is a great need for a larger government to provide more public goods and services. Sections four and five discuss Galbraith's *New Industrial State*. Section four discusses how in modern society, due to technological and organizational needs, big business is a necessity. A powerful technostructure develops to plan and manage these large enterprises; while section five discusses Galbraith's vision for what is and what he hoped to be the relationship between big business, the unions, and the state. Section six outlines the main contours of what has happened in the U.S. economy since Galbraith's *New Industrial State*, and offers criticisms from a general radical (or, indeed, Wobbly or Marxist) perspective. Finally, section seven provides a conclusion. It also gives the last word back to Galbraith himself. Galbraith, at the remarkable age of 96, wrote yet another book on the U.S. system, and it turned out to be a very critical, caustic one indeed.

American capitalism and the need for big labor

Already in *American Capitalism*,[7] Galbraith emphasized the ubiquity of large corporations in most industries. Most industries have high barriers to entry in terms of cost and economies of experience. Therefore, as old firms die off and few or no firms can enter, most industries will end up with a few dominant oligopolistic firms surrounded by a fringe of smaller ones (1956: See ch. 4, "The Abandonment of the Model," 32–49). Thus, "a large share of the productive activity of the United States is carried on by a comparatively small number of corporations" (1956: 7).

In most industries, effective price competition tends not to operate so much on the same side of the market, since there are so few dominant firms in each industry. Oligopolists prefer to not compete with each other in terms of price. However, effective competition tends to operate across the market between the buyers and sellers. This can be seen with the growth of strong retail chain stores such as Sears, Roebuck, and the large grocery stores. These large retail stores can use their power to bargain down the prices of the goods sold by the oligopolistic manufacturers of goods. This growth of powerful entities on the other side of the market, so that powerful buyers are confronting powerful sellers, is what Galbraith calls a countervailing power. While this growth of countervailing power may be seen in the retail chain stores, its most important manifestation is in the labor markets with the development of large, powerful unions. Also important is the farm sector, where the farmers have gotten federal price supports for their goods; this, according to Galbraith, is another manifestation of countervailing power.

For Galbraith, there is a tendency for countervailing powers to be a self-generating force and to arise necessarily. Economic power is organized in response to economic power, since "power on one side of a market creates both the need for, and the prospect of reward to, the exercise of countervailing power from the other side" (1956: 113). Countervailing power is needed to counter original economic power. This is seen most clearly in the labor markets where workers form unions for their own protection. Moreover, unions tend to need oligopolistic employers because the oligopolies are able to generate economic profits. These economic profits can then be shared with their unionized employees. Firms in more competitive industries such as farming, or in the theoretical model of perfect competition, have little or no economic profits to share with their employees. Hence, in those real or theoretical situations, there is little incentive or need to form the countervailing power of unions. But in industries characterized by large firms (which are most industries in the U.S.) there is the need and ability to organize unions, to increase worker power, and to raise employee wages.

So Galbraith is generally in favor of unions;[8] for Galbraith it is good that workers and farmers have developed countervailing powers. The development of countervailing power (unions for workers, price supports for farmers) has replaced social inferiority and economic insecurity with a sense of equality and confidence (1956: 146). Thus, for workers and farmers, there are psychological and social, as well as purely economic benefits, from their development of countervailing power. Therefore, there is a positive role for the government to help organize countervailing powers. Indeed, "the provision of state assistance to the development of countervailing power has become a major function of government . . . perhaps *the* domestic function of government" (1956: 128, emphasis in original). The government should help promote countervailing powers such as labor unions to redress the position of the weaker group. Again: "the support of countervailing power has become in modern times perhaps the major domestic peacetime function of the federal government" (1956: 136). So it is good that the U.S. now has strong unions, and Galbraith argues that the government should further help to organize the unorganized rural and urban workers.

Galbraith sought to legitimize government support to the development of countervailing powers. Thus, "the state must be expected to participate in the development of countervailing power" (1956: 168). Thus, we have big business. There is a need for big strong unions to counter big business. There is also the need for a relatively powerful government to help organize countervailing powers. Galbraith had a positive view of government. While, until the nineteenth century in England, and the twentieth century in most of the rest of the Western world, state authority was "at least episodically rapacious or corrupt"; now, "in the United States, as in the parliamentary democracies in general, the great majority of the people have come to regard the government as essentially benevolent" (1956: 29). The need for a relatively large strong government sector would be more fully examined in Galbraith's *The Affluent Society*.

The affluent society and the need for big government

In some ways, *The Affluent Society* is Galbraith's most radical book. There he argues that we live in a relatively affluent society. Therefore, we really do not need an increase in the production of private goods. What we really need is an increase in the production of public goods and services; hence a bigger role for government. Moreover, while our society is relatively affluent, we tend to be governed by an economic theory that was more relevant in a poorer society. Most standard economic theory, or what Galbraith dubbed "the conventional wisdom," is concerned with the efficiency of production. However, in a world where the production of goods is not the central problem, "the efficiency of the process by which they are produced ceases to be an overriding consideration" (1971: 256). Thus, most economic theory is now outdated; hopelessly obsolete.

As Galbraith puts it: "one would not expect that the preoccupations of a poverty-ridden world would be relevant in one where the ordinary individual has access to amenities – foods, entertainment, personal transportation, and plumbing – in which not even the rich enjoyed a century ago" (1971: 2). In the time of Smith, Malthus, and Ricardo, when the world was so poor, nothing was more important than that there be an increase in output and wealth. Now, however, businessmen, farmers, workers, and reformers usually most want more security, not more income. They want to get away from the insecurities of the market: unemployment for the worker; bankruptcy for the farmer and businessman.[9] Farmers want price supports; workers want social security and unemployment compensation. Corporations try to get away from economic insecurity and reduce risk by becoming larger, by diversifying, and by trying to manipulate the demand for their goods.

The goods themselves are not so important; this is one of the reasons why advertising can be so effective in manipulating people's needs and selling superfluous goods. Needs which are truly important and vital cannot be easily manipulated. Indeed, what is important about the production of goods is not so much the goods themselves as the employment that is needed for their production. If the goods are not produced, they will probably not be sorely missed by society. However, the unemployment generated by the lack of production will be a problem, particularly to the unemployed. Thus, the production of goods is needed for the employment it generates. A growth in output can also lessen the tensions which could come about by efforts to redistribute income from the rich to the poor. Increased output then is really needed to ease social tensions between the rich and the poor and to reduce unemployment.[10]

According to Galbraith, there is low marginal utility to society of the privately produced goods (1971: 261). Thus, there is too much private production, and not enough public production. Unfortunately, "we view the production of some of the most frivolous goods with pride. We regard the production of some of the most significant and civilizing services with regret" (1971: 127). Vacuum cleaners, the result of private production, are good. Street cleaners, the result of public production, are not. "Alcohol, comic books and mouthwash all bask under the superior reputation of the market. Schools, judges and municipal swimming pools lie under the evil reputation of bad kings" (1971: 131). With increasing wealth, there is diminishing importance to produce more. Production for the sake of production is frequently a bit of a sham: "to create the demand for new automobiles, we must contrive elaborate and functionless changes each year and then subject the consumer to ruthless psychological pressures to persuade him of their importance" (1971: 271).

Thus arises a social imbalance where there are too many privately produced goods and not enough public services. According to Galbraith, we have poor public schools, police services, parks, and playgrounds. We have dirty streets, empty filthy lots, poor public transportation, and polluted air. More money needs to be spent in these areas by government to correct our social imbalance. Thus the need for a larger government. Therefore, when we need to increase aggregate demand to stimulate the economy, we should increase government spending to provide for various needed public services, rather than decrease taxes which then increase spending on less needed private goods.

The correction of the social imbalance will increase social stability. Better schools, public health services, recreation, housing, and mass transportation systems would help attack the social and cultural causes of much poverty. For Galbraith, "an affluent society, that is also both compassionate and rational, would, no doubt, secure to all who needed it the minimum income essential for decency and comfort" (1971: 292). Again, this would most likely entail an increase in the responsibility and size of the government.

Moreover, since what is most important about production is not what is produced but in providing a job and being a source of income, we need to divorce production from economic security. Let us not worry so much about voluntary idleness among the workers, and be more generous in unemployment compensation. Since production itself is not so important, efficiency is not so important; we must find other goals in life than mere efficient production. This de-emphasis in the importance of production will also de-emphasize the importance of the businessman, who is in charge of production.

There has been a drastic decline in the length of the work week. In 1850 it was just under 70 hours; in 1950 about 40 hours. According to Galbraith, this makes sense given the decline in the marginal urgency of the product. So it is good to have more leisure.[11] Let us also make work itself easier and more pleasant. We can do this partly by drying up the supply of undereducated, unskilled labor at the bottom of the ladder. Indeed, we should eliminate economic/manual toil as much as possible. Yet, for other people, a new class, work may be a source of satisfaction and enjoyment. They have a good working environment, use their brains and their creativity; their work is interesting and rewarding. This new class is further elaborated upon in *The New Industrial State*.

The new industrial state and the need for big business

Although always a central concern in his writings, Galbraith explores in most detail the nature and role of big business in *The New Industrial State*. Big business arises because of the importance and sophistication of technology, as well as the need to plan to try to escape as much as possible from the vagaries of the market. Galbraith points out that "the five hundred largest corporations produce close to half of all the goods and services that are available in the United States" (1967: 1–2). These huge firms tend to be run by managers. At the time of his writing, "the men who now run the large corporations own no appreciable share of the enterprise" (1967: 2). The managers are selected by a Board of Directors which is selected by the managers themselves. The U.S. economic system thus has a core economy composed of big business. There are also, of course, many small firms as well: thus, the U.S. may be viewed to have a dual economy.[12] Nonetheless, to really understand the U.S. economy and its dynamics, we should focus our attention on the large corporations, not teeny enterprises.

The large firms try to plan their own future. The planning is needed because of complicated, specialized technology. This requires specialized knowledge and specialized people; hence organizations. There are long lead times between the research and development of new products and their actual appearance on the market. The large firms try to anticipate the needs of the consumer. They try to gain control over what is sold and what is supplied to minimize or get rid of disruptive market influences. They also generate their own savings through retained earnings, thus freeing them from dependency on the capital markets. This also frees the managers from the suppliers of capital and contributes to the shift in power from the owners to the managers of large businesses.

According to Galbraith, "power goes to the factor which is hardest to obtain or replace" (1967: 56). Due to the importance of food production, until about 200 years ago, power was associated with ownership of land. With the rise of industrial capitalism, the person who controlled capital became most powerful; that capitalist could get the needed labor and land. Now, with plentiful capital, there is a shift in power to the current scarce resource – talented people.

With the large corporation necessarily comes the need for organization. There arises the need to organize the specialists who organize the information to do the planning and coordination. People need to obtain, digest, pool, and test information. This is done through committees; there is too much information needed for one person to stay abreast of. Hence the need for a technical planning staff; thus arises what Galbraith calls the technostructure. The technostructure includes management; but also other various participants, people who contribute information to group decisions. It includes engineers, sales executives, scientists, technicians, designers, and other specialists. The technostructure is the brain of the enterprise.

The technostructure needs to plan; to do this effectively it needs to exclude outsiders from the planning process; that is, the government. Galbraith points out that the country banker can interfere with the decisions of the farmer. However, bankers are generally not a problem for the technostructure of big business, which gets most of its capital from retained earnings. With advanced technology, large amounts of capital, comprehensive planning, and increasing size and complexity of the organization, entrepreneurs are replaced by people, by committees, by the technostructure.

In this state, "management does not go out ruthlessly to reward itself – a sound management is expected to exercise restraint" (1967: 115). Stockholding by management is small, often non-existent. Managers do not abuse their position and ability to be bandits: "more pay, more deferred compensation or pension rights, more stock options . . . would require only the routine blessing of counsel" (1967: 117). Therefore, management does not maximize profits, and they are not united with the owners of the corporation. Rather, they tend to unite with the rest of the technostructure.

The technostructure is motivated not so much by compulsion or money. Rather, members identify with the goals of the organization and/or try to improve that organization. The organization itself needs a certain minimum level of earnings to keep the stockholders happy and to provide a supply of savings for reinvestment. The technostructure will put the "prevention of loss ahead of maximum return. Loss can destroy the technostructure; high revenues accrue to others" (1967: 168). The technostructure is for growth; expansion of output means expansion of the technostructure, expansion of their own kind. Thus, the technostructure wants a secure level of earnings, a maximum rate of growth and, of course, technological advance (1967: 175).

By Galbraith's reading of history, "power in economic life has over time passed from its ancient association with land to association with capital and then on, in recent times, to the composite of knowledge and skills which comprises the technostructure" (1967: 140). When the landowners were in power, people ruled largely through force and compulsion. With rule by capital, the capitalists and wage earners were ruled or motivated by money. Not so with the technostructure. As long as their pay is adequate, they have other concerns. They identify with the goals of the organization, or try to improve the organization. The attempt to improve the organization is called by Galbraith adaptation: "the association with organization in the hope of influencing its goals to accord more closely with one's own" (1967: 158). This tendency to identify with the corporation could have bad effects on the union movement.

The new industrial state and unions, government, and the future

We saw above that in *American Capitalism* Galbraith emphasized the need for unions to form a countervailing power to big business, to raise worker wages, and to enhance the dignity of the workers. In *The New Industrial State* Galbraith still sees this to some extent. Unions, though, are now more clearly a junior partner to businesses: "By helping to frame the rules and by participating in their administration through the grievance machinery, the union serves invaluably to mitigate the feeling that such systems for their administration are arbitrary or unjust" (1967: 277). Unions can standardize wage costs between different firms, insure that changes in wages occur at about the same time, and assist in price controls by the industry. No firm can reduce prices because of lower wage rates for their particular workers. The union contract introduces stability for the duration of the contract and is binding on all its members (1967: 278–9).

But unions could also be swallowed up or eliminated by kinder, technocratic enterprises. Workers will tend to identify more with the goals of the corporation rather than with the union itself. The blue-collar proletarian will decline sharply, replaced by white-collar workers. Higher educated, part of the technostructure, hence part of the decision-making process itself, they will have fewer incentives to join or form unions. The technostructure will more likely give in to pay demands than the old-fashioned entrepreneur-owner. It can give high pay without union pressure, or to avoid having a union at all. Moreover, high employment from the regulation of aggregate demand and comparative affluence reduces the dependence of the individual worker on the union; the worker can easily quit and get another job. Galbraith thus sees the unions as gradually losing ground and in the earlier stages of a permanent decline. So Galbraith can be read as of two minds concerning the unions. Unions are on the way down, but relatively slowly, due to the benignity of the corporations. Yet, they could also (in his previous work) be viewed as a countervailing power, or now at least as a junior partner to big business.

Similarly with big government. As in *The Affluent Society*, Galbraith still wants and sees the need for big government. However, now, instead of acting as a countervailing power to big business, he sees the state more, or rather, too accommodating to the needs of the industrial system. Furthermore, "the line dividing the state from what is called private enterprise, or at least from the highly organized part of it, is a traditional fiction" (1967: 232); indeed, "the industrial system, in fact, is inextricably associated with the state" (1967: 296). The state is largely serving the needs of the industrial sector: it provides the educated workers so desperately needed by industry; it provides the highways and air traffic management; it regulates aggregate demand; and it supports much research and development. Much or most of the regulation of demand and research and development goes to the military-industrial complex, as well as space exploration. There is a bit of a sham here: "that defense requirements are set purely by national interest, that they are independent of any needs of the industrial system, is a useful formula. It sanctifies expenditures that could not be defended for their support to the industrial system" (1967: 232). War, and the threat of war, meets the needs of the industrial system, keeping up aggregate demand and promoting technological change. Thus, the image of a nation beset by enemies is encouraged. This is a very dangerous game.

Yet, Galbraith (1967: 345) also envisions the potential for a different kind of state. He would like to see more

> care of the ill, aged and physically or mentally infirm, the provision of health services in general, the provision of parks and recreation areas, the removal of rubbish, the provision of agreeable public structures, assistance to the impoverished and many other services [that] are not of particular importance to the industrial system.

There are still too many privately produced goods and services, and not enough public goods and services which do not serve the needs of the industrial system. The government also needs to preserve and promote architecture and urban and environmental design. "Far more than the test of production, which is far too easy, the test of aesthetic achievement is the one that, one day, the progressive community will apply" (1967: 353). We need to win emancipation from the corporate management of our wants, and "there is no intrinsic reason why work must be more unpleasant than non-work" (1967: 365). The modern educational system, which so extensively accommodates to the needs of the industrial system, should also lead the way to emancipation from that industrial system – toward aesthetic and intellectual values rather than vocational needs.

Galbraith feels that we live in "a world of great corporations in which people increasingly served the convenience of these organizations which were meant to serve *them*" (vii, emphasis in original). Right now, "large economic organizations shape social attitudes to their ends" (1967: 167). This needs to be reversed. Instead, "the expansion of public services that are not sponsored by the industrial system, the assertion of the aesthetic dimension of life, widened choice as between income and leisure, the emancipation of education – require that the monopoly of the industrial system on social purpose be broken" (1967: 379–80). Galbraith hopes that the intellectual and educated class will be able to bring about this reform, this taming, this putting the industrial system into its proper, subservient place. Thus, it would seem that there is a positive role for a more enlightened, more socially responsive big government. Or, as Galbraith explicitly stated in a little political tract written a few years after *The New Industrial State*, there is a need for a large public bureaucracy to police a powerful private bureaucracy (1970: 73).

So what happened?

One of the most noteworthy changes since Galbraith wrote these works culminating in *The New Industrial State* is that our managerial class has been making out like bandits. So, for example, we read in the newspapers how a president of Disney received US$140 million in severance pay after 14 months on the job (Glater 2005); or how a co-president for Morgan Stanley for three months received US$32 million (Thomas 2005). On the one hand, these anecdotal stories reported in our news media make for entertaining reading. On the other hand, there is a real systemic problem here for capitalists (and others). The managerial class is appropriating a significant amount of surplus value. In a recent study on executive pay, Bebchuk and Grinstein found that "aggregate compensation paid by public firms to top-five executives during the period 1993–2003 added up to about $350 billion . . . aggregate compensation paid by public firms to their top-five executives was 9.8 percent of the aggregate earnings of these firms during 2001–2003, up from 5 percent during 1993–1995" (2005: 1).[13] So the amount of surplus value being appropriated by the top managers is significant and in recent years has been getting larger. In addition, if anything, this study underestimates the value of executive compensation since, while including "salary, bonuses, long-term incentive plans, the grant-date value of restricted stock awards and the (grant-date) Black-Scholes value of granted options" it does not include the value of executives' pension plans (2005: 2).

Meanwhile, big business, their managers, and time have not been kind toward the U.S. labor movement. In the 1950s and 1960s around 30 percent of U.S. workers were union members (Greenhouse 2005). In 2004, 12.5 percent of wage and salary workers were union members; 36.4 percent of government workers were union members. Only 7.9 percent of workers in private-sector industries were unionized (United States Department of Labor 2005). The decline of unions has been much more than Galbraith thought would occur. Moreover, as Wal-Mart, America's largest corporation epitomizes, U.S. firms now do compete with one another by keeping out unions to lower their employee expenses, thus allowing them to either lower their output prices, increase their profits, or both.[14]

Finally, as is well known, there have been stagnant living standards for the average U.S. worker. Basically all gains in productivity in the U.S. since Galbraith wrote *The New Industrial State* have gone to the capitalists and their hired managers. The real wage, the median average hourly wages and salaries of production and non-supervisory workers in the total private sector, adjusted for inflation, has been falling since 1973. According to Wolff, "Between 1973 and 1993, the real wage declined by 14 percent, though it has since risen by 7 percent from 1993 to 2000, for a net change of –8 percent" (2004: 3). From 1947 to 1973 real wages grew by 75 percent. However, "in 2000, the hourly wage was $14.08 per hour, about the same level as in 1968 (in real terms)" (2004: 7). Both the relative and absolute share of income to the bottom half of people fell in the last quarter of the twentieth century (2004: 3–4). Between 1959 and 1973 the poverty rate declined by more than half, from 22.4 to 11.1 percent. In 1998 it was 11.3 percent, still above its low point in 1973 (2004: 6).

Meanwhile, according to Wolff, the percentage of college graduates in the adult population soared from 5.4 percent in 1947 to 26.2 percent in 2000. Between 1947 and 1973 the percentage of adults who had graduated from college rose by 7.2 percentage points, while between 1973 and 2000 it grew by 13.6 percentage points (2004: 11–12). So, the system was able to produce new members of the technostructure. Workers' wages did not skyrocket as a result of scarcity of skilled labor.[15]

So what went wrong with Galbraith's vision/hopes for the future of what he saw as the new industrial state? I think from a radical position,[16] Galbraith, in spite of his towering genius, made two key mistakes. First, he underestimated the intensity of the class struggle and the power of the capitalists, the formal owners of the means of production. Second, he neglected the fact that capitalism is by its nature a worldwide international system; he essentially treated the U.S. economy as a closed economic system.[17] Yet, as the 1905 Industrial Workers of the World Manifesto asserted, "universal economic evils afflicting the working class can be eradicated only by a universal working class movement" (1905 [1972]: 9). And the universal working class movement "must be founded on the class struggle, and its general administration must be conducted in harmony with the recognition of the irrepressible conflict between the capitalist class and the working class."[18]

A strong liberal welfare state, such as Galbraith wanted, either to act as a countervailing power to big business; or to control and transcend; or to put big business in its proper place, subservient to the needs of the rest of society, requires a firm, large tax base to support its activities. It will also most likely need to put a lot of rules and regulations on big business. Capitalism, being an international system, will try to move to those parts of the world where taxes are lower and rules and regulations are fewer or less adequately enforced. This is what the finance textbooks call tax and regulatory arbitrage. In an international world, with a tendency toward the so-called law of one price, capital flees high taxes and expensive (from their point of view) regulations to lands of lower taxes and less expensive regulations. Of course, since taxes are based largely on profits, the firms do not necessarily have to move their physical operations to low tax locales. With the employment of clever, skilled accountants, they can move as much as possible their accounting profits to these locales through the adroit use of paper (profits). Thus, there is and has been a tendency to starve the liberal welfare state of its financial resources; as well as pressure to reduce regulations, or to "deregulate" industries which are able to move (or threaten to move) abroad.[19]

The case is similar with regard to unions and workers' wages and standard of living. Capital is able to avoid and/or destroy unions by threatening or actually going abroad where wages are cheaper; an example of what may be called "wage arbitrage." Hence the need, as the Wobblies (and, of course, Marx and many radical economists) so clearly saw, to try to organize workers worldwide. Workers of the world indeed need to unite, or the capitalists will divide and subjugate them.

The grasping of a significant chunk of workers' surplus value by the managerial class has and is no doubt upsetting to the capitalist class; and the dynamics of this is being currently being played out in contemporary society. Nonetheless, I think it is clear that the managerial class, as representative of capitalist interests, has also successfully moved against most of the rest of what Galbraith termed the technostructure, as well as the working class as a whole. They have successfully kept the power of the rest of the technostructure, as well as the rest of the working class clearly in check, which has manifested itself in a drastic weakening of the union movement as well as a generally stagnant (or worsening) standard of living for the average worker.

Moreover, the aggressive capitalist class since the 1960s has successfully been trying to promote its own hegemony. It is as if they have read their Gramsci (1971) on the need to develop conscious class cultural hegemony,[20] or keenly studied the social movements of the 1960s with an eye to using their financial power to help create, nurture, and promote their own pro-capitalist cultural hegemony and movements. As indeed they have. So they have and finance their clever buffoons and entertainers such as Rush Limbaugh; they have created conservative research centers such as the Heritage Foundation and the Cato Institute to promote their agendas; they have studied people such as Joseph Schumpeter on the inherent weaknesses of capitalists as a ruling class (1950; especially Part II, "Can Capitalism Survive?," 59–163) and have tried to promote correctives to these weaknesses (Pack 1987, 1995); they have their partisan news media and commentators, as well as their political operatives and strategists (See Bradley 2005; Frank 2004: 195, 246–9). As Paul Krugman (2005) has pointed out, to some degree they have set up their own parallel universe of bogus scholars and research institutes, putting out studies favorable to their (short-run) financial interests, consciously creating and promoting all sorts of confusions.[21] And, of course, they have and will continue to go after the relative independence of academia itself. As James Piereson, long-time director of the John M. Olin Foundation has delicately put it, liberal academics "don't like American capitalism, American culture, and they don't like American history – they see it as a history of oppression. . . . There are some people who are prepared to spend large sums of money to address this problem" (quoted in DeParle 2005).[22] Indeed, Galbraith's vision/hope itself, that a new class of honest, critical scholars, intellectuals, and students could help lead the way to tame and control the power of big business is, of course, under attack, both now and in the past, by these capitalist-financed cultural warriors.[23]

Conclusion, and Galbraith's parting riposte

Now, some 40 years after *The New Industrial State* was published, there is not much left of big labor in the United States. Big government, outside of the military industrial complex, is also not so big and/or it is under danger of getting whittled down: witness, for example, efforts to privatize social security. Big business remains, in some ways, bigger and more powerful than ever. The class struggle has largely gone in favor of the capitalist side. As many radical economists, Wobblies, and Marxists have argued, there is a desperate need for a strong worldwide union movement to help workers worldwide. In the absence of a worldwide movement, through the workings of so-called tax, regulation, and wage arbitrage, there will be continued downward pressure on the ability of governments to collect taxes, to enforce strong regulations on business, and on workers' standard of living. The liberal welfare state will continue to be under attack. Capital will continue to go, or threaten to go, to those parts of the world where effective taxes are lower, regulations either fewer and less costly or easier to evade, and where wages are lower.

Yet, I think the last word here should no doubt go to John Kenneth Galbraith himself, who passed away in spring 2006; for Galbraith was well aware of many if not most of these issues. For example, in the 1985 introduction to the fourth edition of *The New Industrial State*, Galbraith admitted that he had overemphasized the competence and ability of the technostructure (1985: xxxi). He also acknowledged that "in the first edition of this book I urged that in the long run there would be a decline in union power, and this has proceeded much more rapidly than I foresaw" (1985: xxxiv). And he was "somewhat less confident as to the influence of the educational and scientific estate than in the days before President Reagan took office" (ibid.). A few years later, at a session of the American Economic Association on "*The New Industrial State* After Twenty Years," Galbraith again conceded that he had "unduly emphasized the intelligence and efficiency of the technostructure" (1988: 375). He also touched on the international aspect (or relative lack thereof) in his earlier work:

> In 1967, my view was, in some measure, of a closed America-dominated corporate structure extending its reach internationally by way of American multinational or transnational enterprises. I did not foresee the invasive thrust into this structure by Japan and other countries.

Yet, perhaps the most astonishing and astute updating of his analysis of the new industrial state came in 2004. At the remarkable age of 96, Galbraith published a final book, *The Economics of Innocent Fraud: Truth for Our Time*. In it, he said that the U.S. should now be accurately characterized as "The Corporate System" (2004: 8, 59). He knew that the management of this system is making out like bandits: "Legal self-enrichment in the millions of dollars is a common feature of modern corporate government. This is not surprising; managers set their own compensation" (2004: 27). The corporation is a private bureaucracy, and "corporate power lies with management – a bureaucracy in control of its task and its compensation. Rewards that can verge on larceny. This is wholly evident" (2004: 31).

In terms of the U.S. government, there is currently corporate control of defense and weapons development, hence of the military industrial complex; of the Treasury; and of environmental policy. Galbraith (2004: 35–6) wrote,

> Management having full authority in the modern great corporation, it was natural that it would extend its role to politics and to government. At this writing, corporate managers are in close alliance with the President, the Vice President and the Secretary of Defense. Major corporate figures are also in senior positions elsewhere in the federal government; one came from the bankrupt and thieving Enron to preside over the Army.

There continues to be a blurring of the difference between the private and the corporate sector, along with a diminishing public sphere. Private firms are even getting closer to combat in Iraq. Thus, "in war command as in peace, the private becomes the public sector" (2004: 37). Speaking of Iraq, it is "the greatest military misadventure in American history"; the second greatest being the war in Vietnam (2004: 55).[24] Now, as some 40 years ago, there is a deep need for "independent honest, professionally competent regulation"; but that will be "a difficult thing to achieve in a world of corporate dominance" (2004: 51). Instead, we live in a world where "the corporate power has shaped the public purpose to its own ability and need" (2004: 58). The problem is this: "As the corporate interest moves to power in what was the public sector, it serves, predictably, the corporate interest. That is its purpose" (2004: 53).

So, in the U.S., we now have a vastly weakened union movement, and a government largely subservient to or taken over by the corporate interest, by big business. Again, as in the 1960s, our leaders have taken us into a gross military misadventure. Again, the image of a nation beset by powerful enemies is being encouraged by our leaders. By temperament, Galbraith was not a radical[25] and was certainly never a Wobbly or a Marxist.[26] Yet, at the very end of the day, Galbraith and a radical, Wobbly, or Marxist view of the state of the world may not be that far apart.[27]

Acknowledgements

I would like to thank Eric Schliesser, Tony Aspromourgos, and two anonymous referees for their helpful comments on earlier versions of this chapter.

Notes

1 For a recent intellectual biography of Galbraith, see Parker 2005. A labor of love and deep scholarship and erudition, I doubt it will be superseded for a long time.
2 For a discussion emphasizing the differences between these books, see Sharpe 1974. This chapter emphasizes more how these three works complemented each other and developed a relatively coherent vision of U.S. society.
3 Here Galbraith echoed and developed ideas from Keynes's "Economic Possibilities for our Grandchildren" where, among other things, Keynes concluded that we should "not let us overestimate the importance of the economic problem, or sacrifice to its supposed necessities other matters of greater and more permanent significance. It should be a matter for specialists – like dentistry" (Keynes 1932: 373).
4 Or Wobbly or Marxist perspective; indeed, for this purposes of the chapter, I basically consider the Wobbly and Marxist perspectives to be part (or variants) of a general radical perspective.
5 For a recent thorough and persuasive demonstration that Galbraith should be viewed as a major foundational thinker integrating institutionalist and post-Keynesian schools of thought see Dunn and Pressman 2005. I would classify Galbraith as a heterodox economist, but not necessarily a radical economist. As with Keynes whom Galbraith greatly admired, Galbraith was more interested in saving and preserving capitalism than in overthrowing it; in becoming part of the establishment than in smashing the establishment.
6 See, for example, Shapiro 1991: 337–8; also Greider 1997, ch. 4, "Gleiche Arbeit, gleicher Lohn," 57–80.
7 In this chapter references are to the second 1956 edition. As far as I am aware, there are no significant differences between the editions which would affect the substance of my arguments. On the differences between the two editions, see Hession 1972: 57–8. Similarly, below, I used the second revised 1971 edition of *The Affluent Society*.
8 He may have had some reservations concerning certain building trade unions which may not confront original economic power (1956: 138).
9 This is reminiscent of Polanyi's (1957) argument that to preserve itself society had to move away from the gross instabilities of unregulated economic markets.
10 In recent decades it seems there has been more of a redistribution of income to the rich (particularly through changes in the tax laws – see, for example, Johnston 2005) in the guise of increasing output (supply-side economics). In addition, efforts have been made to periodically increase unemployment to discipline workers and reduce wage demands. (This, I think, has been the primary practical effect of the monetarists and their wars on inflation.)
11 Since Galbraith wrote this, there have been few or no gains in the shortening of the work week. Moreover, there has been an increase in labor force participation, especially of women (see Parker 2005: 292 and the references in fn. 45, 719–20). This could be partly due to declining and/or stagnating wages (suggesting families are on the "perverse" or backward bending part of their labor supply function); as well as the stimulating of our wants and needs for privately produced goods through corporate advertising and other means; and the continuing paucity or inadequacy of public services. For an argument that the lack of public services stimulates/forces people to purchase more private goods and services see Bartolini 2005.

12 For more on the dual economy see Averitt 1968, published the year after *The New Industrial State*.

13 Page references are to the June 2005 Olin Discussion paper, not to the 2005 *Oxford Review of Economic Policy* version.

14 See Frank (2004: 51–5) for a description of how the beef-packing industry is creating sad "rural boomtowns" in Western Kansas based on cheap labor, as they leave the unionized stockyards in Chicago and Kansas City.

15 Economists imbued with the principles of neoclassical economic theory could attribute the larcenous pay of our managerial class to their scarcity and productivity. Thus, for example, Ben Stein, in an otherwise sympathetic article explaining that the people who really take risks in our society are our soldiers, not hedge fund managers, thinks that hedge and commodity fund managers who are getting $250 to $500 million a year "do something very useful, helping to allocate capital and to make money for the shareholders and for the people who invest with them" (2005). How pathetic.

16 Or Wobbly or Marxist position.

17 Indeed, from reading Galbraith's economics and political works, one would scarcely realize that he was born and raised a Canadian, or realize how interrelated the U.S. and Canadian socio-economic systems are. He does, however, affectionately describe his Canadian rural upbringing in *The Scotch*, which he warns the reader is not a book of "serious economics or grave politics" (Galbraith 1964: 9).

18 Of course, the importance of the class struggle and that capitalism is by its very nature an international system was also stressed by Marx. To select just a few paragraphs from his (and Engels's) influential *Communist Manifesto*: "The history of all hitherto society is the history of class struggles" (I, 1); "Our epoch, the epoch of the bourgeoisie, possesses, however, this distinctive feature: it has simplified the class antagonisms. Society as a whole is more and more splitting up into two great hostile camps, into two great classes directly facing each other: bourgeoisie and proletariat" (I, 15); "The need of a constantly expanding market for its products chases the bourgeoisie over the whole surface of the globe. It must nestle everywhere, settle everywhere, establish connections everywhere" (I, 19). The quotes are taken from Gasper 2005: 39, 40 and 44.

19 Here the so-called financial services industry, or the sector of finance capital, has been adept at leading the way to deregulation, and to helping other industries avoid regulations and taxes. See, for example, Smith and Walter 1990, 1997, especially ch. 6, "Regulatory Issues," 153–84). For an entertaining (albeit at times nauseating) insider look at some of these accounting scams through the creative use of derivatives, see Partnoy 1997.

20 Which, of course, some of their hired hands (or, to be more accurate, hired heads) have done.

21 Pundits often say that we live in the information age. It would be at least as and probably more accurate to say that we live in the age of disinformation.

22 On the financial support and backing of the 2002 Nobel Laureate for Economics Vernon L. Smith by conservative Kansas money, see Frank 2004: 80–2.

23 Galbraith himself had trouble acquiring a permanent appointment at Harvard due to his outspoken, forthright, critical views; see Galbraith 2004: 55. Parker (2005: 222–32) tells a more complete story.

24 I think the fiasco in Iraq to some extent radicalized Galbraith at the end of his life; just as the fiasco in Vietnam had made him more radical in the late 1960s and early 1970s.

25 See, for example, Galbraith 1994 ch. 9, "The New Deal," 83–95; and Galbraith 1964: 144–5.

26 Although, as is well known, he personally supported many Marxist and radical economists.

27 The key difference between the various positions would probably be who or what group can be looked forward to as the agent for progressive, positive social change; no small problem.

References

Averitt, R.T. (1968) *The Dual Economy: The Dynamics of American Industry Structure*, New York: Norton.

Bartolini, S. (2005) "The Happiness Paradox: Explanations and Policy," paper presented to the Capabilities and Happiness Conference, Milano, Italy, June.

Bebchuk, L. and Grinstein, Y. (2005) "The Growth of Executive Pay," Discussion Paper No. 510, Revised 06/2005, The Harvard John M. Olin Discussion Paper Series. Available at http://www.law.harvard.edu/programs/olin_center/papers/510_Bebchuk_et%20al.php (accessed June 26, 2008), also in *Oxford Review of Economic Policy* (2005), 21(2): 283–303.

Bradley, B. (2005) "A Party Inverted," *New York Times*, March 30, A17.

DeParle, J. (2005) "Goals Reached, Donor on Right Closes up Shop," *New York Times*, May 29, A1+.

Dunn, S.P. and Pressman, S. (2005) "The Economic Contributions of John Kenneth Galbraith," *Review of Political Economy*, 17(2): 161–209.

Frank, T. (2004) *What's the Matter With Kansas?* New York: Metropolitan Books.

Galbraith, J. K. (1956) *American Capitalism: The Concept of Countervailing Power* (2nd edn), Boston, MA: Houghton Mifflin. First published in 1952.

—— (1964) *The Scotch*, Boston, MA: Houghton Mifflin.

—— (1967) *The New Industrial State*, Boston, MA: Houghton Mifflin.

—— (1970) *Who Needs the Democrats and What it Takes to be Needed*, New York: Signet Classics.

—— (1971) *The Affluent Society* (2nd edn), Boston, MA: Houghton Mifflin. First published in 1958.

—— (1985) "Introduction to the 4th edn," *The New Industrial State*, xi–xxxv, Boston, MA: Houghton Mifflin.

—— (1988) "Time and the New Industrial State," *The American Economic Review*, 78 (2): 373–6.

—— (1994) *A Journey Through Economic Time: A Firsthand View*, Boston, MA: Houghton Mifflin.

—— (2004) *The Economics of Innocent Fraud: Truth for Our Time*, Boston, MA: Houghton Mifflin.

Gasper, P. (ed.) (2005) *The Communist Manifesto: A Road Map to History's Most Important Political Document*, Chicago, IL: Haymarket Books.

Glater, J.D. (2005) "Big Bucks May Stop Here," *New York Times*, August 10, C1+.

Gramsci, A. (1971) *Prison Notebooks*, New York: International Publishers.

Greenhouse, S. (2005) "Are Unions Still Relevant?," *New York Times*, July 30, C1.

Greider, W. (1997) *One World, Ready or Not*, New York: Simon & Schuster.

Hession, C.H. (1972) *John Kenneth Galbraith and His Critics*, New York: New American Library.

Industrial Workers of the World (1905 [1972]) "Industrial Workers of the World Manifesto," reprinted in J.L. Kornbluh (ed.) *Rebel Voices, An I. W. W. Anthology*, (pp. 7–9), Ann Arbor: University of Michigan Press.

Johnston, D.C. (2005) "Richest are Leaving Even the Rich Far Behind: Tax Laws Help to Widen Gap at Very Top," *New York Times*, June 5, A1+.

Keynes, J. M. (1932) "Economics Possibilities for Our Grandchildren," in *Essays in Persuasion* (pp. 358–73), New York: Harcourt Brace.

Krugman, P. (2005) "Design for Confusion," *New York Times*, August 5, A15.

Pack, S.J. (1987) "Schumpeter Plus Optimism Equals Gilder (Ceteris Paribus)," *History of Political Economy*, 19(3): 469–80.

—— (1995) "Schumpeter Plus Optimism Equals Gilder (Ceteris Paribus) Part II: Schumpeter and the 'Laffer Curve,'" Paper presented at History of Economics Society Meeting, Notre Dame, June.

Parker, R. (2005) *John Kenneth Galbraith: His Life, His Politics, His Economics*, New York: Farrar, Straus & Giroux.

Partnoy, F. (1997) *F.I.A.S.C.O.: Blood in the Water on Wall Street*, New York: W.W. Norton.

Polanyi, K. (1957) *The Great Transformation: The Political and Economic Origins of Our Time*, Boston, MA: Beacon Press.

Schumpeter, J. (1950) *Capitalism, Socialism and Democracy (3rd edn), New York: Harper & Row.*

Shapiro, A.C. (1991) Foundations of Multinational Financial Management, Boston, MA: Allyn & Bacon.

Sharpe, M.E. (1974) *John Kenneth Galbraith and the Lower Economics* (2nd edn), White Plains, NY: International Arts and Sciences Press.

Smith, R.C. and Walter, I. (1990) *Global Financial Services: Strategies for Building Competitive Strengths in International Commercial and Investment Banking*, Philadelphia, PA: Harper Business.

—— (1997) *Global Banking*, New York: Oxford University Press.

Stein, B. (2005) "We Were Soldiers Once, and Broke," *New York Times*, July 17, BU3.

Thomas, L. (2005) "Morgan Payoff for Short Stint is 32 Million," *New York Times*, July 12, A1+.

United States Department of Labor (2005) "Union Members Summary," January 27. Available at http://www.bls.gov/news.release/union2.nr0htm (accessed August 2, 2005).

Wolff, E.N. (2004) "Recent Trends in Living Standards in the United States," in Wolff (ed.) *What Has Happened to the Quality of Life in the Advanced Industrialized Nations?* (pp. 3–26), Northampton, MA: Edward Elgar.

7 A radical critique and alternative to U.S. industrial relations theory and practice

Richard McIntyre and Michael Hillard

Introduction

We have developed a militant practice as academics who participate in university life as authors, teachers, and administrators of our institutions, but also stand with exploited and oppressed groups. We do not see our job as bringing the truth to the unschooled masses, nor are we naive enough to believe that all wisdom lies "with the people." We do not believe that by going among the people we lose our status as petty bourgeois. Instead, we feel comfortable functioning as what Gramsci called "organic intellectuals" and doing what Staughton Lynd calls the work of accompaniment (Lynd 1997).

In previous work together we argued that the crisis of the academic field of industrial relations (IR) has occurred largely because the industrial relations expert has lost his (or occasionally her) subsumed class position as an assuager of conflict due to the change in the balance of power between organized labor and management/ownership, especially in the United States. In the early 1990s we had argued that employer complaints about the quality of available labor power in the U.S. were related to the change in the nature of the labor process (social skills and acculturation becoming more important) and the crisis of the American family that together made entrants into the wage labor market decreasingly able to cope with this change (McIntyre and Hillard 1992, 1995; Hillard and McIntyre 1999).

We welcome the opportunity to develop these arguments further with fresh empirical material. We will also argue that these issues are intertwined, in that the declining influence of industrial relations (or labor and employment relations as it has now been renamed in the U.S.) scholars on social change is partly a result of the limited attention given to the household as a site of both work and class relations and also to a continuing inability (or unwillingness) of industrial relations scholars to see class, in the sense of surplus production, appropriation and distribution, as a significant concept.

As against industrial relations orthodoxy, and in spite of our admiration for the IWW, we do not suggest that "One Big Union," or its postmodern equivalent, "One Big Multitude," is or should be the rallying cry of the local, national and transnational movements for social justice. But recent work in Marxian class analysis can, we think, help people like us engaged in the work of accompaniment to propose meaningful ways for differentiated groups of working people to be together.

The IWW did have a keen sense of the importance of gender in organizing. Their masculinist rhetoric is not something we would return to but we do think that gender and its relation to class has been in the past and is now critical for militants to understand. Some of the most successful recent organizing on many issues has paid attention to and constructed such relationships and we think their examples are telling.

We mostly want to encourage our comrades to move with us to what we see as both a more radical and Marxist vision than is generally on call in industrial relations, albeit one that joins with feminism in a serious way and so is willing to decenter the exploitation of waged labor as the *key* contradiction in capitalist societies.

In the following section we outline the central traditions in the industrial relations field, discuss the relationship of the post-1970s wave of radical economics to those traditions, and examine how a Marxist-feminist approach differs from both of these. The third section examines how globalization, the growth of immaterial labor, and neoliberal politics have affected the labor process and labor markets, and how these effects relate to the contemporary crisis of the American family and working-class culture more generally. We suggest that these changes point to the need for very different kinds of organizations than those that the U.S. labor movement and its allies in industrial relations have been traditionally willing to support. In the final section we examine the new feminist organizing as a reaction to and cause of these theoretical and ontological shifts. Standing the IWW on its head, we argue that a new and very different set of gender identities and class conflicts can be the basis for a new solidarity.

Industrial relations, radical labor economics, and Marx

This section critically examines the academic field of industrial relations (IR), and compares and contrasts it with feminist, radical political economy (RPE), and Marxist views of the capitalist employment relationship. We illustrate the variety and continually evolving strengths of IR and the institutionalist tradition from which it springs, and comment on why it has been of interest to us and to many radical economists. We also criticize its politics and theory of history, showing that IR has generally ignored gender and the specific ways this omission is of importance, and we describe what we see as the class position and class politics of IR experts. Put bluntly, IR has a class-accommodationist agenda that ignores both class and patriarchy. Responding to a recent broadening of the scope of the field, we suggest that IR scholars have neglected/avoided insights from Marx, Marx-influenced and feminist scholars, and might benefit from their inclusion. We will lay out a class analysis of changes in the labor process and rising female labor force participation that, we believe, both explains these major changes and links them to recent and successful organizing.

Industrial relations and radical political economy[1]

Industrial relations began as a subset of institutional economics, focused on the question of capital-labor conflict and compromise solutions to that conflict.[2]

Beginning with Richard Ely and especially with the work of John R. Commons and his students in the Wisconsin School in the late nineteenth and early twentieth century an evolutionary line of descent can be traced through a second generation of scholar/policy-makers from the 1930s to the 1990s (John Dunlop, Clark Kerr, Richard Lester, Arthur Ross). This group differed from the first in being somewhat friendlier to orthodox (neoclassical) economics. A third generation., sometimes students of the mid-twentieth-century group, but at least heavily influenced by them, are active and influential today (Michael Piore, Richard Freeman, Eileen Applebaum, Barry Bluestone, Thomas Kochan, Paul Osterman, Bruce Kaufman). Some in this third generation differed from the second in their greater concern for problems of urban poverty, racism, and sexism.

Commons and some of his students, notably Selig Perlman, devised the IR tradition's "corporatist" vision of interest-group industrial democracy. This vision included the very influential doctrine of American exceptionalism and business unionism.[3] This analytical and policy vision and related values are the core of the IR tradition, and remained largely unchanged until the 1980s, with only minor modifications at that time. The second generation of institutional labor economists continued the multiple focus on labor markets, social insurance, and capital-labor conflict. But they inhabited a different world, where the labor movement was well established, had some power and limited state backing, and they had tremendous resources and a role in state regulation of capital-labor conflict from the New Deal through the 1970s. IR theorists/practitioners flourished, and they embraced the notion that their vision had become the enduring structure of American society, a structure to which other societies were expected to converge.

This turned out to be wildly incorrect of course, and IR went into something of a crisis in the 1980s. This is a problem for radicals also because both Institutional thought and industrial relations have been of interest to radical economists because they largely rejected the values and methods of neoclassical economics. Michael Piore and Sean Safford (2005:17) capture this sensibility well:

> In many ways, the (increasingly few) scholars who remain identified with the field of industrial relations do so out of a commitment to its "old institutionalist" roots: that is to say, its emphasis on history and on a rationale for action and institutional development that is inherently non-rational, but rather based on differences of power, cognition, and morality.

Commons explicitly hoped to develop a practice that made Marx unnecessary. IR scholars have shown sporadic interest in radical economics, and recently there have been some tentative attempts to take radical thought more seriously.[4] If IR has been reluctant to learn from radicals though, the opposite is not true.

Radical political economy (RPE) emerged in the 1970s by creatively adapting existing institutional economics, Marx, and what was then the "new labor history."[5] At its best, this work offered a new and fresh critique of American capitalism and joined in an international Left discussion. But insofar as late 1970s to early 1980s radicals assumed that "planning" (certainly of the indicative type) was inevitable in the face of economic crisis, they fell into the same trap as IR did (McIntyre and Hillard 1995).[6]

Institutional economics and industrial relations have both been rich sources of empirical material, with a fundamentally "social" (vs. methodologically individualist) orientation that makes their work compatible in some ways with Marxist analysis.[7] The preference for qualitative and historical research and attention to norms and power are fully consistent with Marx's class analysis in our view. But none of these authors deal explicitly with class in the Marxian sense, that is, the way some people live off the labor of others, and the consequences of this "exploitation" not only within the employment relations system but throughout society. What we do here is to ask, as few IR scholars have, what does it mean to start explicitly from a Marxist *and* feminist perspective in looking at the capitalist employment relationship?

The IR concept of class struggle, the state and leadership

As we (Hillard and McIntyre 1999), and others before us (see, for example, Ramirez 1978; Schatz 1993), have noted, the second-generation IR authors (Kerr *et al.*) held a "corporatist" view of modern capitalist society, one containing a clear politics and notion of the professional role of IR experts. Bruce Kaufman summarizes this ethos well: "The watchword of the institutionalists is *compromise*" (Kaufman 1993: 38, emphasis in original).

Such compromise is imagined to be at least partly dependent on the work of state-supported mediation experts. About the purpose and result of creating such a state machinery of IR experts, Commons famously said: "in dealing with the momentous conflict of 'capital and labor' . . . I was trying . . . to save Wisconsin and the nation from politics, socialism, or anarchy" (Ramirez 1978:188). In other words, IR experts were to provide capitalists with a condition of their existence – workplace and political stability – by making labor revolt and anti-capitalist political expressions by the working class less likely. Thus, Commons's goal was to *depoliticize* the working class *as a class*. In its place, he wanted a neutral-technical/scientific subsumed class to provide technically determined compromises between interests. While Commons was unusually explicit in espousing this political vision, it runs as a thread throughout many later statements of the IR field, notably *Industrialism and Industrial Man* (Kerr *et al.* 1960).

In advocating a corporatist version of capitalism, the IR tradition implicitly (and, at many points, explicitly) argued against worker militancy and radicalism in working-class politics and supported state interventions to this end. In some cases these arguments and actions might have been reasonable but they were (and are) always arrived at without any attention to exploitation. If, instead of a collection of "interest groups" whose interests are to be balanced, we see class as being about who lives off the labor (and land) of whom, then we IR scholars might have (and might now) come to different conclusions about the kinds of institutions and politics that are reasonable.

For us, historically, IR scholars and practitioners may be seen as a subsumed class, one of many contending and struggling for a cut of the surplus produced in capitalist enterprises.[8] Its rise came at a time of heightened U.S. class struggle in the early twentieth century. It was one of many "expert" groups – scientific managers, personnel and human resource managers, "detective agencies" (for example, the Pinkerton Agency) – that proposed solutions to capitalists' difficulty in suppressing labor militancy and establishing an enduring hegemony over the industrial working class. IR experts were at a disadvantage *vis-à-vis* these other subsumed class groups in that they advocated societal recognition and support for trade unionism, albeit of the "bread-and-butter" kind. Only at times of crisis – World War I, the Great Depression, and World War II and its immediate aftermath – could the IR field extract a cut of the surplus, and then only through sponsorship by the state (both federal and state governments). While scholars always could (and do) find a home in the tenured world of academia, access and influence over policy, not to mention funding of academic IR programs, was sensitive to whether IR scholars could sell themselves as fixers of workplace and political conflict. This contradiction in the historic identity of the field – advocating a bitter medicine for capitalists while embracing an arms'-length advocacy for improving the lives of, and even empowering (within certain strict limits) workers – had limited success, but once these conflicts were over, so was the thriving existence of IR as a subsumed class.[9]

Leading IR scholars are keenly aware that their field went into decline, along with the New Deal industrial relations system, in the 1980s. This has created much soul-searching. Some of this soul-searching has produced a more coherent theoretical identity for the field, while acknowledging and trying to remedy political weakness.[10] This opens up new possibilities for radicals and institutionalists to work together more broadly and systematically both in scholarly and political pursuits (as has sometimes happened since the 1960s and does now especially at the local level). We welcome this, and at the same time call for caution and self-conscious awareness of where goals overlap, and where they do not.

The capitalist–employment relationship

Volume I of *Capital* was published twenty years prior to Ely's founding of U.S. institutional economics, a history consistently ignored by industrial relations scholars in the U.S.[11] Marx's analysis in *Capital* incorporates Ely's three distinctive characteristics of the labor market (inequality of bargaining power, management authoritarianism, and workers' economic insecurity) while going beyond Ely to highlight the separate processes by which surplus labor is performed, appropriated, and distributed.

Beginning with Marx, and elaborated extensively by radicals from the 1970s forward, is a theory and narrative of the inherent presence of class conflict in capitalist employment relations. For example, *Capital* Volume I's richest and most extended narrative is devoted to the struggle over the length of the working day. British capitalists, seeking an advantage in competition, are shown pushing the working day past all physical and moral limits including cruelties that dramatically shorten the lives of workers and rob children of a meaningful childhood.[12] Workers, seeking to preserve their "property" (themselves) and their humanity, demand a working day that does not physically destroy them and leaves time for cultivation of their physical, intellectual, and cultural powers.[13]

The institutional and Marxist traditions thus share the common assumption that class conflict under capitalism is to be expected. Where they part ways is on what is the appropriate *resolution* of this conflict. For Institutionalists, class conflict is seen as a threat to social order, a "primitive democracy" to be channeled and ultimately tempered.[14] Marx proposed different notions.

Of course, Marx is infamous for predictions of a proletarian-led revolution that, in the outlines he proposed, never came to fruition. Less famously, Marx proposes that the working class could, through struggle, improve its position within an existing economic system *without* overthrowing it. His prime example in *Capital* was the British working class's victorious struggle to shorten the working day and reduce child labor in the 50 years up to and including the 1860s.[15] It has been the political quest of working-class parties in advanced capitalist countries to accomplish that very goal of improving the quality of life for workers and for society, seeking to "humanize" capitalism by minimizing economic insecurity and discrimination, reducing/eliminating poverty, increasing safety and health standards (for example, limiting hours worked, eliminating child labor) and provision of public goods (for example, education, childcare, public space). The labor movements of various countries have also sought regulatory and union agreements that decrease property rights for capital, and expanded workers' rights such as legal guarantees over the right to a job, workplace decision-making power, and a significant stake in corporate governance.

Thus, a common place for the Left has been the conclusion that the quality of economic and social life for working people in a particular nation is a reflection of the strength and degree of past and current success of its labor movement. Why is XYZ (childcare, retirement, health care, social security, length of the working week, weeks of paid vacations) better in Sweden or Germany than in the U.S.? Simple answer: Their labor movements succeeded economically and politically where the U.S. labor movement either failed, or won more modest improvements that a now far weaker (comparatively) labor movement has been unable to protect. There is of course no reason to believe that these improvements will lead to revolutionary change, but such improvements are, we would argue, good in themselves.

Marx and Engels were careful to stress that within capitalism, the state *could* be pressed by circumstance into opposition to the interests of capitalists.[16] A politically empowered working-class movement can, and has, shaped capitalist societies to be different from each other. Marx's (1977: 416) conclusion about the struggle over the length of the working day is instructive on "reformist" possibilities within capitalism:

> For 'protection' against the serpent of their agonies, the workers have to put their heads together and, *as a class*, compel the passing of a law, an all-powerful

> social barrier by which they can be prevented from selling themselves and their families into slavery and death by voluntary contract with capital.

Industrial relations scholars in the U.S. have largely ignored the Marxian IR tradition, though Marx often seems to haunt their work as absence.[17] But Richard Hyman and other European scholars have had an active and evolving research program in Marxist industrial relations since the 1960s. Hyman's work is useful in part because it is an antidote to IR thinking framed and limited by the particular view of unions put forward by the Webbs. Hyman (1971) sought in a more encompassing way to investigate the revolutionary *and* non-revolutionary possibilities of trade unionism and to come to some kind of dialectical synthesis. For the former, he drew on the young Marx and Engels, who often discussed the limits of trade unions as defensive organizations, but also called them military schools for class warfare and saw them as a stage in the transition from the workers being a class in themselves to being a class for themselves. There is the especially evocative imagery of the gravediggers of capitalism in the *Communist Manifesto*: capital accumulation brings about industrial concentration, which in turn brings about the combination of low-wage workers with low wages, with these combinations engaging in industrial and political action to overthrow private property, putting an end to their enslavement.

The moderation of the British trade unions after the mid-nineteenth century led Marx and Engels to qualify their optimistic view, but they retained their general theory of the relation between trade unions and revolutionary struggle. They saw in the British case that unionization was limited to the most privileged, skilled part of the working class (the labor aristocracy). Combined with the ideological and material corruption of the trade union leadership, and the benefits of empire, which could partly be used to buy off the working class, this produced trade union moderation.

While Marx and Engels were more than willing to criticize trade unions in practice, they believed that each of these hindrances to revolutionary unionism would pass in time. Lenin and Trotsky were more pessimistic. Lenin thought that unions had learned to achieve their economic objectives within capitalism, and were becoming integrated into its institutions (Hyman 1975: 14). This was understood as an organic rather than a planned process, and in fact Lenin was influenced by his reading of the Webbs on this issue, seeing this incorporation as a normal tendency in bourgeois societies (Lynd 1996: 206–31). Trotsky agreed about incorporation, but thought that this flowed partly from intentional and deliberate cooptation strategies of states and corporations (Hyman 1975: 17).

Ironically, the pessimistic twentieth-century Marxist view of trade unionism is quite similar to the corporatist view of unions and class conflict espoused by mainstream U.S. industrial relations (Hyman 1971: 21–2). Dunlop, Kerr and other postwar IR scholars argued that in "higher stages" of capitalism, contrary to Marx, the level of industrial conflict declines as conflict itself becomes institutionalized, predictable, and ritualized (Kerr *et al.* 1960). Further, the legitimacy of business unions would reduce the gross inequalities that led to conflict in the first place.

Hyman, writing as industrial conflict in England was heading toward its post-World War II peak in the 1970s, criticized the pessimistic approach as one-sided and undialectical. He thought that counter-tendencies to integration must be attended to as well as historical contingency to create a conjunctural and dialectical analysis combining the revolutionary and non-revolutionary tendencies of the trade unions. What are these contingent factors? Hyman cited the following in the 1970s: the ability of capitalism to satisfy workers' economic demands, the aspiration levels of workers, the depth and level of their organization, their attitudes toward democracy, and the success of the bourgeoisie and their state allies in creating bourgeois cultural hegemony. He still sees these factors as key (Hyman 2004).

As we have argued elsewhere, industrial relations orthodoxy added to the pessimism of Lenin a smooth and one-way understanding of historical evolution in which all countries would eventually become well-governed, corporatist social democracies featuring an established, and conservative unionized working class (Hillard and McIntyre 1999). But Hyman's main concern was with the Marxian tradition, and here he argued that neither the pessimistic nor optimistic views could be accepted wholesale. Rather, they should be dialectically combined to guide concrete research. More radical union activity will always run somewhat ahead of workers' consciousness especially as the latter is dominated by bourgeois ideology, but concrete analysis of the conjuncture might present opportunities for normalizing such radical activity. This is precisely what we are arguing here, although the radicalism we are looking at flows as much from a feminist as from a Marxist perspective. We agree with Hyman that the Marxist classics (whether optimistic or pessimistic) do not provide us with an adequate theory of the role of trade unions today. New practical and theoretical work in Marxism and feminism however has provided us with the tools to analyze contemporary labor and employment relations that take advantage of the strengths of both positions.

Gender and industrial relations

Gender was not an explicit category in industrial relations analysis prior to the 1960s. Still, the focus of New Deal industrial relations, and advocacy for "responsible" business unionism, put a "masculine" signature on the IR field.[18] Business unionism, as it came to be practiced from the 1930s forward, featured top-down, hierarchical, *worksite* unions. Within the New Deal IR system, tremendous pressure existed for leaders to be compromise-deal-making leaders, membership was passive, national pattern bargaining framed issues, and unions acted as service providers, with a focus on "bread-and-butter" issues – largely establishment and protection of a "family wage" for a male bread-winner.

Even the "progressive" CIO favored and successfully implemented a centralized, top-down, bureaucratic unionism that delegitimized dissent, absorbed male activists into the bureaucracy (or cast them out), and systematically excluded women who had been central to organizing and strike victories during the early to mid-1930s (Fraser 1983; Faue 1996; Lynd 1996). Faue and Lynd write about the community-based unionism that sparked the labor movement in 1933 to 1937, creating militancy that made both the CIO and the NLRA possible. Faue notes, as have others, that women participating as both workers and as wives of workers were central to this community-based movement, and the movement itself leveraged, if for a brief time, a gender-neutral language of labor solidarity that relied on community spaces where women had, or asserted, a prominent role.[19] "Celebrating a political role for women, it built on their social activism in both neighborhood and workplace. Women had a clear, aggressive role that was legitimized in the context of community and family" (Faue 1996: 174).

When both AFL and CIO unions began to eliminate bottom-up unionism in the late 1930s, the "context of community and family" was delegitimized and treated at part of a "private" realm separate from the legitimate realm of the workplace. Crucial entities such as women's auxiliaries and labor schools that taught women political and leadership skills were demoted or eliminated, and participation in union hierarchies by women was closed by a reassertion of gendered notions of the appropriate role of women in democracy.

Later, when faced with a frontal attack by capital in the 1970s and 1980s, many labor leaders were caught unable to respond and generally fought off efforts to refocus tactics, increase participation, or look to new strategies and issues to organize and resist (Kochan *et al.* 1994; Getman 1998; Kellman 2004). A return to a militant unionism that organically involved women and emphasized community solidarity, tactics that may have been part of an effective response to this attack was seen by the male leadership of unions such as the UFCW and the UPIU as threats to be crushed, which they were. In turn, as the labor movement has faced a crisis of membership and a need to organize, it has been at least partially stuck in a traditional business-unionism organizing model. This model is rooted in selective lessons from the 1930s and 1940s, and reflects the centralized and patriarchical ethos of centralized worksite unionism. The ultimate aim of this model is to "*incorporate*" new union workers passively into existing institutions versus workers *creating* their own institutions.

With the third generation of IR more attention was paid to gender issues, but this has generally taken the form of explaining the gender wage gap or work-family balance without any explicit consideration of how gender is *produced* within and in turn influences the labor process,[20] and certainly without attention to the ways gender conditions exploitation differently in the workplace and the household. In the following section we deploy a Marxian class analysis of the workplace *and* the household to investigate significant changes in contemporary capitalism. In the final section we will return to community unionism and argue for the centrality of a gendered vision for the transformation of the labor movement and the capitalist employment relationship in the U.S.

Decentering wage labor in contemporary capitalism

We think it useful to consider labor – whether it be in the workplace and employment relationship, the labor process itself, or working-class agency inside and outside of the workplace – in its broadest context. "Workers" are participants in a series of social processes, including labor, that exist in a variety of sites. The characteristics of social life in capitalism have evolved from the nineteenth-century "factory society" to the twenty-first-century network society. We thus seek to describe here new ontological realities for labor, and to refocus Marxist industrial relations on them.

As labor studies became increasingly comparative and linguistic in the 1980s it was clear that there was no generalizable process of working-class formation that flowed simply from the dynamics of capitalism itself.[21] We can no longer essentialize the labor process in thinking about the social existence and identity of the working class. Once we take the problem of *re*production seriously, households, community institutions, education, the media and (in the U.S. especially) churches have to be taken a whole lot more seriously. Especially since Althusser's essay on ideological state apparatuses, Marxists have begun to decenter the labor process as *the* site for the production of ideologies of resistance to capitalism.[22]

We believe these studies point to a needed broadening of the discourse in Marxist industrial relations. Other important recent work in the Marxist critique of political economy does not do this. On the one hand, the most careful students of globalization and the labor movement such as Beverly Silver take us "back to the future," arguing that today's "neoliberal" capitalism is in important respects like the liberal capitalism of Marx's time and so can be analyzed with the same tools.[23] Postmodern analysts of "Empire," such as Michael Hardt and Antonio Negri, reject much of the Marxian conceptual apparatus while producing in theory the classical Marxian revolutionary agent, now not the working class, but the "multitude."

Silver (2003: 64) shows that in every case but one (Japan) the movement of the automobile companies to greenfield sites, first in Europe, then in Europe's periphery, and finally in "newly industrializing countries" such as South Africa, Argentina, and Korea, has led to a typical cycle of unrest, class formation, and resistance:

> In sum, it appears that corporations in the automobile industry have been chasing the mirage of cheap and disciplined labor around the world, only to find themselves continuously recreating militant labor organizations in the new locations. Rather than providing a permanent spatial fix to the problems of profitability and labor control, relocation has only succeeded in geographically relocating the contradictions from one site of production to another.

If Silver is right, she expects to see strong, independent auto-workers' movements forming in Mexico and China over the next decade.[24]

There is a sense in her description that we are going back to the future.[25] We find this cyclical analysis convincing in some ways, and more hopeful than much of the contemporary labor studies literature, but by abstracting from changes in the household we think it misses important points of social tension that will feed back on the labor process and class formation, as we explain in more detail below. We worry also that this is all too mechanical. Industrialization in Europe and North America reduced the effectiveness of older forms of popular protest and resistance while creating new ones. In particular, individual workers' power in the labor market was reduced but they developed new powers of association and found new collective forms of resistance within the workplace. It is to the reconstruction of this (now lost) moment that much of the "how do we rebuild the labor movement" literature is addressed. We find this nostalgic. The current moment should be expected to have an uneven effect on workers' capacities as old forms of bargaining power are undermined while new ones are formed on a potentially larger and more disruptive scale.

We like the optimism of Silver's book but are cautious. Changes in the labor process itself, such as the prevalence of temporary and subcontracted work (to which we will return), have disorganized the working class. Thus the politics of resentment and hate are as possible as the politics of trade unionism and solidarity.

Remarkably, some of those who argue the most fervently that a new stage of capitalism is upon us, requiring a whole set of new concepts, are often also the ones who think we can go back to the future. For instance, Hardt and Negri evoke the IWW as not only among but in the center of a list of models of militant change in the age of Empire (Hardt and Negri 2000, esp. 410–13).

They base this on a close and provocative reading of the transition from mid-twentieth-century capitalism to today. The shift from manufacturing to services is read by Hardt and Negri as of an equal order to that of the Industrial Revolution and marks the end of modernization: there is now no outside to capitalism. Not only has employment growth migrated to services, but industry and agriculture have both also been changed by the informatization of production. "Just as through the process of modernization all production tended to become industrialized, so too through the process of postmodernization all production tends toward the production of services, toward becoming informationalized" (Hardt and Negri 2000: 286).[26]

Just as the Industrial Revolution created new ways of working and being human, so has the passage to an informational economy. The logic of immaterial labor – labor that does not produce a durable material good such as most services and cultural products, or that is supposed to produce an affect, that is, emotional labor – has come to dominate all forms of work they claim.[27] Immaterial labor is like "women's work" in that time solving a problem or creating an idea or relationship can expand to fill the entire day in a way that assembly-line work simply does not.

The tendency for all labor to take on the characteristics of immaterial labor has led to a real homogenization, they claim. For Hardt and Negri (2000: 294), the hegemony of immaterial labor breaks down the difference between the industrial worker, the service worker, and the peasant. The heightened role of cooperation in work increasingly allows cooperative activity to be controlled by labor without the participation or orchestration of the capitalist.

> Today, productivity, wealth and the creation of social surpluses take the form of cooperative interactivity through linguistic, communicational and affective networks. In the expression of its own creative energies, immaterial labor thus seems to provide the potential for a kind of spontaneous and elementary communism.

Since they see class as a thing that happens through collective acts of resistance, the increasing abstraction of labor provides some support for the possibility for the formation of "one big multitude."[28]

The multitude who (may) resist consists of everyone subordinated to capital and there is no longer a special significance to the industrial working class. Those engaged in affective or emotional labor especially are likely to become alienated.[29]

We accept that the labor process has changed in critical ways, and has become both informationalized and feminized. In the body of their text Hardt and Negri do point to new divisions that are created by changes in the labor process and the networked multinational corporation. But in their programmatic statements (and book titles) they claim that the system is producing unities that we simply do not see.[30]

We prefer to face those divisions more squarely. Primitive accumulation, while treated by Marx mostly as an historical phenomenon, is also in fact a key site of conflict in the contemporary world. The appropriation of biological (indigenous medicines) and man-made resources (the airwaves and cyberspace) are flashpoints of contemporary global conflict. As Harvey (2003) argues, the split between the old (that is, labor-based) and new social movements is at least partly based on the different problems they face: ecologists and indigenous peoples struggling with primitive accumulation while working-class organizations struggle within the realm of the self-expansion of capital. In particular, we want to link these divisions closely to changes in other social sites, especially the household, because while networked capitalism may create a "spontaneous and elementary communism" it could also lead to the most vicious forms of reaction.[31]

Labor and the work of reproduction

Globalization may be producing traditional patterns of class formation in new places. The tendency to immaterial labor may be breaking down old barriers between the labor movement and other movements for social justice. We think though that Marxist analysis of employment relations is impoverished without a more complete analysis of the household and its connection to waged work.

In both households and workplaces, labor is done, technology is used, legal relationships are established, and the performance of surplus labor for some people by others both occurs and is occluded. But households and capitalist enterprises differ in that the labor power of the capitalist worker has an exchange value whereas that of the unpaid household worker does not. This is another way of saying that the enterprise is the site of the capital relationship (with all its attendant consequences – accumulation, technical change, and unemployment) whereas the household is not.

But households and enterprises differ in other ways. The cultural, economic, natural, and political ties that bind workers to capitalists are different from those binding performers and receivers of surplus labor in the household. Unpaid household laborers (engaged in child-rearing, cleaning, planning, and cooking) stand in more of a feudal relation to the head of the household.[32] Legal and patriarchal processes and the ideology of love bind the household more. Whereas in the household the cultural process of engenderment leads to women generally producing surplus labor for men, in the capitalist enterprise it shows up more as pay discrimination and differential access to employment and training.

Capitalists' power over workers stems partly from the fact that the former buy the commodity of the latter. Private property rights and the workings of the market then are critical in explaining surplus extraction in the enterprise. No such exchange occurs in the household so that tradition and nature play a bigger role. In the enterprise it is

> the socially contrived *equality* between buyers and sellers of labor power as contractual partners that becomes a condition of existence of capitalist exploitation. In household relationships, on the other hand, the differently contrived inequality between men and women helps to foster feudal relationships.
> (Fraad *et al.* 1994: 92)

Within the household, women control (or have influence over) the means of production, giving women influence that capitalist workers do not have. Capitalist workers on the other hand may have their situation enhanced by forming unions, through state legal actions, and being able to exit their exploitive relationship more easily than wives can. So the effectivity of various cultural, economic, natural, and political processes is not the same in both sites, but work is done and surplus is produced, appropriated, and distributed in each. The interaction between the state, capitalist enterprises, and the household after 1980 is, we think, critical to understanding the possibilities for radical organizing today.

Arlie Hochschild identified a "second shift" that proletarianized women have to do at home once their wage work is over for the day and even a third shift of emotional labor that falls mainly on women. Women are disproportionately employed in jobs that require emotional work and generally carry the majority of the emotional labor in the home.

Hochschild (1997: 43) has also studied the blurring of home and work. Employers have increasingly tried to make the workplace feel like home, "a site of benign social engineering where workers came to feel appreciated, honored, and liked. On the other hand, how many recognition ceremonies for competent performance were going on at home? Who was valuing the internal customer there?" Company-sponsored ritual gatherings replace extended family reunions, and parents in many cases look forward to fleeing to work from their physical labor and emotional distress at home. The ever longer work day hides pockets of sociability, so that many workers develop a sense of control over their time at work which they no longer feel at home.

At home, family time has become industrialized, with parents seeking ever more efficient ways to save time and substituting "quality time" with children for the long, slow time of parenting. Of course, outsourcing household labor has been going on for some time, especially among wealthy families (e.g., piano lessons, summer camps, boarding-schools). Education, health care, and productive labor left the family home long ago. Now family time, shrunk and Taylorized, has been given another burden:

> the emotional work necessary to repair the damage caused by time pressures at home. . . . The emotional work of adjusting children to the Taylorized home and making up to them for its stresses and strains is the most painful part of a growing third shift at home.
>
> (Hochschild 1997: 51)[33]

This is hardly a lament for the lost social world of the "wonder years" family.[34] But just as the family-friendly workplace makes it easier for workers to collude with their employers to deny their own exploitation, so the effects of that exploitation and the ever mounting tensions of family life are displaced on to a set of social enemies: gay marriage, Arab terrorists, or effete intellectual East Coast snobs.

Recent developments in Marxian class analysis allow us to analyze the crisis of the household in class terms and relate it to problems in the capitalist enterprise. This linking, along with the heightened importance of immaterial and especially emotional labor, we will argue, has important implications for organizing and class formation.

Crisis in the family as displacement of crisis in the capitalist economy

Industrial relations scholars have documented the extent to which the labor relations environment changed after the 1980s: non-enforcement of the NLRA, increasing global capital mobility, the management offensive against unions, and so on. What has been less noticed is the impact of this on families and the consequent feedback effect in the workplace. This is partly because IR does not see the family as a site of work, only as a supplier of labor power. In this section we argue that the Reagan-Bush-Clinton shift in the U.S. sent already fragile households into a crisis which has had ramifications throughout society, including in the workplace.

Capitalists in the U.S. at the end of the 1970s faced a problem in that their revenues were being squeezed by rising commodity prices, wages rising faster than productivity growth, and demands by managers for higher rates of capital accumulation to meet growing foreign competition. High and growing wages throughout the post-World War II period alleviated pressure on families and strengthened traditional/feudal families in the major industrialized and unionized cities of the Northeast and Midwest. High wages had also maintained high levels of demand. But in the face of growing foreign competition and rising input prices, this deal came to seem intolerable to many capitalists.

A chorus of complaints about the American economy peaked in the late 1970s and early 1980s: unions were too restrictive, managers were incompetent, regulation was too heavy, and the overly permissive culture discouraged hard work. The Reagan and Bush administrations were able to articulate and play on these analyses to create (or resurrect) a hegemonic bloc and a politics of back-to-basics schools, traditional families, and fundamentalist churches.

First, taxes were shifted away from corporations and on to individuals. Second, government spending was shifted from social programs to military production, directly benefiting at least some industrial capitalists and allowing for a rhetoric of nationalism under which social spending cuts could be sold to the public as something that would in the end benefit all (by allowing more capital accumulation and increasing national security) despite some short-term pain for some people.

The 1970s marked the end of the long postwar increase in wages (Mishel *et al.* 2005: 120). The decrease in the rate of growth of government employment (which continued through the Clinton period) and the massive proletarianization of women increased the supply of labor power to corporations and, along with the combined capitalist/state offensive against unions, depressed wages. With output per hour increasing, profits soared. It was, all in all, a remarkable capitalist success.[35]

This sent traditional households, already reeling from the cultural changes of the 1960s and 1970s, into crisis. In fact, if we were to identify the most dramatic shift in American society over the past 30 years it would probably be the transitional conjuncture that occurred as the prevalent feudal form of household organization broke up into independent, communist, and feudal forms.

Women were increasingly unable or unwilling to perform surplus labor for their husbands. Those who entered the paid labor force confronted the kinds of psychological and physical limits in maintaining their status as producers of feudal surplus labor that Hochschild identifies in *The Second Shift*. Access to wage incomes reduced women's dependence, and their experience of at least a limited form of equality at work clashed with their socially constructed inequality in the household. Many men and women began to find family life increasingly uncomfortable or even intolerable.

The Reagan-era policies that resolved many of the problems of capitalist enterprises shifted new expenses on to already psychologically and economically overburdened families. A deteriorating transportation network, reduced services to children, the poor, the sick and the elderly, along with declining private sector wages and employment opportunities threw households into crisis and a transition to new forms of living.[36] At the same time, Reagan's statement that government was the problem not the solution became literally true as most workers experienced an increase in tax expenditures with declining social services. One reason why ordinary people express such rage against the state in the U.S. is that (as opposed to some other capitalist countries) they get very little from it.

As unions found it more difficult to protect their members, many workers began to see their union dues as money for nothing. This was particularly the case because most U.S. unions had limited themselves to bread-and-butter issues. It was certainly easier for workers to reduce union dues than to increase wages. Households accumulated debt and male workers pressed their wives to fulfill their traditional roles even as those wives had added wage labor and increased emotional labor to their day. Women's exodus into wage labor undercut surplus and in some cases necessary labor in the household, and could not come close to meeting the new demands for emotional labor.

How did this crisis of the family react back on the capitalist workplace? In the late 1980s a chorus of complaints arose in business magazines and academic monographs about the preparation of the U.S. labor force. Part of this was due to increased requirements for social and some technical skills given the trend toward immaterial labor. But a socialization gap also played a role. The transmission of social interaction skills was threatened in all families, and cognitive skills transmission was threatened in impoverished families (McIntyre and Hillard 1992). In other words, in addition to a complex shift in the quality of labor demanded there was a decline in the proportion of the population that could effectively sell its labor power.

It is no accident, as they used to say, that complaints about the "American worker" accelerated in the very years that the cohort who went through early childhood in the late 1970s and 1980s – the social products of the years of economic stagnation, fiscal crisis, and the crisis in the household – were entering the labor market.

The shortfall of household labor time could have been made up if women had reduced necessary labor time for their own maintenance or commodity purchases for that purpose, by increasing the length of their working day or the intensity of their household labor, by adding more workers. In general this did not happen. The high rate of divorce that developed in the 1970s was maintained, reports of domestic abuse among children and adults exploded, drug and alcohol use and eating disorders reached epidemic levels, and a rising tide of anxiety about family life was perhaps nowhere better exemplified than in the hysteria over missing and kidnapped children when clearly it was not the stranger on the street but the uncle in the attic who had to be feared. More and more individuals turned to AA-type groups and to burgeoning revivalist and fundamentalist churches. The advent of a kinder, gentler conservatism under Bush I, the economics of hope under Clinton, and "compassionate conservatism" under Bush II did little to change things.[37]

While IR scholars have documented the impact of Reaganomics on the capitalist employment relation, they have paid less attention to the ways in which the solution to the revenue squeeze of capitalist enterprises, displaced on to households, has caused enormous social change which has and will react back on that solution. The issue for political activity and organizing then is not to rebuild the New Deal system, the union movement, or anything like it, but to analyze the class conflicts that are most likely to result from this conjuncture so as to inform political and organizing activity. What does the transitional conjunucture in the household mean for class conflict in the enterprise and for working-class organization?

What are we struggling over and what kinds of alliances are possible?

Liberal observers of politics seem stunned that "the working class" in the United States votes so regularly against its own economic interest. This analysis presumes that there is a direct and simple connection between some objectively perceived economic condition and the obvious political response. Nothing could be further from the truth, and this kind of soft determinism both disguises the real dangers in the current situation and obscures the real possibilities for movement and action.

The response to the crisis of the patriarchal family, the decline in the value of labor power, and transubstantiation of family and work need not lead to a Left political shift as this has traditionally been defined. Take William Finnegan's illuminating study of the Antelope Valley in Northern Los Angeles County. Finnegan (1998: 62) grew up there himself a generation earlier when it had been an outer suburb of L.A. but returned in the mid-1990s to find schools chaotic and parents collapsing, and the simple dream of economic advancement replaced by drugs, neo-Nazism, and despair. Because of high housing prices, commutes to work are longer, and attachment to the local community has declined even among those able to maintain any energy outside of wage labor and driving to and from it:

> The teen pregnancy rate is also alarmingly high. Juvenile crime is a major problem, usually attributed to 'unsupervised children' – to, that is, the huge number of kids whose parents can't afford after-care and often don't return from their epic commutes until long after dark. With neighborhoods devoid of adults from early morning until night, the most popular youth crime is, naturally, burglary. A sheriff's department spokesman in Lancaster estimated that fully half the Valley's children are unsupervised after school. He also said that there are now, not coincidentally, more than 200 youth gangs represented in the Valley.

Many of these are neo-Nazi groups. Governed by "conservative Republicans of the Pro-growth, anti-tax stripe," this is still a majority white area in a county where whites are a minority, but most of those moving to the valley are non-white and some of the strongest youth leaders are in racially based hate groups that use Nazi imagery, often fueling their cause with a steady diet of methamphetamine.

Finnegan's is a dramatized portrait of changes in family and community life that are typical of many places in the U.S. The conjuncture of the crisis of the household, the decline in the value of labor power, and the change in the nature of work are signs of a strong mutation in social forms in the U.S.

The question for us then is whether the severe human costs of maintaining while denying the existence of capitalist exploitation will feed back on work performance or worker ideologies in ways that endanger capitalists' appropriation of the surplus. The successful push by capitalists and their state allies to secure the conditions of existence for appropriating and distributing surplus value has led to a disintegration of household class structures that has so deeply damaged so many people that we should expect and analyze significant economic and ideological *opportunities* as well as *problems*.

These issues are completely off the radar screen for most industrial relations scholars and trade unionists, but they strike us as being of the utmost importance. The Christian Right has noticed but cannot fully process these shifts. "Family values" has spoken to the pain and misery that many Americans feel about their personal and family lives, but offers only reactionary rhetoric about abortion, homosexuality, and reconstituting women's position as feudal serfs. This rhetoric raises an opportunity, in that the fundamentalist Christian's simultaneous embrace of family values and "free market capitalism" is unstable and tenuous, since it is the latter that destroys the former. It is incumbent on Left scholars to discuss and analyze this, or that contradiction will continue to be papered over and manipulated by corporate intellectuals who see it and recognize it for what it is.

Making the link between the crisis of the household and changes in the labor process can, we believe, provide the basis for a new socialist politics in the U.S. In fact, as we show in the following section, certain labor organizers have already acted on this link. In doing so they are not presuming that changes in the labor process have created the objective conditions for "one big union" or "one big multitude," but they are finding language to reach across the class and non-class barriers that separate exploited and oppressed peoples. They are not abandoning the concept of the working class, but they do not presume that the meaning of that term is constructed, not given. To engage in class struggle today is partly to engage in struggle over what we mean by class.

Learning from practice

Work under capitalism is not simply about what happens inside capitalist workplaces nor are class struggles rooted only *at* the workplace. In this section we discuss the centrality of a feminist model of organizing that takes these insights into account and responds to the transformations within capitalism discussed in the previous section. As our earlier discussion of community unionism suggests, there is nothing new about a labor movement model that starts from this premise. Rather, we can point to a *tradition* of community-based struggles, struggles that have emerged from women's spaces, included women in leadership roles, and reflected women's experience and practice. This tradition offers a continuing potential for transformation of the capitalist–employment relationship, and perhaps for creating a broader anti-capitalist movement.

Rosa Luxemburg – in direct opposition to both Lenin *and* the Webbs – was perhaps the first and most important radical to understand and advocate for community-based militancy, one that included women and eschewed centralism in either communist or social democratic/labor varieties. Rather than centralism, she put forth the notion of *self-activity* (Lynd 1997: 213):

> [W]orkers would in the course of their own self-directed activity come into fundamental opposition to existing institutions and be radicalized in the process. Unorganized workers, outside the trade unions, would have a central role. And intellectual radicals like herself would also play an essential part, not by injecting political ideas into working-class consciousness from the outside, but by accompanying workers and helping to articulate the goals implicit in the struggle.

In her celebration of the worker mobilization broadly and the general strike in particular, Luxembourg sided with the syndicalist practice of the IWW. The male leaders of the IWW discovered in places like Lawrence that the self-activity of women workers gave shape *and leadership* to their struggles, a self-activity that the IWW was wise not to suppress or sideline (Cameron 1993).

Outside observers frequently blamed the Wobblies for both the militancy and solidarity that characterized the 1912 strike, and historians have generally accepted this view, arguing that leaders like Joe Ettor "infused the immigrants with his own militancy."

> Yet by accepting the national form of organization, the IWW was acknowledging its own lack of control over the neighborhoods, where the real bases of power firmly rested. This situation often frustrated Wobbly leaders who frequently found themselves pressing strikers to curb their emotions, to practice nonviolence, and . . . to accept the March 13 settlement, an act that infuriated large segments of the neighborhoods, especially its most militant women.
>
> (Cameron 1993: 135)

The "feminist" chords being struck now were central to the self-activity of Lawrence working women a century ago:

> The strikes of 1882 and 1912 suggest the importance of these connections [between consumption and "the so-called point of production, particularly in actions like boycotts] for worker militancy and class consciousness. Calling for a "fair days wages for a fair days work," female strikers *also asserted their right to clean water, proper health care, decent housing, schools, even time "which belonged to us."* In the industrial upheaval of 1912, *housewives and operatives blended and mixed to form a great human chain of marching strikers, merging issues of the home with those the workplace*. Who could tell where the outrage of low wages ended and the "lash of youthful hunger" began? By what alchemy were poor health, child mortality, and filthy streets separated from shop floor issues of overwork, poor conditions, and declining wages? Linking arms and pressing their claims shoulder to shoulder, *women gave a totality to worker militancy*, which they themselves defined as a "fight for bread and roses."
>
> (Cameron 1993: 3; emphasis added)

Contemporary labor scholars and activists, including labor geographers, have come to describe this alternative to business unionism as community-based unionism.[38]

Some, particularly Cobble (1993b), Savage (2005a), and Dan Clawson (2003: 51–89), highlight a specifically contemporary *feminist* model that extends the example of "spontaneous" community-based militancy of the 1910s and 1930s as described by Cameron, Faue and Lynd.[39] While we see continuity with earlier community unionism, what has changed is the new "ontological reality" described in the previous section.

The crisis in the household and full entry of women into the labor force has broken down the "alchemy" separating the household and workplace. In turn, it means that the "class" aims of a new labor movement involve humanizing capitalism in ways that address issues confronted by women, because it is largely women who connect this household crisis to the capitalist workplace. We find evidence for this in some of the more successful organizing campaigns of recent years, such as the "Justice for Janitors" campaign, sponsored initially by the Service Employees International Union (SEIU) and the organization of clerical and technical workers at Harvard (HUCTW). These and other recent campaigns emphasize rank-and-file participation, using deep connections in the community, and the potentialities for organizing people of color and immigrants (a large proportion of whom are female), and the creation of community *within* the workplace among women workers, and especially among educated, white-collar workers.

These examples do not constitute a complete vision of a movement to transform capitalism.[40] SEIU may well be replicating the worst top-down features of the early CIO. Tactics used by HUCTW and HERE may work with some groups of white-collar workers but not others. Entire potentially anti-capitalist social groups, such as young radical environmentalists, exist outside of the current or envisionable framework for labor organizing.

Organizing the unemployed, the poor, temporary workers, and shifting from an economistic to a more cultural and political focus makes sense from a Marxist-feminist perspective and may in fact be reasonable responses to actually existing capitalism. The unemployed workers' movement in Argentina and the "intérmaires," the part-time workers in entertainment and the media who struck in France in 2003, are additional examples of this new way of being union. The strikes and demonstrations of nurses in France in the early 1990s and the militancy of the California Nurses Association demonstrate that emotional wage labor can be extremely alienating in that what is being sold is the ability to create human relationships, something very intimate which is drawn under the command of the boss or the client.

But even some of the most free-thinking U.S. trade unionists struggle with these new images of being union, as they do with calls to open unions to new sectors of society and to broader social movements (DeMartino 2004; Moody 1997). "Accompaniment" by radicals with an analysis of the underlying forces shaping capitalism, and articulating a vision of human/social possibility may help to make such radical changes palatable.

IWW and militancy today

After Lawrence, the militant syndicalism of the IWW was rooted in a masculine vision of worker solidarity. Syndicalism arose at the time of early mass production, when conditions at work were oppressive and employer powers often dictatorial in both the workplace and "community." Syndicalism – with its obsession with direct action and sabotage – was both a critique/response to class power and to the "respectable reformism of craft-based labor unions" (Schor 1999: 65). But, Francis Schor argues, it was also a "vestigial gendered form of protest." He quotes Peter Stearns (1990: 100): "For many in the working class, uncertain about their manly status in the workplace, periodic protest, shared among brothers, was a vital way to claim their masculinity, a reward in itself."

> The IWW's assertion of the imagery of sabotage – often a virile metaphor of resistance to speed-up and industrial discipline – unleashed a torrent of reformist labor and even socialist criticism. This was a debate within the working class over what it means to be a man in capitalist society, both at work and in society at large. In short, for the IWW, promotion of sabotage constituted "a kind of masculine posturing which directly challenged individualizing techniques of power mobilized by industrial capitalism."
>
> (Stearns 1990: 67)[41]

It is not surprising that this male-gendered identity emerged given material conditions. In the U.S. the IWW's base shifted during the 1910s from eastern, urban, multi-gendered cities to primary industries (wheat fields, mines, timber ranges) in the west, where men in migratory camp situations predominated. This created a "gendered solidarity" described by one writer as follows:

> Working together a thousand feet below the ground, living together in crowded bunkhouses, and drinking, gambling, and whoring together far from the ties of conventional society, the miners developed bonds that most men never know, a brotherhood forged in blood.
>
> (Carlson 1983: 47)

The IWW "established brotherly bonds of solidarity" for these men and gave them a "form of cultural empowerment that signaled to many wandering men that they were more than hired hands or mere cogs in a machine"(Carlson 1983: 69).

The battle over wartime conscription shows how the contending notions of masculinity were the central cultural materials in the battle. Particularly interesting is that much of the IWW's rhetoric was about claiming ownership of one's body and dignity *as a man* against the backdrop of the dehumanizing tendencies of industrial society and the interventionist state. The Wobbly newspaper *Direct Action* asserted that the "IWW is the most virile labour union in existence. . . . Fellow worker if you want to be a man and not a slave get into the IWW and do your share in the Fight for Freedom" (Carlson 1983: 72). Combating oppressive workplace routines also became a "ritualistic test by which one could claim one's own manhood."

We propose to stand this notion on its head, and suggest that the examples of HUCTW and labor feminism in general point to possibilities for a gendered solidarity against capital today. The radical militancy of the IWW was based on a gendered solidarity, albeit a "virile masculine" one. Looking critically at the IWW in Lawrence and the "Wobbly-like" community unionism of the early 1930s, we see a gendered solidarity – based on women's networks and labor movements willing to allow women to move forward as leaders, "breaking down the alchemy that separated household and workplace."

Today, there is a clear connection between crisis in the household and labor conflict. We see new forms of organizing that create – or re-create – that connection as a way forward for both theory and practice in Marxist industrial relations.

Notes

1 For a more extended discussion of the history of industrial relations see Kaufman (1993); Hillard and McIntyre (1999).

2 We recognize that, especially today, IR and institutional labor economics are overlapping sets rather than the former being nested within the latter, but we abstract from this due to space constraints.

3 In this and other things the Commons school was strongly influenced by Sydney and Beatrice Webb's (1894, 1897) work on British trade unionism.

4 Kaufman in particular seems to be more interested in including radical views in the industrial relations dialogue. See Kaufman (2004a, 2004b). Marx often functions as an absence in institutional industrial relations theory.

5 Braverman (1974), Marglin (1974) and Bowles and Gintis (1976) were some of the key texts of this period. The "new labor history" (Thompson, Montgomery, Gutman) provided an implicitly Marxist perspective for understanding U.S. history, albeit one emphasizing culture and class-consciousness, not Marx's class analysis. Just as we have been influenced by but would now distance ourselves from the determinism of the neo-Marxists, we appreciate the contribution of Thompson and his students but also that of the postmodern critics of "New Labor History" (such as Joan Scott and Jacques Ranciere) who have put gender and discourse squarely on the table. See, for instance, Berlanstein (1992: 1–54).

6 Some of this radical work on labor relations drew mostly on Marx, but much of it (such as Bluestone and Harrison's (1982) widely influential *The Deindustrialization of America*) was clearly institutionalist, avoiding altogether any explicit connection to anything Marxist while telling a story of "class struggle" waged by capital on workers and communities. Many authors, including ourselves, seeking to speak to different audiences in different journals at different times, would vary their "paradigmatic identity" from paper to paper. Much of this stems from the requirements of academic and political life (measured by what and where you publish or, conversely, how do you get a broad message out to a local political/policy audience?). Other radicals, caught in a kind of gravitational pull, sought to minimize methodological and philosophical-political differences with neoclassical economics (Rebitzer 1993). See McIntyre and Hillard (1995) and Spencer (2000) for a critique of this move.

7 Ramstad (1996: 20–8) makes this point very clearly.

8 Marx analyzes the role in capitalism of groups that receive distributions of already produced surplus value in exchange for provision of conditions of existence for capitalist exploitation; this analysis is found in volume II and especially in volume III of *Capital*. For the most complete contemporary analysis of the distribution of surplus value to "subsumed classes" see Resnick and Wolff (1987: chs 3–5).

9 See Hillard and McIntyre (1999) where this argument is laid out in detail. We do not revel in this decline because, from Ely and the Webbs forward, institutionally oriented IR scholars have seen capitalism as harsh and unfair to workers absent coercive limitations from worker collectivities (trade unions, works councils) and the state. Their research and practice improved and improves the lives of working people in the United States in dramatic ways.

10 The work of Thomas Kochan is particularly instructive. It was Kochan who first effectively recognized (in his book with Katz and McKersie 1994) the flaws with and negative implications of the Kerr/Dunlop generation's teleology. As an important voice on the Dunlop Commission (1994) he witnessed the inability of that commission to enable any kind of labor law reform given the political weakness of the labor movement national policy and the ascendance of the New Right in Washington. Thus, since 1994, Kochan (2000: 22) has moved to a position of direct political advocacy, calling for the construction of a *new* social contract that creates (or re-creates) labor "rights," greater "voice" and equity:

> In short, if we are to build a new set of social contracts suited to the economy and workforce of the twenty-first century, we must *lead in generating the necessary political discourse* involving the full range of voices with a stake in the issues and produce the ideas and pragmatic experimental evidence that demonstrates a new social contract is achievable and worth pursuing for the good of society.

11 A grudging awareness of this alternative creeps in during the 1980s in some IR texts (see, for example, Kochan *et al.* 1994: 257, note 3). Kaufman, in his history of U.S. IR, notes that earlier U.S. Marxists and radicals were suspicious of the hegemonic aims of Commons's version of IR, and that the current "paucity" of Marxists in the field reflects the dominance of economists and the decision of sociologists who were influenced by Marx to leave the IR field in the 1960s (Kaufman 1993: 200, 238). Marx and Marxian analysis receives a more sustained treatment in Kaufman's recent history of "global" IR, though much of this still leans on the Marx of the *Communist Manifesto* rather than the Marx of *Capital*, and claims distinctly Marxist insights such as the extraction of labor from labor power for the favored institutional tradition (Kaufman 2004a). Still, we see here the possibility for a dialogue between Marxists and institutionalists that was impossible during most of the twentieth century.

12 Marx (1977: 381) argues that the incentive for every capitalist to use up labor power without worrying about their being a tragedy of the commons can only be limited by society itself placing absolute constraints on the capitalist: "*Aprés moi le deluge!* is the watchword of very capitalist and of every capitalist nation. Capital therefore takes no account of the health and the length of life of the worker, unless society forces him to do so."

13 "Time for education, for intellectual development, for the fulfillment of social functions for social intercourse, for the free play of the vital forces of his body and mind, even rest time of Sunday (and that in a country of Sabbatarians!) – what foolishness!" (Marx 1977: 375). Marx's words were used directly by the U.S. labor movement in its struggle for the eight-hour day. See Glickman (1997: 11–34).

14 The notion comes from the Webbs, and was picked up immediately in the U.S. by Commons in the late 1880s. For a critical discussion of this view, see Montgomery (1993) and Lynd, "The Webbs, Lenin, and Rosa Luxemborg," in Lynd (1997: 206–31).

15 Marx (1977, ch. 10, "The Working Day": 340–416). On the victory of this labor movement, Marx says:

> Nevertheless, the principle had triumphed with its victory in those great branches of industry which form the most characteristic creation of the modern mode of production. Their wonderful development from 1853 to 1860, hand-in-hand with physical and moral regeneration of the factory workers, was visible to the weakest eyes. The very manufacturers from who the legal limitation and regulation of the working day had been wrung step by step in the course of a civil war lasting a half a century now pointed boastfully to the contrast with the areas of exploitation which were still 'free'. The Pharisees of 'political economy' now proclaimed that their newly won insight into the necessity for a legally regulated working day was a characteristic achievement of their 'science.' *It will be easily understood that after the factory magnates had resigned themselves and submitted to the inevitable, capital's power of resistance gradually weakened, while at the same time the working class's power of attack grew with the number of its allies in those social layers not directly interested in the question.* Hence the comparatively rapid progress since 1860.
>
> (Marx 1977: 408–9, emphasis added)

16 From Engels's famous *Letter to Bloch* (Tucker 1978: 760–5):

> If Barth therefore supposes that we deny any and every reaction of the political, etc., reflexes of the economic movement upon the movement itself, he is simply tilting at windmills. He has only got to look at Marx's *Eighteenth Brumaire*, which deals almost exclusively with the *particular* part played by political struggles and events; of course, within their *general* dependence upon economic conditions. Or *Capital*, the section on the working day, for instance, where legislation, which is surely a political act, has such a trenchant effect. Or the section on the history of the bourgeoisie.
>
> (Tucker 1978: 765)

Beside Marx's treatment of the circumstances surrounding the passage of the 1844 Factory Act (Marx 1977: 394), see Finegold and Scocpol (1984) on the forces leading to the passage of the Wagner Act and other aspects of the New Deal, in the face of concerted opposition by business interests:

> These measures were made possible by a conjunction of working class pressures with a willingness of state managers to increase their own institutional power at a time when capitalists' veto power was unusually weak. The reforms provided benefits to many members of the working class, strengthened the state in relation to the working class, and increased the state's capacity to intervene in the capitalist economy. The eventual result was that working class struggle ended up contributing to the development of American capitalism.
>
> (Finegold and Scocpol 1984: 167)

Even where the state acts against those interests it is not therefore "anti-capitalist." For example, a long-run effect of the creation of the NLRB - for which was Roosevelt was called anti-capitalist - was to quell and suppress militant expressions and radical politics in the labor movement. See Lynd (1996), Fraser (1983), and Lichtenstein (1993).

17 See McIntyre (2008: ch. 2) for a development of this point. Kaufman's recent work is the notable exception, with the caveats mentioned in note 10 above.

18 We are indebted to Lydia Savage (2005a) for this insight.

19 The Lawrence "Bread and Roses" strike of 1912 is perhaps the best example of this type of unionism in the early twentieth century, based thoroughly on the strengths of women's community networks that provided the strength for leadership and solidarity in the strike. See Cameron (1993).

20 See, for example, Bailyn *et al.* (2001). A notable exception here is the recent work of Michael Piore. See especially Piore and Safford (2005).

21 Portelli's (1991: 195–237) two essays on Harlan County in the 1930s provide a devastating picture of the limitations put on the introduction of either militancy or radicalism in certain cultural and geographical places within the U.S. For the broad argument against a general pattern of working-class formation see Katznelson and Zolberg (1990), and for the linguistic turn, Berlanstein (1992).

22 See, for instance, Fraad *et al.* (1994); Gibson-Graham and O'Neill (2001).

23 Silver (2003). See also Cowie (1999); Klein (2000).

24 There were 74,000 reported mass incidents, or demonstrations and riots in China in 2004, an increase from 10,000 a decade ago (French 2005). We note that these are as, if not more, likely to be against environmental deterioration as they are against labor conditions or wages.

25 Silver recognizes that cars may not be the center of working-class formation in the twenty-first century as it was in the twentieth, identifying and analyzing potential new centers of unrest: semiconductors, producer services, educational services, and personal services.

26 Heavily influenced by the work of Manuel Castells, they argue that there remain varieties

of capitalism, in the sense that there are differences between the service economy model of the Anglo countries and the info-industrial model of Germany and Japan, but both models tend toward the heightened salience of information flows and networks. Much of the former third world is inside this system, but unlike in Silver's cyclical story, the Brazilian auto plant of the 1990s occupies a very different technological and social space than does the Detroit plant of the 1930s. "The geographical differences in the global economy are not signs of the co-presence of different stages of development but lines of the new global hierarchy of production" (Hardt and Negri 2000: 288).

27 In other words, for Hardt and Negri, immaterial labor dominates as a tendency that comes to influence and shape all other forms of labor in the same way Marx claimed that with factory labor would come the factory *society*.

28 This is our term not theirs. The Confederation Paysanne in France and Brazil's Landless Workers Movement are examples for them of open struggles that welcome the participation of all sectors on the basis of new knowledge of ecology, sustainability, and so on. These are "singular modes of being bringing forth a common laboring substance" (Hardt and Negri 2004: 125).

29 This alienation is most effectively analyzed in the work of Arlie Hochschild, especially in *The Managed Heart*. It is significant to us that she begins that book with a quote from Chapter 10 of the first volume of *Capital*, the chapter on the length of the working day. While labor process theory presumed that it was relative surplus value that was the more advanced form of exploitation, Hochschild and other analysts of emotional labor demonstrate that it is the lengthening of the work day and control over time and emotions that is becoming critical.

30 Much like Piore and Sabel, whose *Second Industrial Divide* in the mid-1980s was consciously intended to provide theory for the burgeoning progressive urban redevelopment movement, so Hardt and Negri seem to want their books to appeal to the global movements for social justice that arose in the late 1990s, and so they seek to wash away troubling divisions that might distract and hinder that movement.

31 We do not necessarily disagree with Hardt and Negri's prescriptions for actually existing trade unions, but we do not think these will flow easily from changes in the labor process. They argue especially for unions' inclusion of the unemployed, the poor, and temporary workers, the irrelevance of craft distinctions in a world where labor has really become abstract, and the need for labor organizations to represent not the economic interests of a limited category of workers but the cultural, political, and economic (and we would add, ecological) interests of all. In other words they would open unions to new sectors of society and to broader social movements in ways suggested by a number of people (such as DeMartino 2004; Moody 1997) and exemplified by the movement of the unemployed in Argentina and the "intérmaires," the part-time workers in entertainment and the media who struck in France in 2003.

32 See Fraad *et al.* (1994) for a detailed analysis of feudal class relations in the household. Children should probably be characterized differently from spouses. As Harriet Fraad (2000: 75) notes, it is no accident that "the legal release of children from parents' custody is expressed in the legal vocabulary for freeing slaves."

33 In the language of time management we "spend time" with loved ones as if we were investing capital. This is the wrong metaphor according to Hochschild: (1997), since time is to relationships what shelters are to families. That is, time is not capital to be invested in familes but to social/familial habitat in which to live. Of course, with the recent real estate craze, families may no longer see shelters as habitat but as part of an investment portfolio.

34 As Fraad (2003) puts it, the crisis of the patriarchal/feudal/"traditional" household is both a problem and an opportunity.

35 "This success in treating the problems of capitalist enterprises occurred under the banner of a crusade against big, wasteful, inefficient and intrusive government in the name of individual enterprise, freedom, initiative and prosperity" (Fraad *et al.* 1994).

36 Resnick and Wolff (2003) argue that, in this conjuncture, with eroding union power and slack labor power markets, capitalists and their state allies were able to reduce the moral and historical element in the value of labor power; that is, to reduce the socially constructed norm for an adequate standard of living. In this historically unusual shift, the impersonal rules of international competition were explained as requiring that the lower real wages of the 1970s become a permanent phenomenon and the only choice was either lower wages or higher unemployment. Workers were encouraged to share the burden of competing in the world economy, and many workers as well as their trade union leaders swallowed and continue to swallow this. Even as the intensity of labor and the length of the working day increased, the value of labor power fell and exploitation rose.

37 One big difference is that while spending was restrained under Reagan and Clinton it has not been under Bush II. This and the (important) effects of the invasion of Iraq on class formation are beyond our scope here.

38 See Cobble (1993a); Piore (1991); Wial (1993). Labor geographers have developed an important contribution to the study of the CER, a contribution little noted in IR literature. See Herod (1997, 1998); Savage (2005); Savage and Wills (2004).

39 In truth, there was nothing spontaneous about this militancy, based as it was on relationships forged in neighborhood and community over many years. Labor history literature connecting the early twentieth century to the present is quite extensive. An excellent new look at the continuity of "labor feminism" over the past 70 years is Cobble (2004).

40 Savage (2005b). Savage points to the difficult contradictions faced by the wedding of top-down and bottom-up strategies posed by SEIU's overall approach, contradictions that loom even larger since the recent split of SEIU, HERE, and the Teamsters from the AFL-CIO. As Savage (2004: 549) notes elsewhere, "Community unionism faces challenges, however, in attempting to gain local autonomy for local unions, to access community-based networks, and to integrate those networks into the political structure." See also Clawson (2003: 124–30); DeMartino (1991).

41 Schor also notes that gendered networks that included women, or that were predominantly female, produced militant protest connected to the IWW. But the IWW did not recognize or embrace a women's or feminist version of "posturing" in response to capitalist industrial discipline.

Bibliography

Althusser, L. (1996) *For Marx*, New York: Verso.

Bailyn, L., Drago, R. and Kochan, T. (2001) *Integrating Work and Family Life: A Holistic Approach*, Cambridge, MA: Sloan/MIT Press.

Barker, C., Johnson, A. and Lavalette, M. (2001) *Leadership and Social Movements*, New York: Manchester University Press.

Berlanstein, L. (1992) *Rethinking Labor History: Essays on Discourse and Class Analysis*, Urbana: University of Illinois Press.

Bluestone, B. and Harrison, B. (1982) *The Deindustrialization of America*, New York: Basic Books.

Bowles, S. and Gintis, H. (1976) *Schooling in Capitalist America: Educational Reform and the Contradictions of Economic Life*, New York: Basic Books.

Braverman, H. (1974) *Labor and Monopoly Capital*, New York: Monthly Review Press.

Cameron, A. (1993) *Radicals of the Worst Sort: Laboring Women in Lawrence, Massachusetts: 1860–1912*, Urbana: University of Illinois Press.

Carlson, P. (1983) *Roughneck: The Life and Times of Big Bill Haywood*, New York: W.W. Norton.

Clawson, D. (2003) *Labor's Next Upsurge: Labor and the New Social Movements*, Ithaca, NY: ILR/Cornell University Press.

Cobble, D.S. (1993a) "Organizing the Post Industrial Work Force: Lessons from the History of Waitress Unionism," *Industrial and Labor Relations Review*, 44: 419–36.

—— (1993b) "Introduction: Remaking Unions for the New Majority," in D.S. Cobble (ed.) *Women and Unions: Forging a Partnership*, (pp. 3–18), Ithaca, NY: ILR Press.

—— (2004) *The Other Women's Movement: Workplace Justice and Social Rights in Modern America*, Princeton, NJ: Princeton University Press.

Cowie, J. (1999) *Capital Moves: RCA's Seventy Year Quest for Cheap Labor*, New York: The New Press.

DeMartino, G. (1991) "Trade Union Isolation and the Catechism of the Left," *Rethinking Marxism*, 4(3): 29–51.

—— (2004) "Organizing the Service Sector: From 'Labor' to 'Stakeholder' Unionism," D. Champlin and J. Knoedler (eds) *The Institutionalist Tradition in Labor Economics* (pp. 240–52), Armonk, NY: M.E. Sharpe.

Faue, E. (1996) "Paths of Unionization: Community, Bureacracy, and Gender in the Minneapolis Labor Movement of the 1930s," in S. Lynd (ed.) *We are all Leaders: The Alternative Unionism of the Early 1930s* (pp. 172–98), Urbana: University of Illinois Press.

Finegold, K. and Scocpol, T. (1984) "State, Party, and Industry: From Business Recovery to Wagner Act in America's New Deal," in C. Bright and S. Harding (eds) *Statemaking and Social Movements: Essay in History and Theory* (pp. 159–92), Ann Arbor: University of Michigan Press.

Finnegan, W. (1998) *Cold New World: Growing Up in a Harder County*, New York: Random House.

Fraad, H. (2000) "Exploitation in the Labor of Love," in J.K. Gibson-Graham, S. Resnick and R. Wolff (eds) *Class and its Others* (pp. 69–86), Minneapolis: University of Minnesota Press.

—— (2003) "Class Transformation in the Household: An Opportunity and a Threat," *Critical Sociology*, 29(1): 47–65.

Fraad, H., Resnick, S. and Wolff, R. (1994) *Bringing It All Back Home: Class, Gender & Power in the Modern Household*, Boulder, CO: Pluto Press.

Fraser, S. (1983) "Industrial Democracy in the 1980s," *Socialist Review*, 72: 98–111.

French, H. (2005) "Rioting in a Village in China as Pollution Protest Heats Up," *New York Times*, July 9: A3.

Getman, J. (1998) *The Betrayal of Local 14*, Ithaca, NY: ILR/Cornell University Press.

Gibson-Graham, J.K. and O'Neill, P. (2001) "Toward a New Class Politics of the Enterprise," in J.K. Gibson-Graham, S. Resnick and R. Wolff (eds) *Re/presenting Class: Essays in Postmodern Marxism* (pp. 56–80), Durham, NC: Duke University Press.

Glickman, L. (1997) *A Living Wage: American Workers and the Making of Consumer Society*, Ithaca, NY: ILR/Cornell University Press.

Green, J. and Tilly, C. (1987) "Service Unionism: Directions for Organizing," *Labor Law Journal*, 38(8): 486–95.

Hardt, M. and Negri, A. (2000) *Empire*, Cambridge, MA: Harvard University Press.

—— (2004) *Multitude: War and Democracy in the Age of Empire*, New York: Penguin Books.

Harvey, D. (2003) *The New Imperialism*, Oxford: Oxford University Press.

Herod, A. (1997) "From a Geography of Labor to a Labor Geography," *Antipode*, 29(1): 1–31.

—— (1998) *Organizing the Landscape: Geographical Perspectives on Labor Unionism*, Minneapolis: University of Minnesota Press.

Hillard, M. and McIntyre, R. (1988) "The 'Labor Shortage' and the Crisis in the Reproduction of the United States Working Class," *Review of Radical Political Economics*, 20 (2 & 3): 196–202.

—— (1999) "The Crises of Industrial Relations as an Academic Discipline in the United States," *Historical Studies in Industrial Relations*, 7: 75–98.

Hochschild, A. (1983) *The Managed Heart: The Commercialization of Human Feeling*, Berkeley: University of California Press.

—— (1997) *The Time Bind: When Work Becomes Home and Home Becomes Work*, New York: Metropolitan Books.

Hochschild, A. and Machung, A. (1990) *The Second Shift: Working Parents and the Revolution at Home*, New York: Avon Books.

Hyman, R. (1971) *Marxism and the Sociology of Trade Unionism*, London: Pluto Press.

—— (1975) *Industrial Relations: A Marxist Introduction*, London: Macmillan.

—— (1989) *Strikes*, (4th edn), London: Macmillan.

—— (2004) "Working Draft of 'Marxist Thought and the Analysis of Work,'" in P. Edwards, M. Korcynski and R. Hodson (eds) *Social Theory at Work* (pp. 56–87), Oxford: Oxford University Press.

Jacobson, J. and Newman, A. (2003) "Do Women and Non-economists Add Diversity to Research in Industrial Relations and Labor Economics?," *Eastern Economic Journal*, 45(4): 575–91.

Jacoby, S. (1997) *Modern Manors: Welfare Capitalism Since the New Deal*, Princeton, NJ: Princeton University Press.

Katznelson, I. and Zolberg A.R. (1990) *Working Class Formation*, Princeton, NJ: Princeton University Press.

Kaufman, B. (1993) *The Origins and Evolution of the Field of Industrial Relations in the United States*, Ithaca, NY: ILR/Cornell University Press.

—— (2004a) *Theoretical Perspectives on Work and the Employment Relationship*, Urbana, IL: Industrial Relations Research Association.

—— (2004b) *The Global Evolution of Industrial Relations*, Washington, DC: Brookings Institution Press.

Kellman, P. (2004) *Divided We Fall: The Story of the Paperworkers' Union and the Future of Labor*, New York: The Apex Press.

Kerr, C., Dunlop, J., Harbison, F. and Myers, C. (1960) *Industrialism and Industrial Man*, New York: Harvard University Press.

Klein, N. (2000) *No Logo*, New York: Picador.

Kochan, T. (2000) "Building a New Social Contract at Work: A Call to Action," *Proceedings of 52nd Annual Meeting*, Urbana, IL: Industrial Relations Research Association.

Kochan, T. and Osterman, P. (1994) *The Mutual Gains Enterprise*, Ithaca, NY: ILR/Cornell University Press.

Kochan, T., Katz, H. and McKersie, R. (1994) *The Transformation of Industrial Relations*, Ithaca, NY: ILR/Cornell University Press.

Levine, D. (1998) *Working in the Twenty-first Century*, Armonk, NY: M.E. Sharpe.

Lichtenstein, N. (1993) "Great Expectations: The Promise of Industrial Jurispudence and its Demise, 1930–1960," in N. Lichtenstein and H.J. Harris (eds) *Industrial Democracy in America: The Ambiguous Promise* (pp. 113–41), Cambridge: Cambridge University Press.

Lynd, S. (1996) "Introduction," in S. Lynd (ed.) *We Are All Leaders: The Alternative Unionism of the Early 1930s* (pp. 1–26), Urbana: University of Illinois Press.

Lynd, S. (1997) *Living Inside Our Hope: A Steadfast Radical's Thoughts on Rebuilding Movement*, Ithaca, NY: ILR/Cornell University Press.

McIntyre, R. (2008) *Are Worker Rights Human Rights?* Ann Arbor: University of Michigan Press.

McIntyre, R. and Hillard, M. (1992) "Stressed Families, Impoverished Families: Crises in the Household and in the Reproduction of the Working Class," *Review of Radical Political Economics*, 24(2): 17–25.

—— (1995) "The Peculiar Marriage of Marxian and Neoclassical Labor Economics," *Review of Radical Political Economics*, 27(3): 22–30.

McIntyre, R. and Ramstad, Y. (2004) "Not Just Nike is Doing It: 'Sweating' and the Contemporary Labor Market," in D. Champlin and J. Knoedler (eds) *The Institutionalist Tradition in Labor Economics* (pp. 297–314), Armonk, NY: M.E.

Marglin, S. (1974) "What Do Bosses Do? The Origins and Functions of Hierarchy in Capitalist Production," *Review of Radical Political Economics*, 6: 60–112.

Marx, K. (1977) *Capital*, vol. I, New York: Vintage Books.

Mishel, L., Bernstein, J. and Allegretto, S. (2005) *State of Working America, 2004–2005*, Ithaca, NY: Cornell University Press.

Sharpe.

Montgomery, D. (1980) *Workers' Control in America: Studies in the History of Work, Technology, and Labor Struggle*, Cambridge: Cambridge University Press.

—— (1987) *The Fall of the House of Labor: The Workplace, the State, and American Labor Activism: 1865–1925*, Cambridge: Cambridge University Press.

—— (1993) "Industrial Democracy, or Democracy in Industry?: The Theory and Practice of the Labor Movement, 1870–1925," in N. Lichtenstein and H.J. Harris (eds) *Industrial Democracy in America: The Ambiguous Promise* (pp. 20–42), Cambridge: Cambridge University Press.

Moody, K. (1997) *Workers in a Lean World: Unions in the International Economy*, New York: Verso.

Osterman, P. (1998) *Securing Prosperity – The American Labor Market: How it Has Changed and What to Do About It*, Princeton, NJ: Princeton University Press.

Osterman, P., Kochan, T., Locke, R. and Piore, M. (2001) *Working in America: A Blueprint for the New Labor Market*, Cambridge, MA: MIT Press.

Piore, M. (1991) "The Future of Unions," in G. Strauss, D. Gallagher and J. Fiorito (eds) *The State of the Unions* (pp. 387–410), Madison, WI: Industrial Relations Research Association Series.

Piore, M. and Safford, S. (2005) "Changing Regimes of Workplace Governance: Shifting Axes of Mobilization and the Challenge to Industrial Relations Theory," unpublished paper.

Portelli, A. (1991) *The Death of Luigi Trastulli and Other Stories*, Albany, NY: SUNY Press.

Ramirez, B. (1978) *When Workers Fight: The Politics of Industrial Relations in the Progressive Era: 1898–1916*, Westport, CT: Greenwood Press.

Ramstad, Y. (1996) "The California School versus the Harvard School: Reinterpreting the 1950s Labor Economics," unpublished paper.

Rebitzer, J. (1993) "Radical Political Economy and the Economics of Labor Markets," *Journal of Economic Literature*, 31(3): 1394–434.

Resnick, S. and Wolff, R. (1987) *Knowledge and Class: A Marxian Critique of Political Economy*, Chicago, IL: The University of Chicago Press.

Ross, R. (2004) *Slaves to Fashion: Poverty and Abuse in the New Sweatshops*, Ann Arbor, MI: University of Michigan Press.

Rubenstein, S. and Kochan, T. (2001) *Learning From Saturn*, Ithaca, NY: ILR/Cornell University Press.

—— (2003) "Exploitation, Consumption, and the Uniqueness of U.S. Capitlism," *Historical Materialism*, 11(4): 209–26.

Salvatore, N. (1982) *Debs: Citizen and Socialist*, Urbana: University of Illinois Press.

Savage, L. (1998) "Geographies of Organizing: Justice for Janitors in Los Angeles," in A. Herod (ed.) *Organizing the Landscape: Geographical Perspectives on Labor Unionism* (pp. 225–52), Minneapolis: University of Minnesota Press.

—— (2004) "Public Sector Unions Shaping Hospital Privatization: The Creation of the Boston Medical Center," *Environment and Planning*, 36: 547–68.

—— (2005a) "Changing Organizing, Organizing Change: The Harvard Union of Clerical and Technical Workers," unpublished paper.

—— (2005b) "Justice for Janitors: Scales of Organizing and Representing Workers," unpublished paper.

Savage, L. and Wilis, J. (2004) "New Geographies of Trade Unionism," *Geoforum*, 35(1): 5–7.

Schatz, R.W. (1993) "From Commons to Dunlop: Rethinking the Field and Theory of Industrial Relations," in N. Lichtenstein and H.J. Harris (eds) *Industrial Democracy in America: The Ambiguous Promise* (pp. 87–112), Cambridge: Cambridge University Press.

Schor, F. (1999) "'Virile Syndicalism' in Comparative Perspective: A Gender Analysis of the IWW in the United States and Australia," *International Labor and Working-Class History*, 56: 65–77.

Silver, B. (2003) *Forces of Labor: Workers Movements and Globalization Since 1870*, Cambridge: Cambridge University Press.

Spencer, D.A. (2000) "The Demise of Radical Political Economics? An Essay on the Evolution of a Theory of Capitalist Production," *Cambridge Journal of Economics*, 25(4): 543–64.

Stearns, P. (1990) *Be a Man! Males in Modern Society*, New York: Holmes & Meier.

Thompson, P. and Newsome, K. (2004) "Labor Process Theory, Work, and The Employment Relation," in B. Kaufman (ed.) *Theoretical Perspectives on Work and the Employment Relationship* (pp. 133–62), Urbana, IL: IRRA Series.

Tucker, R. (1978) *The Marx-Engels Reader* (2nd edn), New York: W.W. Norton.

Waldinger, R., Erickson, C., Milkman, C.R., Milkman, R., Mitchell, D.J.B., Valenzuala, A., Wong, K. and Zeitlan, M. (1998) "Helots No More: A Case Study of the Justice for Janitors Campaign in Los Angeles," in K. Bronfenbrenner, S. Friedman, R.W. Hurd, R. Oswald and R. Seeber (eds) Organizing to *Win: New Research on Union Strategies* (pp. 102–20), Ithaca, NY: ILR/Cornell University Press.

Webb, S. and Webb, B. (1894) *A History of Trade Unionism*, London: Longmans, Green.

—— (1897) *Industrial Democracy*, London: Longmans, Green.

Wial, H. (1993) "The Emerging Organizational Structure of Unionism in Low-wage Services," *Rutgers Law Review*, 45: 671–738.

Williams, R. (1978) *Marxism and Literature*, New York: Oxford University Press.

8 Labor during transition

A radical institutional approach

John Marangos

Introduction

Institutional changes in the labor market were crucial for a successful transition from a centrally administered economy to a market economy in Russia, the former Soviet Union, and Eastern Europe. However, the failure to create the requisite labor institutions – labor relations, employment policy, and labor law – during transition had detrimental affects on labor. This meant that in the name of "economic restructuring" and "creative destruction," the labor market experienced rising unemployment, declining real wages, increasing polarization of income and wealth, growing poverty, and a declining life expectancy.

This chapter argues that we cannot adequately interpret the shortcomings of the troubled "transition" to capitalism in Russia, the former Soviet Union, and Eastern Europe using neoclassical economics. The orthodox model of transition in either the shock therapy or the gradualist form portrayed the decline in working conditions as an indispensable requirement for the labor market to equilibrate. This chapter rejects this contention. In turn, using a radical institutional approach, I argue that the traumatic labor market conditions of transition were unnecessary, and where a direct consequence of the orthodox neoclassical assumptions deployed by Western policy makers (for example, by the International Monetary Fund and the World Bank) who shaped this harsh transition. Such approach also recognizes the preconditions that would have been necessary for a less costly transition. Moreover, the introduction of market relations and the development of the foreign-corporate-dominated economy in Russia, the former Soviet Union, and Eastern Europe required the simultaneous development of culture and emulation in supporting the ceremonial and instrumental side of the institutional dichotomy.[1] The cultural framework had to both secure that ambitious people do not pose a threat to the evolving system, while affirming their desire to be part of the system and hence subdue any feelings of injustice. A process of disembeddedment had to be initiated in the transition economies in order for market economic relationships to dominate over custom, trust, morals, and culture. The fact that these cultural and institutional conditions of existence were ignored accounts for the disastrous results which followed. A more promising pathway may have been possible if policy makers had been willing to embrace radical institutionalism, which acknowledges and gives credence to the importance of culture, history, working rules, conflict, power, inequality, and government.

The purpose of this chapter is to determine and develop an understanding of the shifting of workers' rights and working conditions during the transition process by using a radical institutional approach. The radical institutionalist methodology adopted is indispensable for the transition process: the transition process, on the one hand, essentially entailed institutional development appropriate to the market process and, on the other hand, "all institutional analysis, when properly done, should be radical" (Waller 1989: 39). Hence, the terms radical institutionalism and institutionalism are used interchangeably in this chapter. Students of transition and economics, in general, will benefit from these findings as the employment of a radical institutionalist approach will shed light on the consequences of transition on the working people, consequences which orthodoxy depicts as needful.

The chapter is organized as follows. The first section explains radical institutionalism and its relevance to the transition process. The second section expands the radical institutionalist approach to the labor market with an application to the transition process. The third section utilizes the aforementioned developed concepts to the labor market during transition. The final section, presents both the findings in the conclusions.

What is radical institutionalism and its relevance to the transition process?

In orthodox economic analysis of the market-based economy, the market becomes a powerful enabling myth. "Where the mainstream economist sees an effective market, the institutionalist sees a market rife with imperfection" (Woodbury 1987: 1791). Hence, we need a different approach to economics that disassociates socially desirable outcomes from market outcomes. According to Allan Gruchy (1987: xix), "institutionalists define economics to be the science of social provisioning." Furthermore, radical institutionalists attempt to improve the flow of goods and services to everybody, especially the poor: "We cast our lot with the wretched of the earth" (Dugger 1989a: vii). Unlike orthodox economics, institutionalism does not study static efficiency and market equilibrium. Rather, institutional economics is the economics of change, of cultural evolution, and social provisioning. This contrasts with mainstream economics in which resources, technology, values, preferences and the institutionalized distribution of power that structures values and preferences is taken as given (Stanfield 1989: 99). Institutionalists concentrate on social processes – process of change – for which their concepts are compatible. Given that institutionalism is troubled with social change, by definition institutionalism can only be radical.

Being the study of social change, institutionalism is the economics of societal transformation and not "transition," as orthodoxy defined the movement to a market economy in Russia, the former Soviet Union, and Eastern Europe. Hence, in this context, institutionalism appears an appropriate (radical) methodology to examine the so-called "transition" process. Institutionalism is a procedural paradigm that "addresses itself to an explanation of human behavior in economic systems embedded in actual cultural circumstances" (Gruchy 1987: 4). A central feature of the procedural paradigm is the study of dynamic economic processes, processes that require a historical, aggregative, and holistic perspective. As Commons (1950 [1970]: 118) affirmed, "I have never been able to think of the various social sciences as separate fields of history, political science, law, economics, ethics and administration." This statement is quite consistent with the transition process.

Radical institutionalism is based on the works of Thorstein Veblen, John Dewey, and John R. Commons. It blends the methodology of original institutional economics with radical analysis by incorporating class, consciousness, and conflict as articulated by Karl Marx and his followers. Hence it is compatible with Marxism (Dugger 1989b: 127; Stanfield 1999: 955). As Phillips (1989: 22) explains, the radical institutionalist perspective employs Marx's analysis of class conflict and the contradictions of capitalist development within the Dewey-Veblen-Ayres dichotomy between technological and ceremonial structures. The analysis of economic and social problems requires both perspectives: Marxist and institutionalist. The institutionalist paradigm is consistent with the dialectical theory, because dialectical change is procedural as well (Dugger 1989c: 5). Marxism and radical institutionalism have consistent approaches to social theory and policy. The "synthesis" between Marxism and institutionalism is dialectical: the continual interaction and conflict of opposites. Radical institutionalism, having been influenced by the theories of dependency and imperialism in the Marxist tradition, calls attention to the significance of internal factors in inspiring and constraining the social and economic development of societies. However, there is a disparity between the teleological nature of the class struggle for Marxists and the non-teleological emphasis on process in institutionalism.

Dugger and Waller (1996: 169–70) argue that radical institutionalism does not represent a break with the original institutionalist approach, but rather attempts to move it beyond its current, Ayresian philosophical foundation. In Ayresian institutionalism, value is located in the technological process whereas, in radical institutionalism value is located in the democratic process. Radical institutionalists engage in a systematic critique of the current forms of corporate and cultural hegemony and alienation along the lines of race, ethnicity, gender and class in favor of participatory democracy and self-management along with national planning and cultural reform (Stanfield 1999: 955). Radical institutionalism is radical because it is a critical analysis that accurately describes the workings of an economic system with the intent of altering the system toward more democratic and participatory social structures and procedures (Waller 1989: 39). In this way, institutionalism cannot be incremental, it can only be radical (Dugger 1989c: 16–17).

In contrast to the neoclassical models of transition, the market does not just naturally materialize. It is a set of instituted social relations; a set of rules. Moreover, the market is a result of the exercise of power, frequently by the state itself. As Polanyi (1944 [1975]: 139–40) reveals the paradox:

> the road to the free market was opened and kept open by an enormous increase in continuous, centrally organized, and controlled interventionism. . . . There is nothing natural about laissez-faire. Free markets could never have existed had things been left to take their course . . . laissez-faire was created by the state.

The development of the "disembedded economy"[2] and the creation of labor as a "fictitious commodity"[3] in transition economies could not have been the responsibility of the market, rather there was a need for government action. The state legislates and adjudicates the laws and rules that institute markets, as "the market is the result of class conflict, tradition, legislation, and adjudication. The market is not the cause, but an effect" (Dugger 1989c: 8–9). Polanyi described that the groups who led the protective reaction to the establishment of market relations as classes, reacted to protect their own economic and socio-cultural interests. In this way, by changing the economic structure, concurrently, they protected interests "wider than their own" (Mayhew 1989: 557). Polanyi's concepts of "double movement"[4] and "protective response"[5] to social structures of accumulation allow us to examine how the process of transition and change fits into a larger, culturally defined setting. Nevertheless, while transition implies change, such change creates problems of maladjustment due to internal ignorance or ardent resistance from vested interests. "Such institutional maladjustment can have dramatic consequences for the flow of real income" (Stanfield 1999: 955), as is clearly demonstrated in the case of transition economies. In 14 out of 27 transition economies the projected GDP level for 2005 was less than that of 1989, which is the year prior to the initiation of the transition process (EBRD 2005).

According to Veblen, output is a social product, a result of joint effort, not of individual endeavor. Hence, it should be the responsibility of the community to distribute output. Veblen was trying to construct an absurdist theory of economic process, where the process was based on nothing more that "opaque fact" (Daugert 1950: 26–8). Veblen was opposed to capitalism making him a radical. Like Marx, he believed that a fundamental change in capitalism was required to bring about an egalitarian system based on a socially controlled economy. However, unlike Marx, Veblen was deeply pessimistic, not believing that an egalitarian transformation of capitalism was likely, at least not soon enough (Dugger 1989c: 2). Veblen's pessimism was partly due to his implicit theory of consciousness, which rejected the Marxian assertion that capitalism would produce a class-consciousness capable of carrying out revolutionary change. The explanation he offered in the *Theory of the Leisure Class* was based on the belief that capitalist culture persuades the exploited and more risk-taking members of society to aspire to become exploiters, rather than questioning and rebelling against their current social position. Moreover, incorporating John Dewey's social psychological framework, Commons professed that individual thinking readjusts to institutions and thus, economic behavior experienced individually appears as "voluntary" (McIntyre and Ramstad 2002: 294–5). The dominant perception in society is that the only relief from exploitation is to convert into an exploiter: "The prey emulates the predator" (Dugger 1989c: 7).

Thus, emulation is common among the lower classes of a stratified society. As Dugger (1989c: 8) explains:

> It makes them burn with a desire to mimic the upper strata, to do them one better. So, rather than overturning the system, the lower strata become tightly locked into it, as competition for status and wealth absorb all the energies and emotions of the more aggressive members of the lower classes.

In this way, ambitious people from the lower classes become emulative and do not disturb the status quo. Their desire to be a part of the status quo negates any feelings of injustice within the disembedded economy. The enculturation process teaches the ways of a culture to members of the society. Cultures are historic phenomena. Current cultural practices are the result of historical developmental processes (Waller 1989: 40). It is therefore impossible to perceive a culture in static terms, especially in terms of orthodox economics.

In a similar fashion the emulative culture and ideology transmitted in Russia, the former Soviet Union, and Eastern Europe was that of the triumph of capitalism associated with free markets, consumerism, and people's capitalism. "Proletarian internationalism has given way to liberal universalism" (Sakwa 1998: 73), and "the word imperialism is out of style and no longer to be found in the dominant political lexicon, even though imperialism is present and does pillage and kill" (Galeano 1991: 254). The "propensity to truck and barter" was presented as innate human nature and essential for the spread of global capitalism (Holmstrom and Smith 2000: 4). Although celebrations of the "triumph" of capitalism were questionable, Yunker (1997: 327) suggests that the people in transition economies had been "misled, fooled and bamboozled" and blinded to both their own financial self-interest and the higher social interest.

The cultural hegemony imposed on transition economies stressed that there is no other way of understanding social phenomena than through an understanding of individual actions, which implied disembedding the economy from any social cultural foundation. Individuals should be allowed, within defined limits, to follow their own values and convictions, and individuals should not be subject to coercion. The need to strive for a better economic position, to accumulate wealth and competition, were presented as inherent human behavior and thus cannot be eliminated. They can be suppressed, but not eradicated. As the architect of shock therapy Sachs (1991: 26) argued, individuals in transition economies were "troubled, restive, and impatient," and "it seems that the deadening decades of communism did not dull the acquisitive spirit, but rather sharpened it" (Sachs 1993: xiii).

The slogan: "Towards the market at the expense of the state, not the citizens" was very popular in Russia (Kosmarskii 1992: 31). It dismissed the role of the state in the developmental process of market relations and obviously dismissed the institutionalization of any protective response by the state. Nevertheless, the concept of private ownership was historically and culturally unknown to Russians. The words "private" and "privatization" were not even in the Russian vocabulary. However, over time these words were added, acknowledging the need to articulate the privatization policies imposed by the IMF, the World Bank, and mature market economies. Correspondingly, for orthodox economists, "the cultural barrier had evidently been exaggerated" (Aslund 1995: 271).

For orthodox economists, an ideological foundation for the development of a market system in transition economies already existed based on the values of a long tradition of private enterprise and the deeply rooted rationalism and individualism. Supposedly, these values would foster an effective market system as long as all impediments to individual behavior were removed. Moreover, orthodox economists insisted that there was no legitimacy to the claim that people would not know how to behave in a market economy. For example, small-scale trading can be learned quickly. Thus, the acquisitive spirit was on the rise in Russia, the former Soviet Union and Eastern Europe. As Aslund (1994: 35) explains, "All over Eastern Europe, the entrepreneurial spirit has turned out to be excellent."

Shiller *et al.* (1992) argued that empirical evidence strongly revealed that there were no notable differences between Americans and Russians with respect to economic risks and incentives. Based on their findings, the argument that Russians would not be able to respond immediately to market opportunities due to the suppression of the entrepreneurial spirit did not have any merit. "Predictions that people had forgotten how to set up and run a private enterprise have turned out to be completely wrong" (Aslund 1994: 35). Economic behavior and choices are influenced by situational differences, that is, incentives instead of attitudinal differences. Questionnaire results revealed that young individuals were receptive to radical economic reform (that is, shock therapy), and looked favorably on private ownership of land and enterprises and foreign investment. Russian consumers reacted positively to market reforms, and their behavior was consistent with and predicted by classical economic theory (Boone and Federov 1997: 187). Interviews with Polish consumers revealed that the new capability of planning shopping was one of the most fascinating features of the new economic conditions (Berg 1994: 397). Private enterprises increased dramatically as entrepreneurship was oppressed, but still alive (Aslund 1997: 192), and self-interest and self-help was replacing paternalism and statism (Mau 1992: 266). Consequently, "free markets" and the recommendations of the orthodox transition methodology (that is, fictitious commodities and disembedded economy) were "voluntary," perceived as the only feasible alternative by the people in transition economies. This is because, effectively, "free markets" were the only alternative offered by the IMF, the World Bank and mature market economies. Consequently, rather than rejecting and overturning the imposed capitalist economic system, the people of Russia, the former Soviet Union, and Eastern Europe embraced "free markets" implicitly or explicitly, as competition for status and wealth absorbed their energies and emotions.

In sum, radical institutionalists share a conception of human essence and therefore a common standard of human progress. Therefore, they are interested in identifying the psycho-cultural foundation of the orthodox "transition" prescriptions by exposing their cultural hegemony. This cultural hegemony by powerful interests both within and outside the transition economies dominates the mentality of social life and causes and perpetuates unequal opportunities. Orthodox economic theory is incapable on the one hand of identifying the developmental process of markets by dismissing concepts such as disembedded economy, fictitious commodities, and protective response, and on the other hand in determining the consequences of the transition process for the working people in either the shock therapy or gradualist form. Radical institutionalism concentrates on inequality of income, wealth, and power and the psycho-cultural implications of the market capitalism in transition economies by using a Marxian analysis of class and alienation. Hence, the focus of the transition process should be unavoidably more cultural, more procedural, and more dialectical, hence more radical, in line with radical institutionalism.

The significance of a radical institutional approach to the labor market for the transition process

The institutional paradigm adopts the premise that labor markets cannot be adequately understood in terms of "fictitious commodities" of the market exchange model portrayed under perfect competition. The perseverance of a plethora social phenomena of the disembedded economy, such as internal labor markets, collective bargaining, fixed and efficiency wages and involuntary – not natural – unemployment cannot be rationalized by the neoclassical competitive model. A normative judgment in neoclassical theory is that the presence of the necessary labor market institutions, such as collective bargaining, are perceived as "frictions" that hinder the achievement of equilibrium and result in distorted outcomes (Hillard and McIntyre 1994: 620).

The institutional approach to the labor market originates in the works of Beatrice and Sidney Webb, Richard Ely, Robert Hoxie, John Commons, and Selig Perlman. Institutional economics rejects the methodological individualism of orthodoxy in favor of "social" explanations of economic behavior and labor market outcomes. Institutionalists reject the myopic market-oriented theories advanced by orthodoxy placing labor as a commodity (fictitious commodity) in the production process. Rather, they understand market behavior as an expression of an underlying rule structure embedded in institutions. Therefore, labor market outcomes require uncovering the relevant rule structure of institutions. Unlike orthodox economic theory, no efficient outcome is acknowledged, and no particular institutions are given exclusive remark (Hillard and McIntyre 1994: 620–1). Institutionalists do not view labor as a commodity and they regard the work process as a complex, multidimensional, and cultural phenomenon requiring a methodological approach that is interdisciplinary, highly empirical, rich in description, evolutionary, and applicable to public policy (Gimble 1991: 628), and hence radical.

In addition, transition economies had to pursue a strategy of technological autonomy and culture, which naturally influenced the institutional foundations of the labor market. Lacking a technological culture, social development is impossible as labor would endure unemployment, inadequate social protection, and low living standards. Even if economies can purchase technology, without a corresponding technological culture, as theories of technological diffusion would imply, adaptation of the technology would be ineffective and have negative consequences for social development and labor. Social and economic development is particularly determined, by the relative degree of lateness in fostering economic development together with the presence or not of technological autonomy and culture.

Gerschenkron's (1962, 1968) argument was applied to the experiences of developing countries in the 1960s. The latecomers during this period aspired to narrow the income gap between developed and developing countries and sought to do so as quickly as possible and at any cost. This was extremely difficult given the existing poor economic conditions and lack of technological autonomy and culture, which constrained their growth potential. There appeared to be a contradiction, which resulted in tensions. The more underdeveloped a country was to begin with, the higher the tensions (Ofer 1987: 1769). However, tensions resulted in impatience, and impatience resulted in extremely radical and rapid reforms. In the 1990s the economic perception on economic policy has changed markedly from the 1960s. The dominant worldview consistent with the Washington Consensus is that of free markets, deregulation, privatization, monetary discipline, tax reductions, and trade liberalization. Today's latecomers, in this case the transition economies, aspired to narrow the income gap and to do so as quickly as possible at any expense, thus necessitating the shock therapy process. This was because, as previously mentioned, tensions resulted in impatience which caused much more radical and rapid reforms (that is, shock therapy) than those utilized by the mature market economies when they initiated their own economic development.

The course of economic development initiated by the shock therapy process may be considered radical from a historical perspective, since the experience of mature market economies suggests the appropriate procedure is gradualism (Polanyi 1944 [1975]; Bardhan and Roemer 1993: 16). "Haste, impatience, and radical action translate into a high time preference, a high discount rate for future benefits for the sake of short-term achievements" (Ofer 1987: 1799). Hence, shock therapy may be interpreted as a "voluntary" decision by transition economies due to their need as latecomers to achieve the standard of living of advanced economies. This resulted in the immediate introduction of reforms with the belief that the benefits would be instantaneous as well. Gerschenkron's (1962, 1968) argument appears to explain the "voluntary" nature of the transition economies' decisions to implement shock therapy. However, it is equally possible to argue that the strategy was in fact forced upon transition economies. These economies had to satisfy conditions imposed upon them in order to secure funding from the IMF, the World Bank and mature market economies. This, effectively, left the transition economies with no real choice. For example, the IMF and World Bank loans to Romania were terminated because the privatization strategy adopted limited foreign ownership (Gowan 1995: 34). Notably, though, there is an advantage for the latecomers, in this case transition economies, given that they can borrow technologies from the mature market economies without needing to "reinvent the wheel." However, purchasing technology is not enough; what is also required is technological autonomy and culture and an appropriate labor market in order to exploit such technology. Most importantly, it is not costless.

A technological autonomy and culture which influences the structure of the labor market requires complex progressive institutions that must be developed through the effective state and collective action. Based on the institutionalist analysis, the state in transition economies had to play a progressive and responsible role in fostering social development, specifically in creating and fostering the necessary labor market institutions. Institutionalists tend to be activist and interventionist, in contrast to orthodox economists. The relevance of institutionalism to problem solving often implies revision or refinement of labor institutions and policy. However, this belief was not honored by orthodox transition economists of either variant of shock therapy or neoclassical gradualism.

To summarize, the institutionalist's approach to the labor market differs sharply from that of orthodox economists. Where orthodox economists perceive labor to be simply another self-interested factor of production and creating a fictitious commodity, the institutionalists understands labor as a factor of production that is a social human being. While the orthodox economists notice simply a labor union with monopoly power, the institutionalists reveal a relationship between labor and management that is complex and driven by a variety of practices. Whereas the orthodox economists detect just a transfer and diffusion of technology necessary for economic development, the institutionalists identify technological autonomy and culture as essential for social development. Moreover, while the orthodox economists interpret the adoption of shock therapy as a "voluntary" and desirable decision in transition economies that is essential for economic development, the institutionalist shows that the financial commitments associated with the transfer of technology were only granted by the IMF, the World Bank and mature market economies based on the condition of the implementation of shock therapy. These diverse expositions between orthodoxy and radical institutionalism ensure a different distribution of power between labor and management and distinctive processes in the development of working rules in the labor market in transition economies.

Labor during transition

Collective bargaining is the most important method of handling labor-management relations, which involve collective bargaining agreements dealing with wages, and working conditions. Further, such collective bargaining agreements are backed by legally binding contracts, which include grievance procedures. Importantly, collective bargaining is the only approach that permits the exercise of power by both parties to negotiation given that it is the only approach that grants each party a sanction if agreement cannot be reached (Woodbury 1987: 1786). Collective bargaining recognizes the mutual dependence of labor and management but also realizes their inevitable conflict over the terms of their contract. The solution is a process which recognizes the complexities of labor-management relations. Such a solution requires a process that gives power to both labor and management. Collective bargaining should be viewed as a "protective response" (Polanyi 1944 [1975]), or as a means to institute the capital-labor accord and the social structures of accumulation.

Based on a shock therapy model of transition, an efficiently functioning labor market was a necessary condition of transition. The widespread indexation of wages and the large percentage of the labor force employed in state enterprises were supposedly obstacles to stabilization (Sachs 1997: 248). For instance, state enterprises had a tendency to pay high wages based on political considerations, and restrictions on dismissing workers increased labor's bargaining power. Thus wages had to be market-determined, which naturally gave rise to unemployment and inflicting pain, which was necessary and part of the remedy. Furthermore, market-determined wages, coupled with private ownership of enterprises, would ensure job creation. As Schumpeter states, the fundamental aspect of economic development is "creative destruction." Consequently, the orthodox economists assume that transition necessarily involves some "destruction." Surprisingly, at the beginning of the reform program, to avoid a wage-price spiral due to hyperinflation, Sachs and Lipton (1990: 56) recommended a tax-based wage policy to encourage wage increases below the increases in inflation. Of course, this contradicts the free market ideology of shock therapy. For example, the Polish government initiated penalties on wage increases, the so-called *popiwek* (Balcerowicz *et al.* 1997: 138), under which wages were to increase by 30 percent of the monthly inflation rate in January 1990 and 20 percent thereafter. Enterprises conceding wage increases above the norm were heavily taxed. Nevertheless, shock therapy advocates that in market economies inflation can only be contained by allowing some unemployment.

Based on the neoclassical gradualist approach, while the objective should have been market-determined wages, it was in the interest of the economy in the transition phase to maintain some control over wages and try to avoid the wage-price spiral. As Kornai (1993: 211) claims, "It would be a mistake to work for growth in consumer demand through unbridled wage rises. Though perhaps popular initially, it is a dangerous weapon that can easily overshoot the target." This is because inflation is a dynamic process. It is generated and sustained by price and wage increases. Deregulating wages in an environment of weak profit motive, soft budget constraint, and unemployment would hinder the transition process. The government had to set guidelines for the determination of wages strengthened by tax incentives: a wage and incomes policy. Progressive taxation above the predetermined norm would act as a disincentive to excessive wage increases. Partial indexation of wages, not automatic, would maintain industrial peace and reduce inflation. It was a transitional measure that could speed up the reform process and establish a hard anti-inflationary policy. "A more generous approach would signify a lack of understanding of the requirements of a stabilization policy" (Bim 1992: 185).

Hence, both approaches – shock therapy and neoclassical gradualism – denied collective bargaining as a means of settling disputes and establishing labor-management relations. Effectively centrally determined incomes policy under the transition conditions created the preconditions to oblige workers to "voluntarily" adhere to the specific maximum wage increase. Otherwise any wage increases above the norm would penalize enterprises already in the red and jeopardize future growth and restructuring, ultimately leading to closure. The threat of closure and unemployment was a powerful "incentive" for labor to accept wage increases below the inflationary rate. Incomes policy was introduced in mature market economies as a result of sectors of the economy dominated by monopolies or oligopolies with a significant labor organization to reduce the potential of excessive wage increases causing a flow-on effect to other industries that cannot afford wage increases. Cost-push inflation, the wage-price spiral, and higher levels of unemployment result in less competitive industries increasing prices and reducing labor in an attempt to remain profitable. But under the transition conditions, the economies of Russia, the former Soviet Union, and Eastern Europe were characterized by large, powerful, and eventually private monopolies, with very weak, inexperienced, and unpopular unions. Trade unions were associated with Stalinism. Under Stalinism trade unions were totally controlled by the party and their character was changed so that they could function as an element of the state. Independent trade unions representing the workers' interests were transformed under Stalinism into administrative organs of the state and acted to ensure rapid industrialization. The primary functions of such trade unions revolved around increasing labor productivity through the enforcement of work discipline and conducting emulation campaigns. The command nature of the system was realized through the "representation" of the working class by the state and the party, not trade unions, which were both highly centralized. Hence, incomes policy during transition effectively removed the potential for newly formed independent trade unions to grow and become powerful, as one of the most important incentives to join a union, demanding increases in wages, was effectively eradicated. Incomes policy established management unilateralism resulting in management's power to control wages and the terms of employment. Under the transition conditions incomes policy was a means to curtail the development of embryonic labor unions into strong, popular, independent labor unions and to institutionalize management's power.

The institutionalization of poverty and unemployment during transition resulted in an increase in adult mortality rates and a decrease in life expectancy. People in transition economies had to deal with stress, cardiovascular disease, alcoholism, and occupational injuries and illness. Most transition economies experienced an increase in death rates during transition. In Russia, for example, the standardized death rate increased over 50 percent, in Latvia it reached 50 percent, in Estonia 41 percent, and in Lithuania 34 percent whereas, in Moldova, Kazakhstan, Belarus, and the Kyrgyz Republic the death rate increased over 25 percent. Slovenia and Poland registered slight decreases in standardized death rates, while Czech and Slovak Republics recorded sharp declines. Moreover, Hungary experienced a 9 percent increase in death rates, while in Uzbekistan it reached 9.9 percent and in Turkmenistan it reached 4.9 percent (Brainerd 1998: 2016–17). Economic reforms, in this case transition reforms, affect people's health in a variety of ways: for instance, macro-economic instability causes uncertainty and unemployment. Changes in relative prices influence consumption patents. Increased poverty, cutbacks of the social expenditure and the deterioration of public health infrastructure directly determine the livelihood and well-being of the people. Finally, rising crime rates are necessarily the result of increased poverty.

Shock therapy supporters were not surprised by the link between the rate of reform and a reduction in life expectancy. Sachs (1996: 131) argued that while changes in life expectancy varied between transition countries, they were inversely related to the speed and depth of reforms. In the Czech Republic, Slovakia, and Poland, which introduced shock therapy, life expectancy rates continued to increase during the transition period. However, in countries which introduced a gradual approach, such as Hungary, life expectancy was reduced and it plunged in the Ukraine. Shock therapy supporters blame gradualism for the reduction in life expectancy. The inflation caused and maintained by the gradual approach increased stress and made life unpredictable; thus more people were confronted with difficulties which they could not manage (Aslund 1995: 288).

However, what shock therapy supporters fail to disclose is that at the beginning of the reform program, the Czech and Slovak Republics already had in place guaranteed minimum income schemes which provided social support as a last resort for those individuals falling outside unemployment compensation schemes (Boeri 1997: 131). Surprisingly, the Czech Republic, which implemented shock therapy, registered its highest unemployment rate in 1991, which amounted to only 4.1 percent, with youth unemployment at around 6.5 percent by mid-1996. The Czech Republic's low unemployment rate is associated with the implementation of active labor market policies. These policies include "carrot-and-stick" administration of benefits, subsidies targeted toward additional job creation for the young, unskilled and long-term unemployed, and a well-organized network of employment offices that actively supervise and assist workers and that provide better screening and placement of vacancies and job seekers (Boeri *et al.* 1998: 82). In contrast, the Slovak Republic suffered a large budget imbalance after the split from the federation in 1993, and consequently did not maintain the active labor market policies inherited by the federation. This resulted in a large increase in unemployment. In the case of Poland, although the country implemented restrictive fiscal and monetary policy, it opted for a gradual privatization of state enterprises and banks with the goal of maintaining an acceptable level of employment. Poland never applied the shock therapy privatization program. Strangely enough in contrast to shock therapy, Poland restructured their state enterprises before privatization quite successfully (Fischer and Sahay 2000: 19). Hence, there was an increase in mortality rates in nearly every transition economy independently of the speed of reforms, with the exception of those economies that reduced unemployment rates by either active labor policies or maintained employment by gradual privatization. Neither of these policies was supported by shock therapy advocates.

Brainerd (1998) concludes that the death rates in transition economies were correlated with the rates of GDP growth, inflation, crime, and unemployment. There was a strong correlation between deaths from cardiovascular disease and inflation and also between crime and unemployment. We may easily conclude from the interpretation of these findings that a reduction in macro-economic instability, unemployment and uncertainty, and the establishment of law and order, improves quality of life and life expectancy.

Conclusion

A radical institutionalist approach to the "transition" process emerges as a suitable framework to analyze transition outcomes. A radical institutional approach reveals the psycho-cultural foundation of the orthodox "transition" prescriptions by exposing their cultural hegemony. The transition economies surrounded by mature market economies were determined to achieve the standards of living of advanced economies by adopting the imposed cultural hegemony of "free markets." The orthodox transition prescriptions underline the cultural hegemony of "free markets" by powerful interests within and outside the transition economies. Consequently, the implementation of the "transition orthodoxy" appears and is interpreted as a "voluntary" decision by the people of transition economies. In particular, the implementation of shock therapy in these economies, while "radical" in the sense of contradicting the historical development of capitalism, appears to be a voluntary choice of the governments and people in transition economies. Nevertheless, the cultural framework of the transition process debate was imposed from the IMF, the World Bank and mature market economies. It may easily be argued that transition economies were even bribed into adopting shock therapy. Shock therapy and the orthodox methodology were presented as the only choice given that the state's involvement in economic affairs was already discredited. Therefore, the dominant cultural framework in transition economies persuaded the exploited and risk-takers to desire to become exploiters with whatever means (even illegal) and to suppress any feelings of injustice.

In this chapter, we have concentrated our analysis on the labor market and, due to space limitations, have concentrated only on some issues and outcomes of labor market transitions. Strangely enough, while all markets had to be liberalized based on the orthodox prescription, control in the labor market had to be transferred from the state to management. Incomes policy and privatization were the means to control wages, to suppress labor unions, and to establish management prerogative. The disembedded capitalist labor market required the uninterrupted establishment of management control of the labor process. Without the presence of strong labor unions, real wages declined, working conditions deteriorated, and unemployment and poverty was instituted as a permanent feature of the labor market to serve as a "reserve army."[6] Under these conditions, coupled with the contraction in social and health services and expenditures, there was a substantial decrease in life expectancy among the people in transition economies. Hence, the experience of "transition" reveals that uncontrolled market liberalization may actually be able to reduce poverty and unemployment by creating the necessary conditions for people to depart this life!

Acknowledgments

I would like to thank Jackie Gabriel, Phil O'Hara and the participants of the Conference on Radical Economics in the 20th Century – Radical Economics and The Labor Movement for their useful comments.

Notes

1 The institutional dichotomy is present in capitalist societies as, on the one hand, there are the instrumental activities of human beings based on the instincts of parenthood, workmanship, idle curiosity, industry, and technology, and on the other, ceremonial activities based on non-instrumental, non-technological, and non-scientific behavior. Instrumental behavior is forward-looking while ceremonial behavior is static and past-binding.
2 The concept of the disembedded economy refers to a tendency for economic relationships to become dominant over the social relationships of kinship and polity.
3 "Labor, land, and money are not commodities. . . . None of them is produced for sale. The commodity description of labor, land, and money is entirely fictitious" (Polanyi 1944 [1975]: 176).
4 The expansion of the market in the economy creates a counter-movement to devise forms of collective action by workers and their families who suffer social dislocation. This twofold process is named "double movement."
5 As the expansion of markets in the economy had an increasingly negative impact on social life it stimulated a socially protective response with the goal of limiting the dislocation that workers and their families experienced by market shocks.
6 A pool of unemployed is an inherent feature of the market capitalist economy. Marx calls this pool the "reserve army of labour" or "industrial reserve army."

Bibliography

Aslund, A. (1992) *Post-communist Economic Revolutions. How Big a Bang?*, Washington, DC: Center for Strategic and International Studies.

—— (1994) "Lessons of the First Years of Systematic Change in Eastern Europe," *Journal of Comparative Economics*, 19(1): 22–38.

—— (1995) *How Russia Became a Market Economy*, Washington, DC: The Brookings Institution.

—— (1997) "Observations on the Development of Small Private Enterprise in Russia," *Post-Soviet Geography and Economics*, 38(4): 191–205.

Balcerowicz, L., Blaszczyk B. and Dabrowski M. (1997) "The Polish Way to the Market Economy 1989–1995," in T. Woo, S. Parker and J.D. Sachs (eds) *Economies in Transition. Comparing Asia and Europe* (pp. 131–60), Cambridge, MA: MIT Press.

Bardhan, K. and Roemer, J.E. (1993) "Introduction," in P.K. Bardhan and J.E. Roemer (eds) *Market Socialism: The Current Debate* (pp. 3–17), Oxford: Oxford University Press.

Berg, A. (1994) "Does Macroeconomic Reform Cause Structural Adjustment? Lessons from Poland," *Journal of Comparative Economics*, 18(1): 376–409.

Bim, A. (1992) "The Role of the State in Transitional Postcommunist Economies," in A. Aslund (ed.) *The Post-Soviet Economy. Soviet and Western Perspectives* (pp. 181–95), New York: St. Martin's Press.

Boeri, T. (1997) "Labour-market Reforms in Transition Economies," *Oxford Review of Economic Policy*, 13(2): 126–40.

Boeri, T., Burda, M. and Kollo, J. (1998) *Mediating the Transition: Labour Markets in Central and Eastern Europe*, London: Centre of Economic Policy Research.

Boone, P. and Fedorov, B. (1997) "The Ups and Downs of Russian Economic Reforms," in W.T. Woo, S. Parker and J.D. Sachs (eds) *Economies in Transition. Comparing Asia and Europe (pp. 161–88), Cambridge, MA: MIT Press.*

Brainerd, E. (1998) "Market Reform and Mortality in Transition Economies," World Development, 26(11): 2013–27.

Commons, J.R. (1950 [1970]) *The Economics of Collective Action*, New York: Macmillan.

Daugert, S.M. (1950) *The Philosophy of Thorstein Veblen*, New York: Columbia University Press.

Dugger, W.M. (1989a) "Introduction," in W.M. Dugger (ed.) *Radical Institutionalism. Contemporary Voices* (pp. vii–xii), Westport, CT: Greenwood Press.

—— (1989b) "Radical Institutionalism: Conclusion," in W.M. Dugger (ed.) *Radical Institutionalism. Contemporary Voices* (pp. 125–33), Westport, CT: Greenwood Press.

—— (1989c) "Radical Institutionalism: Basic Concepts," in W.M. Dugger (ed.) *Radical Institutionalism. Contemporary Voices* (pp. 1–20), Westport, CT: Greenwood Press.

Dugger, W.M. and Waller, W. (1996) "Radical Institutionalism: From Technological to Democratic Instrumentalism," *Review of Social Economy*, LIV(2): 169–89.

EBRD (2005) *Transition Report Update*, London: European Bank for Reconstruction and Development.

Fischer, S. and Sahay, R. (2000) *The Transition Economies After Ten Years*, Washington, DC: IMF Working Paper WP/00/30.

Galeano, E. (1991) "A Child Lost in the Storm," in R. Blackburn (ed.) *After the Fall. The Failure of Communism and the Future of Socialism* (pp. 250–4), London: Verso.

Gerschenkron, A. (1962) *Economic Backwardness in a Historical Perspective*, Cambridge, MA: Harvard University Press.

—— (1968) *Continuity in History and Other Essays*, Cambridge, MA: Harvard University Press.

Gimble, D.E. (1991) "Institutionalist Labor Market Theory and the Veblenian Dichotomy," *Journal of Economic Issues*, 25(3): 625–48.

Gowan, P. (1995) "Neo-liberal Theory and Practice for Eastern Europe," *New Left Review*, 213 (September/October): 3–60.

Gruchy, A.G. (1987) *The Reconstruction of Economics: An Analysis of the Fundamentals of Institutional Economics*, Westport, CT: Greenwood Press.

Hillard, M. and McIntyre, R. (1994) "Is There a New Institutional Consensus in Labor Economics?," *Journal of Economic Issues*, XXVIII(2): 619–29.

Holmstrom, N. and Smith, R. (2000) "The Necessity of Gangster Capitalism: Primitive Accumulation in Russia and China," *Monthly Review*, 51(9): 1–15.

Kornai, J. (1993) "Transformational Recession: A General Phenomenon Examined Through the Example of Hungary's Development," *Economic Appliquee*, 46(2): 181–227.

Kosmarskii, V. (1992) "Public Attitudes to the Transition," in A. Aslund (ed.) *The Post-Soviet Economy. Soviet and Western Perspectives* (pp. 25–38), New York: St. Martin's Press.

Mau, V. (1992) "Prospects for Russia's Economic Reforms: Comments and Discussion," *Brookings Papers on Economic Activity*, 2: 266–73.

Mayhew, A. (1989) "Polanyi's Double Movement and Veblen on the Army of the Commonweal," *Journal of Economic Issues*, 23(2): 555–62.

McIntyre, R. and Ramstad, Y. (2002) "John R. Commons and the Problem of International Labor Rights," *Journal of Economic Issues*, 36(2): 293–301.

Ofer, G. (1987) "Soviet Economic Growth: 1928–1985," *Journal of Economic Literature*, 25(4): 1767–833.

Phillips, R. (1989) "Radical Institutionalism and the Texas School of Economics," in W.M. Dugger (ed.) *Radical Institutionalism. Contemporary Voices* (pp. 21–37), Westport, CT: Greenwood Press.

Polanyi, K. (1944 [1975]) *The Great Transformation*, New York: Octagon Books.

Sachs, J. (1991) "Crossing the Valley of Tears in East European Reform," *Challenge*, 34(5): 26–32.

—— (1993) *Poland's Jump to the Market Economy*, Cambridge, MA: MIT Press.
—— (1996) "The Transition in the Mid Decade," *American Economic Review Papers and Proceedings*, 86(2): 128–33.
—— (1997) "An Overview of Stabilisation Issues Facing Economies in Transition," in W.T. Woo, S. Parker and J.D. Sachs (eds) *Economies in Transition. Comparing Asia and Europe* (pp. 243–56), Cambridge, MA: MIT Press.
Sachs, J. and Lipton, D. (1990) "Poland's Economic Reform," *Foreign Affairs*, 69(3): 47–66.
Sakwa, R. (1998) "Russian Political Evolution: A Structural Approach," in M. Cox (ed.) *Rethinking the Soviet Collapse. Sovietology, The Death of Communism and the New Russia* (pp. 181–201), London: BookEns.
Shiller, R.J., Boycko, M. and Korobov, V. (1992) "Hunting for Homo Sovieticus: Situational versus Attitudinal Factors in Economic Behavior," *Brookings Papers on Economic Activity*, 1: 127–81.
Stanfield, J.R. (1989) "Recent U.S. Marxist Economics in Veblenian Perspective," in W.M. Dugger (ed.) *Radical Institutionalism. Contemporary Voices* (pp. 83–104), Westport, CT: Greenwood Press.
Stanfield, R. (1999) "Radical Institutionalism," in P. O'Hara (ed.) *Encyclopedia of Political Economy* (pp. 955–7), London: Routledge.
Waller, W.T. Jr. (1989) "Methodological Aspect of Radical Institutionalism," in W.M. Dugger (ed.) *Radical Institutionalism. Contemporary Voices* (pp. 39–49), Westport, CT: Greenwood Press.
Woodbury, S.A. (1987) "Power in the Labor Market: Institutionalist Approaches to Labor Problems," *Journal of Economic Issues*, 21(4): 1781–807.
Yunker, J.A. (1997) *Economic Justice: The Market Socialist Vision*, Boston, MA: Rowman & Littlefield.

9 Offshore production and global labor arbitrage

A new era of capitalism?

Claude Pottier

Introduction

The increasing magnitude of offshoring and outsourcing production in low-income countries gives rise to a debate on their impact on labor in developed countries. Standard economists (with a few exceptions like Rodrik) have a narrow approach to this phenomenon, measuring the number of jobs affected and concluding that they are few in comparison with the bulk of jobs created and destroyed each year in the developed countries. Radical economists have a broader approach, considering the impact of international capital mobility on the capital-labor relationship. Yet, the effects of the global organization of firms are not well integrated in the analysis of neoliberalism. Offshoring and outsourcing to low-wage countries enable transnational corporations to play workers off against each other. This chapter seeks to demonstrate that this "labor arbitrage" (Roach 2003), or "global auction" (Brown and Lauder 2001, 2003), or "organization of competition between workers" (Pottier 2003), constitutes a new direction in globalization and a new era of capitalism.

In the following section two, it is argued that the impact of globalization on labor and, more specifically, the effects of the global organization of firms are insufficiently taken into account in the analysis of neoliberalism. In the next section, the hypothesis is developed that global labor arbitrage represents a new era of capitalism. Then, empirical evidence is supplied on the magnitude of offshoring and outsourcing in low-wage countries, and on their impact on labor. Next, the notion of "global management of workforce by multinationals" is outlined. The final section offers a brief review of alternatives to global labor arbitrage.

The status of the global organization of firms in the analysis of neoliberalism

It is worth noting first that, starting from the neoclassical framework, Rodrik (1997) emphasizes the impact of the worldwide organization of firms on the nature of bargaining between workers and employers. The economics literature, he says, has focused on the decreasing demand for low-skilled labor in developed countries. But the important point is the increase in the elasticity of demand for production labor since the 1960s (pointed out by Slaughter in the case of the United States). It means that workers can be substituted for each other across national borders, either through foreign direct investment or through international outsourcing. Therefore, Rodrik concludes, workers' bargaining power is weakened.

Now, let us place this bargaining power at the center of the analysis, as it is in the Marxist and regulationist approaches. Most work within these analytical frameworks converges on one point: neoliberalism or global neoliberalism is a new phase in the history of capitalism, in which the postwar capital-labor compromise has been replaced by a new hegemony of capital. This new phase started at the end of the 1970s when the ruling classes reacted to a decline in their relative income and to the weakening of their power (Duménil and Lévy 2004; Wolfson 2003). The two major means of this restoration were the new dominance of finance and a frontal attack against workers and their unions.

But how is globalization integrated into these analyses? Different approaches may be distinguished, according to their increasing ability to allow for the global organization of firms. In one set of works, this organization is seen as a means to restore the profit rate since the rate of surplus value is higher in the countries on the periphery. That is Duménil and Lévy's standpoint, based on their observation of the increase in profits coming from the foreign affiliates of American multinationals, in proportion to their domestic profits. Similarly, Wolfson sees a link between neoliberalism and globalization in the pressures, placed by developed countries on developing countries, to eliminate capital controls and other barriers to foreign investment. Owing to their subject, these analyses do not place the expansion of multinationals abroad in the context of increasing cost competition and of the willingness of firms to escape the labor constraints (cost and legislation) of developed countries. Therefore, they miss an important point: the increasing activity of firms in low-income countries means not only an extension of the area of exploitation in these countries but also a weakening of labor's position in developed countries.

This fact is recognized in a second set of works. Thus, for Crotty and colleagues (1997), the international mobility of capital has contributed to the deterioration in labor's situation in developed countries. Nevertheless, they assert that "foreign investment is neither inherently good nor bad." Only "in the structures of the current neoliberal global regime, increased capital mobility is contributing to a race-to-the-bottom tendency." It is so because this regime has created "a more destructive competitive environment" that led to liberalization of international direct investment in the 1980s and to an increase in capital mobility. Thus, the weakening of workers' bargaining power is not the outcome of the international mobility of capital per se. It is basically the result of the new competitive regime. However, there is an ambiguous element in this argument since, for the authors, this new regime partly results from the pressure of increasingly open borders.

Lipitt (2004: 341) gives a more central place to globalization. A new "Social Structure of Accumulation" was formed in the United States in the 1970s, he says, and globalization is one of the three elements accounting for this major change (the two others being the evolution of political forces and social conflicts). Globalization combines with technological change to explain the deterioration in labor's position: "Companies increasingly gained the option of moving production abroad, outsourcing procurement to foreign suppliers or replacing workers with automatic processes." In the same way, Aglietta (1997) asserts that the combination of technical change and international mobility of capital results in a broadening and deepening of the international division of labor, which is (together with the "exhaustion of gains in productivity" and increased financial openness) one of the main factors explaining the "crisis of Fordism."

The hypothesis of global labor arbitrage as a new era of capitalism

Starting from globalization

Let us consider the relationship between neoliberalism and globalization in the opposite way. Instead of starting from neoliberalism and analyzing how globalization interferes with it, it is worth starting from the globalization process as an independent process and considering how it comes into relation with neoliberalism. Actually, there are two distinct phenomena with two different scales of time. On the one hand, the globalization process is old and rather continuous in time (with the exception of the 1930s). On the other hand, the history of capitalism may be characterized by a succession of periods of regulation and deregulation with variable intensity in the domination of capital over labor. According to this view, neoliberalism is the current phase of deregulation: "a new free market era" for Wolfson, a "second financial hegemony" for Duménil and Lévy.

The hypothesis of this chapter is fourfold:

1. Offshoring and outsourcing in low-wage countries mean a global labor arbitrage by firms, which constitutes both a break in the globalization process and a new era of capitalism.
2. It entails a structural, and not temporary, weakening of labor's position relative to capital.
3. It is the outcome of an evolution which is both prior and external to neoliberalism.
4. However, today the two phenomena are interconnected. In particular, a new phase of regulation should include control of the international mobility of capital.

The validity of this hypothesis has to be backed by empirical analysis of the magnitude of offshoring and outsourcing in low-income countries, and their impact on labor in developed countries. That will be done in the following two sections. In this section, the hypothesis is developed.

The starting point of the argument is the inherently borderless character of capital accumulation. The paradox is that, for a long period of time, the greatest part of the accumulation had taken place within nations, and was subject to the specific capital-labor relationship existing in each country. Today, however, firms are in a position to choose between different countries to locate parts of their production and to play workers off against one another. Thus, the capital-labor relationship tends to operate on a worldwide scale and not only in each country, with a tendency to align with wages and labor standards existing in developing countries (the "race to the bottom"). This is a major change in the accumulation process, supporting the idea of a new era of capitalism.

The question of the impact of globalization on the capital-labor relationship has to be related to that of the historical evolution of foreign direct investment in countries where wages are lower. In 1913, Rosa Luxemburg (1972: 37) wrote: "Capital cannot do without worldwide means of production and labor-power." In Luxemburg's time, capital moved to colonies in order to gain access to raw materials. Thus, the production of affiliates in these countries was integrated with the parent companies, but this integration was limited to raw materials. Subsequently, market penetration became another dominant motivation of foreign direct investment in developing countries. In this latter case, capital takes advantage of a more favorable employment relationship, but this is not a substitute for the relationship existing in developed countries since the production is oriented toward local markets. The situation is completely different when capital moves into low-wage countries in order to serve markets in developed countries. Then capital avoids the constraining employment relationship that has been set, after a long history of social conflicts, in developed countries. This situation is rather new in the everlasting antagonism between capital and labor over sharing out value. Relocation of activities and outsourcing to low-income countries gathered momentum since the 1960s and developed on a large scale since the 1990s. The countries on the periphery are not only new markets but also privileged places for obtaining surplus value.

Offshoring and outsourcing take place in the broader process of production rationalization, on a world scale, led by the transnational corporations. It means a much deeper integration of production than before, as evidenced by intra-firm trade. This fact is overlooked by all those who see nothing new in the current process of globalization. In particular, the division of labor, set by the multinationals between developed and emerging countries, is rapidly evolving. That means an extension of the field in which workers can be played off against one another.

Characteristics of global labor arbitrage

Two characteristics of this labor arbitrage should be underlined. First, for the situation of labor in the developed countries, there is a basic difference between the impact of offshoring and outsourcing in low-wage countries and the effects of "usual trade" with these countries. Here, "usual trade" refers to international trade other than intra-firm. For the greatest part of the history of capitalism, trade between independent firms made up nearly all international trade, but this is no longer the case. Thus, in 2002, intra-firm trade accounted for 31 percent of U.S. exports of goods and 38 percent of U.S. imports. In international trade between independent firms, as delineated by standard theories, competition between workers is limited because the levels of labor productivity between developed and developing nations differ greatly. Things change a lot when workers belong to the same transnational company. All over the world, firms implement similar technologies and types of organization, with variation in the capital–labor combination. Surveys carried out in affiliates of transnational corporations located in developing countries show that their technology levels are not much lower than in the parent companies (Pottier 2003). Their organization is sometimes even more efficient because it is more recent and because its implementation did not have to meet workers' opposition. As a result, the productivity gap within the transnational corporations between plants located in developed countries and those located in developing countries is much lower than the differential in labor costs. Thus, labor costs play a more decisive role in the arbitrage between plants. Therefore, competition between workers according to their location is, by far, much stronger than in the usual trade between nations. The persistent differential between the variations in the cost of labor and the variations in the productivity level within the multinationals shows that the neoclassical hypothesis of a strict relation between wages and labor productivity does not hold. According to the Marxist view, wages are primarily determined by the local conditions of labor-power reproduction.

The second characteristic of the competition between workers is that it is not limited to low-skilled labor, as it is in the Heckscher-Ohlin-Samuelson (HOS) standard theoretical framework. Although it is true that most of the jobs concerned are low-skilled, there is a growing proportion of skilled jobs (Brown and Lauder 2003). That is the case in the manufacturing sector, where the activities performed in low-wage countries are not limited to assembly (Pottier 2003), and it is even more obvious in the service sector. The notion of static comparative advantages of nations is inadequate. Firms create a new international division of labor and part of this creation stems from their effort to lower their labor costs. Under the pressure of oligopolistic competition, firms are involved in a process of reengineering and standardizing their activities so that the related standardized jobs can be sent offshore (Dossani and Kenney 2003). Therefore, the criterion for this relocation moves from the degree of skill to the degree of standardization of jobs. The substance of labor is not static, as standard theories assume, because firms strive to routinize all work, including skilled work, in order to minimize their costs.

Role of the state

New communication technologies and progress in transportation have paved the way for the transfer of activities to low-wage countries. However, the main determinant of this phenomenon was transnational corporations' pressure on states to liberalize international trade. The leading role of multinationals in the General Agreement on Tariffs and Trade (GATT) and World Trade Organization (WTO) rounds need not be demonstrated (George 2004). Their pressure had a double motivation: to gain better access to markets and to be more competitive. Concerning this latter motivation, trade liberalization was a means to build production bases in developing countries in order to serve markets in developed countries. Even before trade barriers were lowered in these countries, in the manufacturing sector, the transnational corporations got two specific policy instruments favoring the imports of products manufactured by their affiliates and subcontractors located in low-wage countries. The first was the General System of Preferences (GSP), providing duty-free quotas of exports for selected products and developing countries. The second was the production-sharing mechanism, setting a duty exemption for the value of components manufactured in developed countries and incorporated in imported goods manufactured abroad in affiliates and subcontractors.

In addition to this assistance by states in developed countries, transnational corporations were aided by states of developing countries, particularly in the establishment of export-processing zones. In these zones, the states put together the various conditions of the accumulation of capital: land, communication and transportation facilities, equipment for the reproduction of labor power, tax exemption. Furthermore, it may be argued that the two main free trade areas in the world, North American Free Trade Agreement (NAFTA) and the European Union (EU), implicitly favor labor arbitrage since they associate countries having very different levels of development and social systems. As a continuation of the creation of maquiladoras and then of the liberalization of the Mexican economy, NAFTA has given a new impulse to establishing cheap production bases for American firms. The enlargement of the EU to low-wage countries is a similar process. A report of the Commission of the European Communities (2003: 10) is very explicit on this matter: "A further enlarged EU, with its increased variety of wage structures and technological skills, will provide European industry with opportunities for competitive reorganization." Moreover, the EU is not a simple free trade agreement, like NAFTA, but also an economic union, that is to say a zone where the conditions of competition are being harmonized. Since all the conditions are subjected to this harmonization, except social (and fiscal) ones, competition between workers is even more intense in the EU enlargement than in the globalization process. Labor arbitrage is the result of the mobility of capital to low-wage countries of the Union, but it is also the outcome of the opposite movement of workers from these countries to European developed countries.[1]

To sum up, the global labor arbitrage by transnational corporations may be viewed as the result of the following sequence:

1. The initial factor was the need for capital to enlarge the space of its accumulation beyond national borders, both for the realization of value and for its creation.
2. Liberalization of international trade in the manufacturing sector was the prerequisite of this enlargement. Consequently, the dominant fraction of capital, namely the large firms submitted to oligopolistic competition, put pressure on states to implement this liberalization.
3. The liberalization of international trade strengthened cost competition, especially between firms of developed countries, because their technological levels converged (Giraud 1996).
4. Faced with this increasing cost competition, firms responded by non-spatial modes of organization, mainly through the rationalization and the externalization of activities.

5 The spatial aspect of their new organization was the establishment of production and export bases in low-wage countries (more precisely, countries offering minimal conditions of skills and industrial environment; that is to say, emerging countries). The liberalization of international direct investment allowed for this evolution.

By no means does this sequence, which focuses on the globalization process, exclude the role of neoliberalism. First, the very purpose of this regime is the weakening of the bargaining position of labor relative to capital. Second, it affects globalization itself. Thus, since the 1980s, free trade areas associating nations with different levels of development have been created and the liberalization of international direct investment has become more marked. However, this evolution is a continuation of a prior process since, at the end of the Tokyo round, in 1979, the average tariff on goods had already been lowered to 4.7 percent. Therefore, the sole dynamics of the internationalization of capital accumulation explains much of the deterioration in labor's situation.

Magnitude of the offshoring and outsourcing process

Global labor arbitrage may be viewed as a new and major feature of capitalism only if offshoring and outsourcing in low-wage countries are large-scale and developing phenomena and if their impact on the labor situation is important. The evolution of foreign direct investment to developing countries is not a good indicator of the magnitude of offshoring because a large part of this investment is market-driven. The only valid indicator is the evolution of imports in developed countries from affiliates and subcontractors located in countries where wages are much lower. In the manufacturing sector, data on the evolution of these imports speak for themselves (Pottier 2003). Thus, imports from affiliates of Japanese firms located in developing countries of Eastern Asia rose from 5.8 percent of total imports of manufactured goods in Japan in 1986 to 22.5 percent in 2004.[2] For the United States, the increase in imports from affiliates of U.S. firms located in developing countries is much lower, as a share of total U.S. imports of goods: from 4 percent in 1986 to almost 7 percent in 2003. But, as a share of imports of goods from foreign affiliates, those coming from developing countries rose from 24 percent in 1983 to 37 percent in 2003.[3] Concerning Western Europe, the inadequacy of the EU database makes a global measurement of the phenomenon impossible. However, a survey of the automobile industry shows a sharp increase in the EU imports from affiliates located in the countries of Central Europe, up to the full membership of these countries. It should be emphasized that, for the whole manufacturing sector, the relocation strategy in this zone has been primarily implemented by German firms, with the explicit goal of reducing the cost of labor. This process followed the debate, which took place in Germany at the end of the 1980s, on the decreasing competitiveness of German territory ("Standort Deutschland"). In the mechanical industry, particularly, the employers set themselves the target of reducing manufacturing costs by standardizing products and relocating part of their production to Central Europe.

With regard to international outsourcing in the manufacturing sector, there are no global data. The only indicator concerns imports coming under the production-sharing mechanism, but this indicator refers to a reality which is larger than outsourcing in some respects and narrower in others. It is larger because it includes imports from affiliates. It is narrower because a large part of outsourcing does not depend on prior exports. Moreover, the significance of this indicator tends to vanish with the liberalization of trade because importers no longer need the benefit of a special tariff. In Europe, for instance, data on these imports to the EU from Central and Eastern European countries have been meaningless since 1998, the year when most trade barriers were removed between the two areas. Nevertheless, the evolution of these imports up until 1997 was spectacular: from 1.9 billion ecus in 1988 to 7.1 billion in 1997. They added to the same type of imports in the EU, coming from the developing countries of the Mediterranean basin, but, in 1997, they were nine times as much (Fabbris and Malanchini 2000).

The conclusion is clear. Since the mid-1980s, transnational corporations have set up export bases in low-wage countries that have become crucial elements of their competitiveness in developed countries' markets. In the manufacturing sector, where transportation costs matter, these bases have been set up at the peripheries: Mexico for U.S. firms, Eastern Asia for Japanese multinationals, Central Europe for West European firms. In the service sector, where the proximity constraint does not exist, firms rely on all the emerging countries. In the United States, the Bureau of Economic Analysis (BEA) provides data on "Business Professional and Technical" (BPT) services, which include services that are likely to be affected by offshoring.[4] These data show that, from 1997 to 2003, U.S. imports from affiliates were much more important and grew much faster than unaffiliated imports (Borga and Mann 2004). Unfortunately, the origin of these imports is known only for the unaffiliated ones. For them, it appears that there is an increase in the share of developing America and Asia, from 17.8 percent in 1992 to 19.5 percent in 2004. In the subsector of computer and data processing, for the sole unaffiliated imports, India's share grew from a little more than 1 percent in 1997 to nearly 18 percent in 2004.

Impact on labor

In the economics literature, the conventional idea is that offshoring and international outsourcing have a weak impact on the labor markets of developed countries. Therefore, it is argued that workers' anxiety in this regard is largely unjustified and irrational. Two arguments may be opposed to this opinion. First, it should be emphasized that the simple fact that offshoring and outsourcing are both a new and rapidly growing phenomenon (as shown in the previous section) is itself a dramatic change for working people. For the first time in the history of capitalism, firms are able to play off workers all over the world and there are good reasons to believe that this tendency will continue to accelerate. The second argument points out that while some of the effects of offshoring on labor are subject to measurement, others are not, although there is every indication that their impact is important.

The first variable which may be taken into account is the number of jobs affected by offshoring and outsourcing. Compared to the total jobs existing in a country, it is obviously low. In the United States, the Bureau of Labor Statistics provides data, since 1996, on "extended mass layoffs" (layoffs of 50 or more employees expected to last at least a month). In the period 2002 to 2003, those layoffs due to "import competition" and "relocation overseas" accounted for around 36,000 a year, which is only 4 percent of the 900,000 layoffs. In comparison with the 14 to 15 million new jobs created and 13 million old jobs destroyed each year in the United States, it is even lower (Schultze 2004). However, the number of layoffs concerned is higher because those that have fewer than 50 employees being laid off are not taken into account. Moreover, one should include the deficit of U.S. jobs due to location (and not only relocation) in low-wage countries in order to export to developed countries. Conversely, offshoring leads to job creation in the United States because the firms concerned are more competitive and because low-income countries increase their imports from the United States. It is impossible to evaluate the resulting balance but the important point is the following: should this balance be equal to zero, the impact on wages, benefits, working conditions and job insecurity would still be important, first, because the workers gaining or losing jobs are not the same, and second, because there are spillover effects on labor markets.

There are several ways to consider measurement of the impact on wages. The first is to refer to the literature on the impact of imports from developing countries, which is a broader subject since it is not limited to imports from affiliates and subcontractors. Most measurements have been done by using the hypotheses of the HOS theory. It says that an increase in imports from low-wage countries leads to reduced wages for low-skilled workers through the diminution of relative prices in the labor-intensive sectors. As the initial measurements showed a weak impact of the imports from developing countries, many economists concluded that the diminution of relative wages, affecting the American production workers, was mainly the result of technical change (Lawrence and Slaughter 1993). However, allowing for outsourcing, Feenstra and Hanson (1995) estimated that the effect of rising imports was important (15 percent to 33 percent of the decrease in the relative wages of U.S. production workers). Wood's criticism of the HOS framework was more radical since he denied the independence between imports and technical change. The effects of rising imports on labor markets have been underestimated, he said, because defensive innovations in sectors where competition with developing countries is intense have not been allowed for (Wood 1995). Another step should be made in the way opened up by Wood, by considering that the strategy of multinationals is not defensive but offensive. In the context of increasing competition, they standardize both their technologies and their activities in order to transfer them to countries where wages are much lower.

In this process, what matters is not only the actual transfer of activities to low-wage countries but also the threat to do it, which means a permanent pressure on labor. Kate Bronfenbrenner (2000) has given some indications on the importance and effects of the relocation threats on labor in the United States. In this country, as in others, the effects are diffuse, but when they come to be concentrated in space or time their importance is striking. That was the case in summer 2004 in Germany, where the employers undertook a large-scale offensive to reduce the cost of labor by threatening to relocate activities to Central and Eastern Europe. The focal point of attack was the extension of labor time without a wage increase. It also meant the diminution of bonuses and the limitation of future wage increases. In exchange, the employers promised to invest in existing German plants rather than in new plants in Central and Eastern Europe. This deal concerned large parts of the manufacturing industry: mainly the sectors of automobile (DaimlerChrysler, Opel, Volkswagen), trucks (Man), pneumatics (Continental, Michelin), electronics (Siemens), and electrical appliances (Bosch). The spillover effects on labor markets were remarkable. In some sectors of construction and services not directly concerned by offshoring, employers and even the state also demanded an extension of labor time without compensation. At the same time, French workers faced similar pressure for the extension of the work week. In conclusion, many "stylized facts" show that the impact of offshoring and outsourcing on labor seem to be important, although it is impossible to measure it thoroughly.

The global management of workforce by the multinationals

The decisive role of labor cost for a given level of skill shows that the notion of comparative advantages of nations should be subordinated to that of absolute advantages. However, that remains a static notion. A major characteristic of the global economy today is that firms are more and more in a position to both use and shape social disparities between nations. That is why the notion of a "global management of workforce by the multinationals" might be put forward. Two features of this management have been pointed out previously in this chapter.

First, firms strive to standardize work. This issue should be set in the contradiction between the development of productive forces and the capitalist relations of production. Competition between firms forces them to innovate and to develop new skills. But skilled work is expensive and hard to control. Worldwide competition increases the constraint of reduction in labor cost. In response, firms standardize and fragment the different activities comprising the process of production and standardize the work in each activity. Thus they have better control of its cost and its use. Second, once the activities have been standardized and fragmented, firms can put workers in competition all over the world. Either they transfer activities to low-wage countries or they maintain them in developed countries in return for a reduction in the cost of labor and an increase in its flexibility.

Two other features of this system of global workforce management should be added. The first element is workforce training. Given the skill shortage in low-wage countries, firms have to develop training programs. They often do so with the cooperation of local authorities, which lowers the cost of training. The pressure for partial privatization of education all over the world does not mean only an extension of the field of capital accumulation; it is also a way to define skills and jobs that suit firms' needs. The second feature is the mobility of labor from low-income to developed countries. The critical issue is the immigration of skilled labor and the enlargement of quotas for different categories of skills. The increase seen in temporary immigration has to be related both to training and offshoring employees coming from low-wage countries are initially trained or employed in developed countries and then return to their home countries, working in the affiliates of multinationals (Saxenian 2002).

The logical consequences to expect from this global management of the workforce by the transnational corporations vary according to countries' levels of development. In developed countries, the relative wages of low-skilled workers should continue to decline, along with those of a growing number of skilled employees, as long as their jobs can be standardized. In emerging countries, the relative wages of skilled employees should continue to increase and will tend to converge with wages in developed countries. But this is no more than a long-term trend. Given the importance of the workforce reservoir in rural areas of developing countries, wages will still be determined mainly by the local conditions of labor-power reproduction. Moreover, competition between developing countries in attracting firms will favor social dumping. Finally, in all countries, both developed and developing, job insecurity should increase.

What are the alternatives?

From what has been said previously, both on the global organization of firms and on the neoliberal regime, it ensues that, today, workers are not in a position to impose a real alternative to this evolution. However, one might speculate on different alternatives, starting from the limited responses currently brought by the social and political movements and, then, considering, more broadly, the contradictions of the global neoliberal regime.

The first limited response lies in the compensation that might be given to workers in developed countries who have been hit by firms' global strategies. It consists in reshaping the social safety net, notably by strengthening the unemployment insurance system, providing health care for laid-off workers and wage insurance for those who have been displaced. This policy of compensation has to be complemented by the development of job training, so that employees are able to find a competitive job. In the United States, these two types of measures could fit into the strengthening of the "Trade Adjustment Assistance" and its extension to laid-off employees in the service sector. According to Atkinson (2004: 10), this policy would lead to the establishment of a new bargain with workers: "If the workforce accepts a rapidly changing and highly competitive economy, government will ensure they have portable employee benefits, fair unemployment insurance benefits . . . access to continuous and affordable life-long education, and expanded opportunities for capital ownership."

Yet, this orientation comes up against a contradiction that has been pointed out by Rodrik (1997: 73): "The mobility of capital and of employers both aggravates the risks immobile groups face and renders it more difficult to generate the public resources needed to finance social insurance schemes." In order to overcome this contradiction, Rodrik considers "taxation of footloose factors at the global level, with revenue sharing among nations." More specifically, Atkinson and the Progressive Policy Institute (2004: 12) propose that "if companies choose to lay off American workers in order to have the work done overseas, they should be asked to pay not only for the unemployment insurance costs incurred, but also for the wage insurance costs." These two proposals lead to the opening of Pandora's box. Significant taxation of firms that set up a global organization of production in order to take advantage of the international disparities in the cost of labor would challenge the international mobility of capital, which has become a crucial element of its accumulation.

Before returning to that point, a second limited response should be considered, that which is supported by the world's labor and social movements. The movement for social accountability of firms is powerful because it mobilizes many people all over the world and because the multinationals are aware that their image has a high value. Based on a moral standpoint, this action can successfully impose the adoption and enforcement of core labor standards in subcontracting plants working for the multinationals. The scope of this movement is limited, though, because it does not fit into the capital-labor relationship and, therefore, does not address the issue of other labor standards. That raises the question of the internationalization of trade unionism and, more specifically, of the role of the works councils set up in the multinationals on a world scale. These councils get information on firms' location plans. Sometimes, they are consulted and get modifications in the restructuring plans, but they cannot cancel them. Eventually, neither the movement for social rights nor that of trade unions for labor standards and corporate restructuring can challenge the ability of firms to transfer jobs to low-wage countries (Anderson and Cavanagh 2004). In the long run, the internationalization of trade unions will probably be the appropriate response to the internationalization of capital (Munck 2002). But firms will remain in a position to benefit from global labor arbitrage for a long time.

That leads to a much broader issue, concerning not only the global organization of firms but also of the neoliberal regime. If it is taken for granted that this regime is not sustainable and that capitalism will need a new regulation, then the control of international capital mobility will be one of its major components. World regulation is conceivable in the long run, but, for the time being, the institutions of regulation remain mainly national. Today, nation-states strive to alleviate, through their budgets, the consequences of an international mobility of capital that they encourage, but they do it in vain because the gap between social needs and fiscal resources keeps increasing. So new regulation would impose a dramatic change in the orientation of national budgets: much less for the international accumulation of capital (with, on the contrary, taxation of capital mobility), much more for the social needs and for the restoration of public utilities. History shows that such regulation cannot arise from rational behavior by the ruling classes, but rather from the chaos of a major crisis.

Notes

1 See the "Proposal for a Directive on Services in the Internal Market" (known as the "Bolkestein directive"), adopted by the European Commission in 2004, giving a legal framework to social dumping.
2 Data on imports from affiliates: METI, "Surveys on Overseas Business Activities."
3 Data on imports from affiliates: BEA, "U.S. Direct Investment Abroad, Operations of U.S. Parents and Their Foreign Affiliates."
4 They include the following subsectors: advertising, computer and information services, research and development, management, consulting, legal services, construction, architectural and engineering services, and industrial engineering.

References

Aglietta, M. (1997) *Régulation et crises du capitalisme*, Paris: Odile Jacob.

Anderson, S. and Cavanagh, J. (2004) "Outsourcing: A policy agenda," *Foreign Policy in Focus*, April.

Atkinson, R. (2004) "Meeting the offshoring challenge," policy report issued by Progressive Policy Institute, Washington, DC, July.

Borga, M. and Mann, M. (2004) "U.S. international services. Cross-border trade in 2003 and sales through affiliates in 2002," *Survey of Current Business*, October.

Bronfenbrenner, K. (2000) "Uneasy terrain: The impact of capital mobility on workers, wages and union organization," commissioned research paper for the U.S. Trade Deficit Review Commission, Washington, DC.

Brown, P. and Lauder, H. (2001) *Capitalism and social progress. The future of society in a global economy*, New York: Palgrave.

—— (2003) "Globalisation and the knowledge economy: Some observations on recent trends in employment, education and the labour market," *Cardiff University, School of Social Sciences Working Papers Series*, no. 43, November.

Commission of the European Communities (2003) "Some key issues in Europe's competitiveness; Towards an integrated approach," communication from the Commission to the Council and the European Parliament, Brussels, November 21, COM(2003) 704 final.

Crotty, J., Epstein, G. and Kelly, P. (1997) "Multinational corporations, capital mobility and the global neo-liberal regime: Effects on northern workers and on growth prospects in the developing world," *Seoul Journal of Economics*, 10(4): 297–341.

Dossani, R. and Kenney, M. (2003) "Went for cost, stayed for quality? Moving the back office to India," University of California, Berkeley: Institute for International Studies, APARC.

Duménil, G. and Lévy, D. (2004) "Neoliberal dynamics: A new phase," research paper issued by Cepremap and Modem, Paris.

Fabbris, T. and Malanchini, F. (2000) "Patterns of vertical specialisation and European Outward Processing Trade (OPT): A comparative analysis between Mediterranean countries and CEEC'S. Is the real competition?," research paper issued by Femise network.

Feenstra, R.C. and Hanson, G.H. (1995) "Foreign investment, outsourcing and relative wages," NBER Working Paper no. 5121, Cambridge, MA.

George, S. (2004) *Another world is possible if. . .*, London: Transnational Institute.

Giraud, P-N. (1996) *L'inégalité du monde*, Paris: Gallimard.

Lawrence, R.Z. and Slaughter, M.J. (1993) "International trade and American wages in the 1980s: Giant sucking sound or small hiccup?," *Brookings Papers on Economic Activity: Microeconomics*, 2.

Lipitt, V.D. (2004) "Class struggles and the reinvention of American capitalism in the second half of the twentieth century," *Review of Radical Political Economics*, 36(3): 336–43.

Luxemburg, R. (1972) *Oeuvres IV, L'accumulation du capital (II)*, Paris: François Maspéro.

Munck, R. (2002) *Globalisation and labour*, London: Zed Books.

Pottier, C. (2003) *Les multinationales et la mise en concurrence des salariés*, Paris: L'harmattan.

Roach, S. (2003) "The global labor arbitrage," paper presented at Global Economic Forum, 6 October.

Rodrik, D. (1997) *Has globalization gone too far?*, Washington, DC: Institute for International Economics.

Saxenian, A. (2002) "Transnational communities and the evolution of global production networks: The Case of Taiwan, China and India," *Industry and Innovation*, 9(3): 183–202.

Schultze, C.L. (2004) "Offshoring, import competition and the jobless recovery," *Brookings Policy Brief*, 136, August.

Wolfson, M.H. (2003) "Neoliberalism and the social structure of accumulation," *Review of Radical Political Economics*, 35(3): 255–62.

Wood, A. (1995) "How Trade Hurt Unskilled Workers," *Journal of Economic Perspectives*, 9(3): 57–80.

10 Financialization, employability and their impacts on the bank workers' union movement in Brazil (1994–2004)

Maria Alejandra Caporale Madi, José Ricardo Barbosa Gonçalves and José Dari Krein

In recent years, after recurrent global crises, there has been broad recognition that the current operation of financial markets does not generate market equilibrium and economic growth, but rather instability and growing poverty. In fact, the indicators of Brazil's economic performance were not satisfactory between 1994 and 2004 (Table 10.1): the process of financial liberalization has instead been associated with stabilization policies and recessive macroeconomic adjustments.

Since the 1990s, the financialization process was nurtured by global liquidity and the fast expansion of private capital flows. The recent economic structural changes in the capitalist system have resulted in increasing concentration, centralization, and capital mobility with decisive impacts on investment decisions. As a result, social vulnerability – higher unemployment and lower earnings – has increased due to price assets instability (also exchange rate instability) and credit crunches in financial markets. In Chesnais's words (1999: 51):

> A pattern of high financial return was universally imposed by financial markets, with local variations, depending on the influence of financial arbitrages on domestic monetary policies. The evaluation of domestic currencies in exchange markets was submitted to this new financial regime, as well as the practices of Central Banks.

Moreover, the financial markets' turbulence and volatility have reinforced a vicious circle that involves increased foreign indebtedness, instability and new crises.[1] In Brazil, the predominance of short-term decisions that impose volatility on interest rates and product levels has provoked stop-and-go movements in the dynamics of economic growth. At the same time, economic openness has restricted the options for investment within a framework of industrial restructuring of product chains. While the importance of export integration advances, domestic production became dependent upon the dynamics of the international economy. This process has not generated structural changes so as to achieve systemic competitiveness.

When considering the decade of the 1990s, the contrast is particularly significant to the period between 1946 and 1975, when Brazil's rate of economic growth placed it in the leadership of developing countries. Since the crisis of the 1970s, the process

Table 10.1 Gross domestic product and population, Brazil 1960–2004, in percentages

Period	*Gross domestic product*	*Population*	*Gross domestic product per capita*
1961–1970	6.17	2.89	3.19
1971–1980	8.63	2.44	6.04
1981–1990	1.57	2.21	–0.63
1991–2000	2.65	1.43	1.20
2001–2003	1.23	1.01	–0.23
2001–2004	2.23	1.01	0.75

Source: Banco Central do Brasil, www.bacen.org.br.

of foreign and domestic economic adjustment has been centered on the contraction of aggregate demand, leading to higher unemployment and strengthening inequality.

Monetary stability and international integration are two concepts that synthesize the debate around economic policy choices in the 1990s. In this context, the concept of "credibility" turned out to be decisive to understanding the interaction between the global and local institutions.[2] In other words, the policy of deregulation of capital flows had the potential of success since governments adopted not only the right macroeconomic policies but also implemented prudent measures and efficient supervision practices in the financial systems.

In contrast to the state-based institutions on which the post-1945 economic development process was based, the new growth agenda turned out to be centered on private economic agents' decisions while the economic role of the state might involve the delineation and protection of property rights and the promotion of legal, judicial and normative efficient systems.[3] This new development pattern promoted the notion that private economic agents would be agents of development. As a result, job market conditions turned out to be decisively influenced by private decisions overwhelmed by short-term expectations. Moreover, the increasing efficiency in enterprise management involved new labor relations that had decisive impacts on social organization.[4] But the new labor relation was overwhelmed by tensions among the results of the policies chosen, the promotion of citizenship, and the achievement of the long-run needs of society. Thus, the impacts of financialization illuminate the contradictions between financial hypertrophy and societal expectations in terms of citizenship, employment, and income. Nevertheless, as Gonçalves and Madi (2005) pointed out, the tensions observed in the new relations among the state, society, and the markets were overwhelmed by processes of homogenization and resistance in labor markets.

In this framework, the future of the bank workers' union movement in Brazil offers an important window to analyze sociability conditions following deregulation. The reason for choosing bank workers is because of their strong tradition of unionism, their capacity to successfully wage strikes, and their active participation in national labor unionism. Unionization of bank workers started in the 1930s[5] but suffered a temporary interruption during the military dictatorship period.

It rebounded in force after 1979 during the process of redemocratization when the expansion of the banking system provided the foundations for the changing composition of the workforce and contributed to the organization of the bank workers in unions. From the 1980s on, bank workers' unionism has been one of the main segments that structure the so-called "new" unionism and has actively participated in the formation of a national central union called CUT (Central Única dos Trabalhadores).[6] As a consequence of national strikes and demonstrations, the bank workers' union was able to negotiate national collective contracts and to extend the negotiated scope of labor relations.[7] Since the 1990s, the bank workers' union has faced challenges to overcome the outcomes of the labor flexibilization process, increasing unemployment, and fall in real incomes. In addition, there were changes in workers' behavior[8] that suggest the adoption of attitudes compatible with the short-run and liquid features of the global financial process. This chapter states that this new framework stimulates individualization, threatens social cohesion, and favors fragmentation inside the bank workers' union movement. In the first section the changing structure of the Brazilian banking system and its impact on the bank workers' struggle is outlined, while the second section discusses the nexus among employability, sociability, and syndicalism so as to apprehend the consequences of globalization for the bank workers' union movement and its agenda. The third section concludes the chapter.

Bank strategies and labor

Changing structure of the Brazilian banking system in the 1990s

The guidelines of Brazilian macroeconomic policy – based on low inflation, high real interest rates and reduction of public budgets – established the parameters for the processes of capital attraction and portfolio adjustment in the banking system. In particular, the yield, risk, and liquidity conditions imposed by the management of the Brazil's domestic public debt were decisive to the new configuration of all economic sectors.[9] Considering the evolution of the banking system, the process of adjustment involved changes in the market structure and microeconomic strategies, flexibilization in labor relations, reduction in the number of workers, and the redefinition of the bank workers' abilities and required skills.

Under the regulatory perspective, the creation of the universal banks in 1988 institutionalized the existence of financial conglomerates, with consolidated statements and full mobility to operate in money, exchange, capital, and credit markets. Throughout the 1990s, the principal factors that contributed to changes in the Brazilian financial sector structure were price stabilization, internationalization, deregulation, competition, and technology. After 1994, the outcomes of the price stabilization program (Real Plan) were responsible for a reduction of the national financial system's participation in the gross domestic product. The negative effects of the end of inflation on the rates of banking profitability imposed new adjustments on the banking sector. The implementation of the Bank of International Settlements (BIS) requirements of capital adjusted to risk management was also part of this changing context. In addition, the PROER, a program oriented to the liquidity needs of the banking sector after the Real Plan, was established in order to privatize banks. It included administrative, operational, and equity reorganization, previously authorized by the Brazilian Central Bank; financial assistance to achieve the targets proposed by the Basel Accord (CMN Resolution 2099/94); and fiscal facilities to cover costs and expenses originating from the modernization processes. At the same time, the PROES program was implemented in order to privatize public banks.

Following the opening of the Brazilian banking sector to foreign capital in 1995, a growing process of mergers and acquisitions led to a more concentrated market structure. In 1994, there were 243 financial institutions: the ten largest had 60.2 percent of the total active accounts and 66.1 percent of the total deposits. In 2002, there were 180 banks; the ten biggest had 68.3 percent of total active accounts and 75.7 percent of total deposits. One of the main characteristics of this process was the reduction in the total number of banking institutions, while foreign capital increased its share of total active accounts until 2002 (Table 10.2). The reorganization of the financial system thus introduced a more privatized and internationalized market structure.

Internationalization of the Brazilian banking system was justified as necessary in order to strengthen the financial system. The arguments used by the Brazilian government overstated the following advantages of the foreign banks: better access conditions to new technologies, financial innovations and methods of risk management, greater operational efficiency, and lower operational costs. Nevertheless, the opening of the financial system has had no strong effects on the quality and costs of the financial services. In truth, domestic banks reacted to the growth of foreign direct investment in the Brazilian financial system and have been aggressive in the process of acquisitions so as to preserve their relative position in the market.

In spite of the overall institutional changes, the Brazilian financial sector continues to atrophy since the preference for liquid assets predominates in portfolio decisions. Considering the reaction of banks in response to the macroeconomic policies, short-term operations allow them to review their strategies over shorter periods. Thus, the ability of the banking system to adapt itself to changes in vulnerable macroeconomic conditions is justified, in great part, because of the absence of long-term credit positions and as the result of the composition of liabilities concentrated on short-term demands. Risk management has privileged the concentration of short-term assets and liabilities. In the period analyzed, the management of credit risk expressed the signaled atrophy (Table 10.3). The evolution of credit conditions also reflected the transformations observed in the participation of public and private banks. Between 1994 and 2002, the national private banks kept their leadership in the credit market, while the role of the public federal banks declined in contrast to the performance of the foreign private banks (see Figure 10.1).

In this framework, the overall redefinition of strategic plans included the search for new sources of revenue, product diversification, and market segmentation strategies. In the period analyzed, the high level of profitability of the retail banking

Table 10.2 Banking system: total active in Brazil 1993–2003, in percentages

Banking system	*1993*	*1994*	*1995*	*1996*	*1997*	*1998*	*1999*	*2000*	*2001*	*2002*	*2003*
Foreign control	8.35	7.16	8.39	9.79	12.82	18.38	23.19	27.41	29.86	27.38	20.73
National control	40.67	41.21	39.16	39	36.76	35.29	33.11	35.23	37.21	36.93	40.76
Public control	50.85	51.43	52.21	50.91	50.05	45.83	43.04	36.60	32.03	34.65	37.23
Caixa Econômica Federal	14.51	14.98	16.4	16.47	16.57	17.02	17.06	15.35	10.97	11.66	13.04
Banco do Brasil	22.93	18.28	13.91	12.52	14.42	17.44	15.75	15.63	16.76	17.12	18.4
Others	13.41	18.17	21.9	21.92	19.06	11.37	10.23	5.62	4.3	5.87	5.79
Credit cooperatives	0.13	0.2	0.24	0.3	0.37	0.5	0.66	0.76	0.9	1.04	1.28
Total	100	100	100	100	100	100	100	100	100	100	100

Source: Banco Central do Brasil, www.bacen.org.br

Table 10.3 Brazil: participation of credit in gross domestic product 2001–2003, in percentages

Period	*Market-based credit*	*Directed credit (by central bank)*	*Total*
June 01	15.17	8.69	25.66
December 01	15.50	9.30	26.44
June 02	15.86	9.19	26.62
December 02	13.38	9.00	23.83

Source: Banco Central do Brasil, www.bacen.org.br.

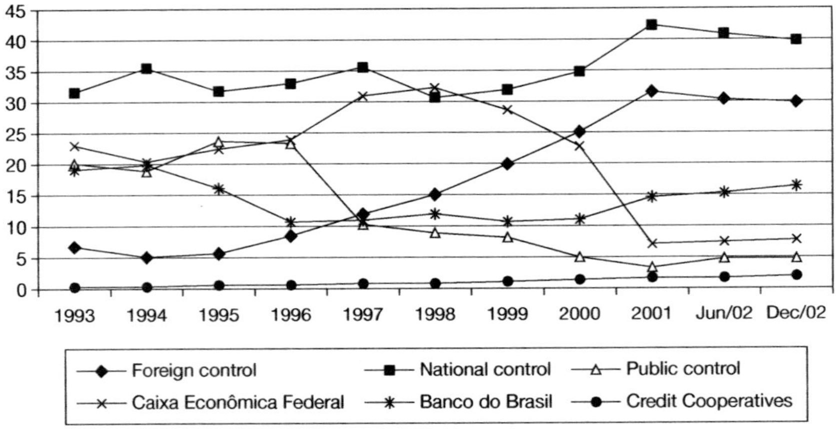

Figure 10.1 Credit, Brazilian banking system, by type of institution 1993–2003, in percentages

sector was centered on asset management, credit revenues nurtured by high spreads, and the expansion of services revenues, such as fees and commissions.[10] Between 1994 and 2003, a new trend was observed: the banks' strategy is to expand the services revenues in order to pay all the expenses with their employees. At the end of the period analyzed, 93.3 percent of these expenses – on average – were paid by the fees and commissions charged on the banks' clients.

New banking system, jobs, and bank workers

In a broader perspective, the banking system, in its search for flexibility and mobility, has not only adopted short-term portfolio strategies but has also developed technological strategies to implement market and operational efficiency targets. After 1995 a technological outbreak was noted, and the year 1996 was an important landmark in terms of technological alternatives. The main changes included decentralization of data processing; more intense use of applications under the Windows platform; consolidation of client-server systems; and outsourcing and reduction of the size of technology development teams. Since the diversification of products and services coexisted with specialization trends, the solutions adopted by each institution stimulated customization. In this context, growing banking competition demanded the adoption of systems so as to support decisions such as data-warehouse and data-mining. The use of innovative programming languages – aimed at reducing marketing costs (for example) and shortening the cycle of development of applications – turned out to speed up the creation and commercialization of products. The use of technologies to quantify risks also grew by means of the utilization of risk management models whose target has been asset management. Finally, technological strategies included the expansion of alternative channels of distribution. Self-service out of traditional branches was stimulated by electronic integration among banks, industry, and commerce. The electronic relationship was mainly affected by requirements to lower costs but also ways to suit clients' convenience (Table 10.4).

All these transformations led to a reduction of jobs and affected bank workers' livelihoods. The sector entered the 1990s with 800,000 jobs, while at the end of the decade this number was reduced by almost half. The reduction in the number of bank workers is associated with outsourcing that has been very intense, especially since the 1990s. According to DIEESE (the Inter-Union Department of Statistics and Socio-economic Studies established by the Brazilian union movement), in 1989 Brazilian banks employed 811,400 people. During 1995 and 1996 banks cut, on average, 174 jobs per day. In the first eight months of 1997, 28,000 jobs were cut. This trend was reinforced by the privatization of the public banks. One remarkable fact is the new composition of the distribution of jobs between private and public banks due to the overall adjustment process. In the state of São Paulo, the main financial center of Brazil, the reduction of the weight of the employment in the financial sector is shown in Table 10.5.

The flexibilization strategies also involved the adoption of cost-reduction policies that included outsourcing, organizational innovations, and new labor relations. Although the outsourcing process presents differences among banks, the main trend has been to consider as core bank activities only those relating to the commercialization of products and services and to promote outsourcing, in greater or lesser degree, involving processes related to the back office, technological support, and remote banking (Table 10.6). The outsourcing trend has been combined with diversification strategies that involve the growth of other institutions rather than banks in the financial conglomerates[11] that turned out to increase the number of

Table 10.4 Channels of distribution, Brazil: 1994–2000, December

Channel of distribution	*1994*	*1998*	*1999*	*2000*
Physical branches	18,760	16,060	16,189	16,396
Banking offices	10,125	7,545	7,117	7,144
ATM network	2,874	6,709	10,808	12,681
ATM network shared among banks	572	1,010	1,369	1,772

Source: DIEESE (2001) *Linha Bancários*, www.dieese.org.br.

Table 10.5 Employment in the financial sector: State of São Paulo 1994–2003, percentage of the total

	1994	*1999*	*2001*	*2003*
City of São Paulo	4.25	4.24	4.35	4.03
Metropolitan region of São Paulo	3.83	3.69	3.62	3.42
State of São Paulo	3.20	2.94	2.80	2.64

Source: Rais/MTE apud Teixeira (2004) *A dinâmica das relações de trabalho no sistema financeiro*, DIEESE/CESIT.

workers in the financial sector who are not considered bank workers because they are not protected by the collective agreement of the bank workers' category (Table 10.7). More recent data from PNAD (2002) indicated that one million workers were employed in the financial system. The challenge faced by the bank workers' union is that of this amount of workers less than 400,000 were bank workers. Considering the data from DIEESE (2003) all these transformations reinforced the diversification of the types of labor contracts in the banking system while the impact of the process of outsourcing in the banking system was higher than the average observed in Brazil at the end of the 1990s.

This framework suggests the emergence of a new configuration of labor relations.[12] In the context of financial deregulation, almost half of finance workers do not belong to the bank workers' category. As a result, they are excluded from bank workers' union representation that has more of a tradition of organization and capacity for negotiation of labor relations. Another important factor responsible for changing labor relations in the banking system has been the adoption of organizational innovations in the workplace, such as the simplification of internal procedures and functional reorganization, that turned out to enhance job reduction. Banks have practiced forms of control of the labor force that make less transparent

Table 10.6 Financial sector: employment by type of institution, State of São Paulo 1994 and 2003, in percentages

Type of institution	*1994*	*2003*
1 Commercial banks	25.1	1.7
2 Universal banks (with commercial activities)	40.3	58.6
3 Savings institutions ("Caixas econômicas")	10.9	11.3
4 Credit cooperatives	0.2	0.7
5 Universal banks (without commercial activities)	0.3	0.2
6 Investment banks	0.4	0.3
7 Others (non-banking financial institutions)	23.0	27.9
Total: Central bank, banking, and non-banking financial institutions	100	100

Source: Rais/MTE apud Teixeira (2004) *A dinâmica das relações de trabalho no sistema financeiro*. DIEESE/CESIT.

Table 10.7 Banking sector: Brazil, outsourcing 2003

Areas of outsourcing	*Percent of responses**
System development	68
Telecommunications	47
Help desk	32
Hardware/software maintenance	32
Asset management	21
Credit cards processing	21
Graphic services	21
Backup site	11
Consulting	11
Central processing data	11
Data communication networks and local networks	11
Services shared with other banks	
EDI – electronic data interchange	37
Bank 24 hours (automatic teller machines)	32
Clearing (payment system)	16

Note: * percent of responses in the FEBRABAN sample

Source: Rais/MTE apud Teixeira (2004) *A dinâmica das relações de trabalho no sistema financeiro*, DIEESE/CESIT.

the coercive mechanisms in order to maximize the discipline and effectiveness of each worker. According to Jinkings (2002), this complex process of transformations that affected in depth the working forms and conditions also produced important modifications in the relations of power inside banks. Those strategies of domination have been expressed in the establishment of wage awards for productivity achievements, the adoption of target plans that serve as parameters for remuneration patterns and the maintenance of jobs,[13] the development of a sophisticated communication system corporation worker (endomarketing), and the creation of "quality" teams. Thus, new forms of control are being developed through techniques of motivation to achieve the corporations' objectives, either through financial incentives, aggregation of functions and status to the bank workers' rank or even the introduction of team groups that make possible a more suitable (from the banks' perspective) level of both individual and collective control.

In particular, the introduction of practices of variable remuneration – that associate workers' incomes to the fulfillment of productivity goals – tends to reveal the enormous pressure or coercion present in the process of adjusting employees' performance to the banks' objectives. These mechanisms have been reinforced by structural changes in the labor market and increased unemployment rates.[14] As a matter of fact, the composition of the category and the profile of the bank worker have changed: (1) by 2003 women had achieved impressive participation in many banking financial institutions (Table 10.8); (2) the time bank workers hold permanent employee status in their institutions has been significantly redefined in the cases *up to five years and more than 20 years* (Table 10.9) and only 5 percent

Table 10.8 Financial sector: employment and gender participation by type of institution, State of São Paulo 2003, in percentages

Type of institution	*Masculine*	*Feminine*
1 Commercial Banks	60.34	39.66
2 Universal banks (with commercial activities)	51.93	48.07
3 Saving institutions ("Caixas econômicas")	42.66	57.34
4 Credit cooperatives	51.46	48.54
5 Universal banks (without commercial activities)	60.09	39.91
6 Investment banks	67.72	32.08
7 Development banks	58.82	41.08
Total: Central bank, banking, and non-banking financial institutions	49.86	50.14

Source: Rais/MTE apud Teixeira (2004) *A dinâmica das relações de trabalho no sistema financeiro*, DIEESE/CESIT.

Table 10.9 Employment in the financial sector: participation by age classification, State of São Paulo 2003, in percentages

Type of institution	*18 to 29 years old*	*30 to 39 years old*	*40 to 49 years old*	*50 or more years old*
1 Commercial banks	27.72	38.91	25.81	7.56
2 Universal banks (with commercial activities)	35.32	36.21	23.63	4.84
3 Savings institutions ("Caixas econômicas")	13.55	24.81	47.87	13.77
4 Credit cooperatives	41.86	29.68	17.89	10.56
5 Universal banks (without commercial activities)	25.69	47.02	22.02	5.28
6 Investment banks	38.76	34.87	20.17	6.19
7 Development banks	5.88	29.41	29.41	35.29
Total: Central bank, banking, and non-banking financial institutions	36.39	33.66	23.88	6.07

Source: Rais/MTE apud Teixeira (2004) *A dinâmica das relações de trabalho no sistema financeiro*, DIEESE/CESIT.

of bank workers are over 50 years of age;[15] (3) the average age of the bank clerk has increased as a consequence of increased requirements for formal education – completion of undergraduate-level or sometimes incomplete undergraduate-level education (Table 10.10).

The increasing use of technology eliminated intermediate ranks and liberated managers to engage in business activities. In fact, there has been an increase in the percentage of workers in management positions justified in order to guarantee a more qualified and customized attendance. At the same time, this trend imposes

Table 10.10 Employment in the financial sector: degree of education, State of São Paulo 2003, in percentages

Type of institution	*First cycle complete*[a]	*Second cycle incomplete*[b]	*Second cycle complete*	*Undergraduate incomplete and complete*
1 Commercial banks	1.0	4.81	15.04	77.69
2 Universal banks (with commercial activities)	0.04	1.73	9.33	88.31
3 Saving institutions ("Caixas econômicas")	1.06	1.02	36.63	60.22
4 Credit cooperatives	2.46	3.24	29.10	62.41
5 Universal banks (without commercial activities)	0.46	1.61	7.80	87.39
6 Investment banks	2.45	1.30	6.48	89.20
7 Development banks	5.88	——	17.65	76.47
Total: Central bank, banking, and non-banking financial institutions	1.86	3.39	19.72	73.94

Notes: [a] Nine years of formal education; [b] between nine and 12 years of formal education

Source: Rais/MTE apud Teixeira (2004) *A dinâmica das relações de trabalho no sistema financeiro*, DIEESE/CESIT.

on workers the need for continuous improvement of their qualifications in an attempt to achieve the banks' demands. According to the transformations verified in the bank workers' category, there has also been observed a reduction in the number of workers in the front office as a result of the intensification of technological resources.

The new requirements demanded to hire professionals, in particular in the banking sector, express the emergence of new abilities that may be apprehended in the scope of the redefinition of the social dimension of labor in Brazil. Thus, in the context of flexibilization of the activities and strategies in the banking system, the dynamics of the accumulation process demanded a new configuration of labor relations, in addition to new qualifications and required abilities that had strong impacts on the bank workers' movement. From the banks' perspective, the human resources policies might be redefined in the context of market deregulation. The selection criteria that guide these rules demand "specialists" in some areas/functions and workers with a broader background in positions of high management. The selection criteria embrace a set of abilities that includes a pattern of behavior (polyvalence, capacity for decision-making, among others) and the adoption of worldwide corporative values (integrity, respect, professionalism, work in teams). In this framework, each employee is considered responsible for his or her career, while cooperation between the employee and the department of human resources could be decisive in guaranteeing professional success in accordance with the individual potential for development in the organization.

Table10.11 Composition of bank workers' remuneration: Brazil 1999–2001, in percentages

Composition of remuneration	*1999*	*2000*	*2001*	*Variation 2001/1999 (%)*
Direct wages	58.29	58.13	57.55	−1.31
Indirect wages (benefits)	9.72	9.69	9.59	−1.31
Social charges	29.15	29.07	28.77	−1.31
Participation in profits and results	2.85	3.11	4.09	–44.7
Total	100.0	100.0	100.0	

Source: FEBRABAN (2002) www.febraban.org.br.

In this context, the programs of variable remuneration that associate individual performance with new standards of remuneration imply transformations in the workers' evaluation process with decisive impacts on the bank workers' union negotiation process. The adoption of performance criteria to guide negotiations between banks and their employees threatens union movement cohesion and may lead to a process of fragmentation inside the category. In fact, as Krein and Gonçalves (2005) noted, some of the largest banks have implemented variable remuneration programs without previous negotiation with the bank workers' union, such as the negotiations involved in the creation of sales clerks' commissions, including equity participation, profit distribution, and participation in the financial results. The variable remuneration programs of banks such as ABN AMRO, ITAU, UNIBANCO, and HSBC cannot be considered as equitable programs of participation in profits and results among workers since they take into account individual or "team" performance.[16]

Table 10.11 confirms the trend that emphasizes the decrease of wages and the growth of variable and individualized remuneration by means of negotiating the employee's participation in the profits and results, and the adoption of awards and commissions for individual and collective performance. Nevertheless, the combination of these possibilities might lead to a smaller portion of banking revenues going towards wages and benefits (Table 10.12).

Table 10.12 Banking system in Brazil: distribution of financial results 2000–2002, in percentages

	2000	*2002*
Human resources	60.6	42.3
Government	22.2	23.1
Shareholders	17.3	34.7

Source: FEBRABAN (2003) www.febraban.org.br.

Employability, sociability, and syndicalism

Between 1950 and 1973, the construction of citizenship became a constitutive aspect of the process of national development where investment and labor had a social dimension.[17] In the Brazilian industrialization framework, the conditions of access to the labor market expressed the possibilities of social integration by means of economic growth.[18] However, as a result of the market deregulation process, the access conditions to the labor market have been transformed. After the 1990s, the impacts of financialization on social organization have been expressed in institutional redefinition, enterprise reorganization, preference for liquid assets in portfolio management, and new labor relations. The social dimension of economic activities seems to have been weakened and society has been overwhelmed by the logic of economic rationality. As a result of the impacts of financial deregulation on industrial society, there has been a reconfiguration of the nexus among employability, sociability, and syndicalism. The fragility of social movements in the face of these recent transformations needs to be understood in the context of redefinition of the role of the state, capital, and labor in the market.

The modifications in the structure and dynamics of the banking system, the changing labor relations, and the unfavorable macroeconomic context to enhance collective action tended to restrain the rate of affiliation to bank workers' unions in Brazil.[19] Consequently, a dramatic fall in the rate of affiliation to bank workers' unions has recently been noted: according to IBGE data, in 2001, 68.2 percent of bank workers were not affiliated to unions.[20]

In order to limit the power of the bank workers' union, very significant changes occurred outside the collective bargaining as a result of the unilateral initiatives of banks. Since the 1990s, many banks initiated practices toward labor relations to implement strategies of cost reduction and efficiency that have bypassed the legal framework of collective contracts. Thus, some aspects relating to working conditions and characteristics of the labor contracts have been transformed without having been subject of collective bargaining, such as technological and organizational innovations, the outsourcing process, the intensification of the working rhythm, and the changes in retirement programs. In fact, these modifications have been imposed by banks in spite of the tradition of the bank workers' unionism in Brazil. For example, the voluntary retirement programs aim to stimulate turnover as a strategy of cost reduction and, as a result, weaken the labor unions' position. Besides, since the outsourcing practices ignored the rules of the bank workers' collective agreements in terms of the number of working hours and remuneration, they also weakened the workers' mobilization.[21]

The establishment of a new pattern of more flexible remuneration was consolidated from 1995 onwards with the introduction of the program of participation in profits and financial results[22] by means of a fixed bonus received by each bank worker during the period of collective bargaining. Considering the new remuneration pattern features, it should be noted that some banks have implemented awards, gratuities, and commissions on behalf of the fulfillment of goals previously established (number of products sold, volume of credit offered, and new accounts opened). Such measures strengthened the importance of individualized and variable remuneration attached to individual performance that is expressed in the following principle: "You make your proper wage."

In 2000, the right that guaranteed to all bank workers a variable bonus for the period of time worked was excluded from the collective agreement after a plebiscite on the "time service gratuity." Although unions tried to resist this concession, in the plebiscite the banks' proposal won a decisive victory that could be justified by the rational behavior of the bank worker who prefers some money at present rather than higher future wages due to the uncertainty related to his or her continuity in the job. Since November 2000, the exclusion of the variable bonus from the labor contract has been compensated by a fixed monetary amount.

The changes in the pattern of remuneration were followed by diminishing real wages. Data from DIEESE (2003) pointed out that, between 1996 and 2003, public sector employees suffered the greatest wage loss among the bank workers although public banks enjoyed record profitability. In fact, the variable remuneration has been used as compensation for the definition of an annual nominal wage readjustment inferior to the last inflation observed between 1995 and 2004 (Table 10.13). In the period analyzed, there have not been negotiations relative to the real increase in remuneration by means of incorporation of the increasing productivity performance.

In relation to the number of working hours (formally six hours daily), there have not been legal alterations, but the emergence of new practices needs to be emphasized. First, the daily working hours have been extended beyond the period legally determined by the collective agreement and, in many cases, the accomplishment of this overtime has not been paid. Second, a redefinition in the classification of a considerable number of bank workers as commissioners (reliable positions or management ranks) so as to extend the daily working hours to eight has been observed. Consequently, the increase in working hours – with the indiscriminate spread of practices that involve overtime and variable remuneration

Table 10.13 Bank workers in Brazil: nominal wage adjustments in relation to inflation

Period	*In percentages*
1995/96	4.2
1996/97	(3.47)
1997/98	0.71
1998/99	(2.38)
1999/2000	0.26
2000/01	0.25
2001/02	(1.81)
2002/03	(2.15)
2003/04	(4.37)
Loss/gain in the period between 1995 and 2004	(8.76)

Source: Rais/MTE apud Teixeira (2004) *A dinâmica das relações de trabalho no sistema financeiro*, DIEESE/CESIT.

– has diminished the real number of jobs. The once typical bank workers' schedule of six daily working hours (settled by the collective agreements) associated with front office activities has diminished their relative weight.

The overall changes suggest the growing challenges faced by the bank workers' unionism owing to the outcomes of the adjustment process in place since the 1990s as banks could achieve almost all their strategic plans in spite of the bank workers' resistance. Recent experience shows that the reduction of the bank workers, the transformations in the profile of the category and in the characteristics of the labor contracts turned out to configure new labor relations in the financial system. Since the 1990s, the bank workers' struggle has been centered around outsourcing practices and toward the incorporation of "non-bank" workers into the bank workers' unions. Nevertheless, until 2005, the results had been restricted in these issues. Besides, the bank workers' union movement has also searched for new forms of representation of the category demands and new forms of participation in society.[23] First, the bank workers' unionism extended the agenda including particular issues defended by groups of interest inside the category, such as gender, race, and culture. Second, the trade unions turned out to offer diversified services to the category.

Taking into account the changing configuration of the bank workers' union movement in contemporary Brazil, the transformations observed in the profile of the category may suggest a weakening that could threaten the historical force and representation of the movement in the current Brazilian modernization process. The bargaining process has increasingly lost its universal dimension and the dynamics of labor relations have become increasingly conditioned by unilateral actions centered on the logic of capital accumulation. The tensions observed between collective negotiations and capital flexibilization policies have characterized the scope of the bank workers' strategies of resistance and efforts for renewal of the movement.

The recent 2004 bank workers' strike is paradigmatic to analyze the trend toward fragmentation. The 30-day strike occurred in all the main cities of the country and was organized in a context characterized by more favorable economic growth indicators and results obtained in other categories' collective negotiations. At the beginning of the movement, the bank workers' assembly that was especially stimulated by the participation of the public bank workers opted to reject the agreement that had been previously negotiated between the centralized direction of the National Confederation of the Bank Workers (CNB) and the National Federation of Banks (FENABAN). As a result, the bank workers' assembly decided to strike for an indeterminate time period.

On behalf of this previous negotiated agreement, the CNB foresaw the possibility of obtaining a real increase in wages (that might average around 25 percent) after 10 years of recurrent losses, and the maintenance of all social benefits achieved in the collective agreements up until then. Nevertheless, the CNB had accepted the exclusion of an additional bonus from the negotiation, a decision that generated dissatisfaction among many bank workers who depended on this bonus to pay debts or purchase goods. Thus, the base of the movement decided to defend the real increase of 25 percent as well as the maintenance of the bonus.

Although the proposal negotiated by the CNB in 2004 was better than those of previous years, its rejection by the base of the movement may be explained by two reasons. First, private bank workers expected to receive a bonus as in recent years – since it corresponded to an additional annual wage of almost 60 percent – while the CNB proposal focused on the real wage increase that might add little to the nominal wages in the short term. Thus, there was a conflict of interests. While the national direction was focused on the evolution of purchasing power over the long run, a significant number of bank workers had short-term expectations because the current transformations prevent them from developing long-term professional expectations in the banks where they work. Second, the public bank workers anticipated that the labor government of the PT (Partido dos Trabalhadores) would reset the significant wage losses that had affected them in the past decade. In the private sector, the strike ended in under two weeks. The movement continued mainly because of the resistance of the public bank workers.

The 2004 strike revealed not only the existence of different expectations between the national central direction and the base of the bank workers' movement but also different expectations and strategies between public and private bank workers. Finally, the bank workers got the fixed bonus, although its amount turned out to be smaller than in previous years. In the private sector, the monetary bonus turned out to be transformed in indirect benefits (food tickets) favoring banks with fiscal subsidies. In the public banks, the value of the bonus was established after judicial determination. Although the results observed were less than expected, the strike could be characterized as a very significant movement, considering the technological transformations in the banking system that turned out to minimize the effectiveness of a strike owing to the diversification of the electronic channels of distribution.[24]

The changes in the collective contracts and in the scope of the union's negotiations illustrate the challenges and transformations of the bank workers' union movement in Brazilian society. In spite of the tradition of the bank workers' union movement, its capacity of mobilization to defend universal demands seems to have diminished because of the emergence of groups of interest that mobilize themselves toward specific demands. In spite of the loss of cohesion observed in the 2004 strike, the bank workers' union movement still looks forward to preserving elements that encompass general interests. The tensions between solidarity and particular interests reveal the different expectations inside the movement. In this context, the bank workers' union movement has adopted a strategy of adaptive resistance whose defensive nature reveals the growing difficulty facing the transformations observed in labor relations.

Conclusion

The tensions in the new relations among state, capital, and labor in the market have been overwhelmed by processes of homogenization and resistance in the labor union movement. The historically consolidated categories with active participation in contemporary Brazilian labor unionism, such as the bank workers, could express the impact of the current tensions on the labor movement. Working conditions were redefined by the new configuration of portfolio and investment conditions in the financial sector. In Brazil, banks turned out to have a key role in the financial conglomerates in the framework of a more privatized and internationalized market structure. Between 1994 and 2004, the changing banking system redefined labor conditions and, consequently, new challenges have been faced by the bank workers' movement.

Since the 1990s, the redefinition of international integration, the context of low growth, and the transformations in the banking system affected labor union power and stimulated the search for new strategies to face the impacts of the deregulation process on Brazilian syndicalism. In this framework, tensions inside the category have characterized the recent evolution of bank workers' trade unionism in Brazil. In the context of the labor market flexibilization and the changes observed in the organization of the banking system, the transformations in the bank workers' labor conditions involved a redefinition of the working and remuneration standards that provoked ruptures and challenges in collective negotiations. A trend toward fragmentation has been observed in the social movements where the collective negotiations tend to relativize the role of the universal dimension of the bank workers' demands.

The overall tensions provoked many changes not only in the process of labor regulation but also in the national bank workers' union organization. On the one hand, these transformations indicated an increasing unreliability in the maintenance of jobs, and a greater flexibility in the allocation of labor and in remuneration standards. In fact, the recent process of labor flexibilization in the banking sector has been overwhelmed by modifications in the abilities socially required. The nature of labor has been deeply transformed and the bank worker redefined on behalf of the new corporative demands that tend to enlarge the control and rhythm of the activities in the workplace. These changes have enhanced the introduction of new issues in the negotiation process, such as outsourcing, target programs, variable remuneration, and longer real working hours. On the other hand, although the bank workers' unionism could not overcome the forces toward the process of labor flexibilization, it preserved itself as an institution by means of the search for new forms of actions, organization, and mobilization. In spite of the pressures, the bank workers' unionism turned out to resist in order to preserve the national collective agreement and to maintain the labor union organization. This fact is decisive in understanding the achievements of the 2004 national strike.

It is undeniable that the recent process of adaptive resistance in the labor movement expressed the social tensions and economic transformations that resulted from the neoliberal adjustment, particularly after the 1990s. For the future, the challenge reveals the difficulty faced by the bank workers' unionism to create new forms of social cohesion in order to establish collective identities in the financial sector and in society.

Notes

1 See, for example, Aküyz (1993) for an analysis of the impacts of financial openness on interest rates and investment.
2 This argument has been developed by Grabel (2000).
3 See, for example, Fligstein (2001) for a survey of the theoretical approaches relating to the transformation and comprehension of the dynamics of the markets in contemporary capitalism.
4 See Kumar (2005) for further analysis of the transformations in labor relations.
5 The first organization of bank workers appeared in the 1920s when the union movement had a philanthropic character. Since the 1930s, it has become a confrontation movement. See, for example, Canêdo (1978); Oliveiras (1990).
6 This central union was created in 1983 and it is now one of the five biggest union entities in the world.
7 The same collective agreement is valid in all regions of the country. The number of clauses in the collective bargaining contract increased from nine in 1979 to more than 60 in 2003.
8 See, for example, Sennet (1999) for an analysis of the behavioral changes in contemporary capitalism.
9 As Minsky (1986) pointed out, banks are always speculating on their ability to refinance their positions in assets (liability management) while they also speculate on the composition of their assets.
10 Data from the Foundation Instituto de Pesquisas Econômicas (FIPE) showed that in 1994 the revenues originated by fees and commissions represented 6.25 percent of total revenues, reaching 11.21 percent at the end of 2003.
11 This process involves the growth in the number of institutions specializing in consumer loans, leasing, factoring, insurance and the management of pension funds, besides credit cooperatives.
12 For further analysis on the impacts of the current transformations on labor relations, see Gorz (1998).
13 Recent research based on one of the biggest national private banks practices found that practically half of the bank workers pointed out that that they develop the target plans on behalf of the coercive practices in order to maintain their jobs. The same research evidenced that these employees have not received additional remuneration but faced an intensification of the working rhythm, an increase in working hours, a worsening of the working environment, and a growth in anxiety and stress. Therefore, the banks' plans and goals are achieved by the bank workers through fear of being dismissed.
14 These structural changes involve the growth in informality, jobs without legal contracts, self-employment, small businesses, family employees, unemployment, and precarious employment. These transformations have reinforced the heterogeneity of the labor force in Brazil.
15 Considering the data from RAIS/MTE (2003), very few workers in the private sector reach retirement age while still working as bank workers.
16 See also DIEESE (2001) for further data relative to the profile of bank workers.
17 See Hobsbawn (1997) for a historical approach to the social and economic reorganization of the Bretton Woods period.
18 For further analysis of the specificities of the Brazilian industrialization process, see Cardoso de Mello (1982) and Tavares (1978).
19 Nevertheless, the bank workers' union of the state of São Paulo is still one of the four most important Brazilian workers' unions. The others are the metalworking union in the cities of São Paulo and São Paulo ABC, and the teachers' union of the public schools of the state of São Paulo.
20 Currently, almost 80 percent of the members of bank workers' unions belong to unions affiliated to the CUT (302,656 bank workers belong to 109 unions). The bank workers have always occupied key positions in the direction of CUT.

21 It is also worth remembering that through the judicial action called "prohibitory interdict" (injunction) banks are able to limit strikes and, therefore, manifestations of the bank workers' movement.

22 Participation in the profits and financial results program (PLR) was stimulated by federal tax benefits and cost reduction programs. The PLR is negotiated during the bank workers' annual wage campaign and it corresponds to a monetary bonus (approximately US$220 in 2004).

23 The bank workers' union movement has tried to include actions relative to social exclusion. For example, the Bank Workers' Union of Santo André has participated in management of the Banco do Povo de Santo André – Crédito Solidário, a non-government organization associated with the city hall of Santo André which receives resources not only from the BNDES (an official development bank) but also from the European Union and associated unions. The objective of these experiences is to expand micro-credit operations toward productive projects in order to stimulate entrepreneurship. Gonçalves and Madi (2005) noted that the recent experience of the Banco do Povo has shown that micro-credit feeds survival strategies that minimize poverty conditions but do not stimulate economic reproduction.

24 This strike did not cause social upheaval. Nevertheless, many people, especially older people, who receive pensions inside the bank branches were negatively affected.

Bibliography

Akyüz, Y. (1993) "Financial Liberalization: The Key Issues," *Unctad Discussion Papers* 56.

Canêdo, L. B. (1978) *Sindicalismo Bancário em São Paulo*, São Paulo: Editora Símbolo.

Cardoso de Mello, J.M. (1982) *O Capitalismo Tardio*, São Paulo. Brasiliense.

Carvalho Neto, A.M. and Carvalho, R.A.A. (1998) *Sindicalismo e Negociação Coletiva nos anos 90*, Belo Horizonte: ITR, PUC-MG.

Chesnais, F. (1999) "Mundialização Financeira e Vulnerabilidade Sistêmica," in F. Chesnais (ed.) *A Mundialização Financeira – Gênese, Custos e Riscos*, São Paulo: Ed. Xamã.

DIEESE (2001) *Linha Bancários*, www.dieese.org.br.

DIEESE (2003) *O Rosto dos Bancários*, www.dieese.org.br/esp/estudos_perfis.xml (accessed June 30, 2008).

FEBRABAN (2003) *Balanço Social*, www.febraban.org.br/Arquivo/Servicos/Dadosdosetor/Balan%E7o_Social_2003.pdf (accessed June 30, 2008).

Fligstein, N. (2001) *The Architecture of Markets*, Princeton, NJ: Princeton University Press.

Gonçalves, J.R.B and Madi, M.A.C. (2005) "Financialization and Employability: The Future of the Bank Workers' Union Movement in Brazil," Paper presented at conference on After Deregulation: The Financial System in the 21st Century, University of Sussex, May.

Gorz, A. (1998) *Metamorfoses do Trabalho*, Petrópolis: Ed. Vozes.

Grabel, I. (2000) "The Political Economy of 'Policy Credibility': The New-classical Macroeconomics and the Remaking of Emerging Economies," *Cambridge Journal of Economics*, 24: 1–9.

Hobsbawn, E. (1997) *A Era dos Extremos*, São Paulo: Cia.das Letras.

Instituto Brasileiro de Geografia e Estatística (2001) *Pesquisa Sindical*, Rio de Janeiro: IBGE.

Jinkings, N. (2002) *Trabalho e Resistência na "fonte misteriosa" – os bancários no mundo da eletrônica e do dinheiro*, São Paulo: Editora Unicamp/Imprensa Oficial.

Krein, J.D. and Gonçalves, J.R. (2005) "Mudanças Tecnológicas e Seus Impactos nas Relações de Trabalho e no Sindicalismo do Setor Terciário," in DIEESE and CESIT *Emprego e Desenvolvimento Tecnológico: Estudos DIEESE/CESIT*, São Paulo: DIEESE.

Kumar, K. (2005) *From Post-industrial to Post-modern Society*, Oxford: Blackwell.

Minsky, H. (1986) *Stabilizing an Unstable Economy*, New Haven, CT: Yale University Press.

Oliveiras, A.L.V. (1990) *Banking Unionism: Origins*, São Paulo: Oboré.

Pesquisa Nacional por Amostra de Domicílio (PNAD) (2002) http://www.ibge.gov.br/home/presidencia/noticias/10102003pnad2002html.shtm (accessed June 30, 2008).

Relação Anual de Informações Sociais/MTE (2003) www.rais.gov.br.

Relação Anual de Informações Sociais/MTE apud Teixeira, M. (2004) *A dinâmica das relações de trabalho no sistema financeiro*, São Paulo: DIEESE/CESIT.

Sennet, R. (1999) *A Corrosão do Caráter*, Rio de Janeiro: Ed. Record.

Tavares, M.C. (1978) *Ciclo e Crise: O Movimento Recente da Industrialização Brasileira*, Campinas: Instituto de Economia, Coleção Teses.

Teixeira, M.O. (2004) *A Dinâmica das Relações de Trabalho no Sistema Financeiro*, research report, Campinas: DIEESE/CESIT.

Index